Praise for Winston Groom's

KEARNY'S MARCH

"An altogether superior read. . . . [Groom] engages, informs and entertains the reader all at once, so that one comes away from his nonfiction books feeling good about what's been so effortlessly learned. . . . The book's main focus is the incredible march West by Gen. Stephen Watts Kearny in 1846, but significant parallel themes include the Mexican War, the Mormon exodus, the Santa Fe and Oregon trails, the Donner Party, and the conquest of California. These are all well-known events and have been oft-related through the years. But Groom's achievement is to interweave them all seamlessly and sweep the reader along like an aspen leaf in a Rocky Mountain stream. . . . Groom is not only a good writer, he's a fine historian in the bargain." —*Mobile Press-Register*

"Groom has done a sprightly job of chronicling this important but little-studied conflict." —Larry McMurtry, *Harper's*

"A grand story. . . . Groom has developed his powers of storytelling— characterization, concision, and scene-by-scene description—to a high art." —*Tuscaloosa News*

"Told wonderfully, drolly by Groom. . . . Informed, reliable, shrewd and insightful, but laid-back. . . . Graceful and succinct. . . . *Kearny's March* is for those who long to relive those exciting and dangerous days—and more particularly for those happy just to read about them. Groom fleshes his story out with enough extravagant, flawed personalities to cast a Shakespearean comedy." —*The Dallas Morning News*

"A vivid recounting of the seminal year that transformed the adolescent United States into a two-ocean nation. . . . [Groom] presents this story with novelistic flair . . . replete with adventure and harrowing tales. . . . There is drama aplenty, with backstabbing by everyone—American, Mexican and Indian. . . . It has all the components needed to make for an epic, and it reads easily. . . . True to his nature, Groom breathes life into the complicated players of his story. . . . An intrigue-filled account. . . . If you like a tale of high adventure, a fun read that is action-packed and informative, then pick up *Kearny's March*. . . . Provides a big-picture view of the motivations of men and the nation writ large at a transformative time in this country's history, while painting a sterling portrait of not only a time but a place—the early American West."
—*The Washington Independent Review of Books*

"Energetic, enthralling narrative history. . . . Written with novelistic appreciation for character and ambition, Groom's military histories are vibrant, kinetic, and popular."   —*Booklist*

"An intriguing, international drama. . . . Groom brings to life the events of 1846–47."   —*Library Journal*

"A masterful blend of scholarly research, colorful description, and a confident, enthusiastic style of narrative writing that adds freshness and immediacy to a true-adventure saga."
—*Alabama Writers' Forum*

"Valuable, lively, brave in scope, and fast-paced. . . . Despite the fact that the subject is a relatively conventional military history, Groom has done it extravagant justice."   —*The Olympian*

"Galloping popular history, guaranteed to entertain. . . . Groom follows Kearny's 2,000-mile march from Fort Leavenworth, Kansas, to California, providing wonderful stories about the soldiers' progress through a rugged, wildly changing landscape."
—*Kirkus Reviews*

Winston Groom
KEARNY'S MARCH

Winston Groom is the author of fifteen previous books, including *Vicksburg, 1863*; *Patriotic Fire*; *Shrouds of Glory*; *Forrest Gump*; and *Conversations with the Enemy* (with Duncan Spencer), which was a Pulitzer Prize finalist. He lives with his wife and daughter in Alabama.

www.winstongroom.com

KEARNY'S
MARCH

KEARNY'S MARCH

*The Epic Creation of the
American West, 1846–1847*

Winston Groom

Vintage Books
A Division of Random House, Inc.
New York

FIRST VINTAGE BOOKS EDITION, NOVEMBER 2012

Copyright © 2011 by Winston Groom

All rights reserved. Published in the United States by Vintage Books, a division of Random House, Inc., New York, and in Canada by Random House of Canada Limited, Toronto. Originally published in hardcover in the United States by Alfred A. Knopf, a division of Random House, Inc., New York, in 2011.

The Library of Congress has cataloged the Knopf edition as follows:
Groom, Winston.
Kearny's march : the epic creation of the American west, 1846–1847 / by Winston Groom. — 1st ed.
p. cm.
Includes bibliographical references.
1. Kearny's Expedition, 1846. 2. Kearny, Stephen Watts, 1794–1848.
I. Title.
E405.2.G76 2011 979'.02—dc22 2011013889

Vintage ISBN: 978-0-307-45574-1

Author photograph © Squire Fox
Book design by Virginia Tan
Maps by Robert Bull

www.vintagebooks.com

Printed in the United States of America
10 9 8 7 6 5 4 3 2 1

To Carolina Montgomery Groom—age twelve

When you were seven and came into my office to ask what I was doing, I was writing *your* book—*Patriotic Fire: Andrew Jackson and Jean Laffite at the Battle of New Orleans,* a tale of pirates, Indians, heroes, and scoundrels.

Here's another story for you with explorers, Indians, generals, and mountain men—and always the heroes and scoundrels—who provide the grace and the disrepute that make our human race at once interesting and unique.

—Your loving papa

If you have no family or friends to aid you, and no prospect opened for you, turn your face to the great West, and there build up a home and fortune. . . . Go West, young man, go West and grow up with the country.

Horace Greeley, 1811–1872

CONTENTS

What's in a Name?

In each of the five military histories I've written previous to this one, there has been some family connection, some near relative of mine involved in the conflict. It wasn't intentional but just sort of happened. In *Shrouds of Glory: From Atlanta to Nashville: The Last Great Campaign of the Civil War* it was my great-grandfather Fremont Sterling Thrower, who fought with the rebel general Joseph Wheeler's cavalry against William T. Sherman in the Battle of Atlanta. In *A Storm in Flanders: The Ypres Salient, 1914–1918: Tragedy and Triumph on the Western Front* it was my grandfather, who served in France with the Thirty-first Infantry (Dixie) Division. In *1942: The Year That Tried Men's Souls* it was my father, a captain in the army during World War II. In *Patriotic Fire: Andrew Jackson and Jean Laffite at the Battle of New Orleans*, it turned out that my great-great-great-grandfather Elijah Montgomery had been a captain with the U.S. Seventh Infantry Regiment during the War of 1812, and during the Battle of New Orleans he had received both a commendation and field promotion to major from Andrew Jackson himself.

When I undertook to write about the Battle of Vicksburg several years ago it was with a slight trepidation because I knew of no link between that terrific event and anyone in my ancestry. It's not that I'm superstitious, but I felt I was somehow breaking a chain, that luck might not be with me. I pacified myself with the fact that on a golf course right behind my home in Point Clear, Alabama, lay a quiet little Civil War cemetery where several hundred Confederate soldiers are buried, most of whom had been wounded during the Battle of Vicksburg. It was the most slender of connections but it would have to do—and did, until one day a distant cousin whom I had never met appeared out of the blue with all manner of genealogical history about the Groom family.

The other sides of the family were pack rats and documented ancestries back to Charlemagne—even to the time of the apes, for that matter—but of the Groom family, beyond my great-grandfather Groom, little was known, and I had always assumed that they must have been criminals, or worse.

Lo and behold, documentation by this genealogist cousin revealed that my great-great-grandfather James Wright Groom had served honorably in the Fourth Mississippi Cavalry Regiment during the Civil War and wound up his life, in 1906, as an engineer and well-respected citizen of Mobile, Alabama, which is where I'm from. Armed with this news, I felt almost uncannily blessed and plunged into my research on the story with renewed vigor and confidence.

Yet here, again, when I planned and proposed *Kearny's March*, there was not a soul in my familial background who had taken the slightest part in that most interesting and acquisitive period in American history. A check of family records turned up no soldiers from the Mexican-American War, and again I began to suffer that sinking sensation you get when something doesn't seem quite right—like starting off a long journey without your lucky penny, rabbit's foot, or what have you.

It hovered over me like a murky pall all through the researching and into the beginnings of the writing, until I had a sudden revelation: there might be a connection after all, however tenuous, between John C. Frémont, the famous Pathfinder of this story, and my great-grandfather Fremont Thrower, who fought in the Civil War.

Because of the widespread publication of his western explorations, Frémont for a time in the mid-1840s was arguably the most celebrated person in America. He had attained such star status that counties, cities, streets, mountains, rivers, parks, libraries, schools, and above all babies were being named after him. I believe it is highly likely that my great-grandfather was among the latter. Fremont Thrower was born in Mobile, Alabama, in 1845, the year that John Frémont's famous explorer's report was published in newspapers throughout the country, and there is no evidence in the family tree of anyone else called Fremont, which is a name of French extraction.

If it is so, an interesting sidelight would be that, eighteen years later, Fremont Thrower found himself serving as a private in the Confederate cavalry, while his namesake, John Frémont, was a general in the Union army.

These small links have become meaningful to me over the course of writing these historical books and lend a sort of immediacy to the work. It's certainly not blood kin, if indeed it's anything at all, but I'll take it, the same way I did the little cemetery behind my house—a feeling that there's something somehow special between yourself and the matter at hand.

Point Clear
December 11, 2010

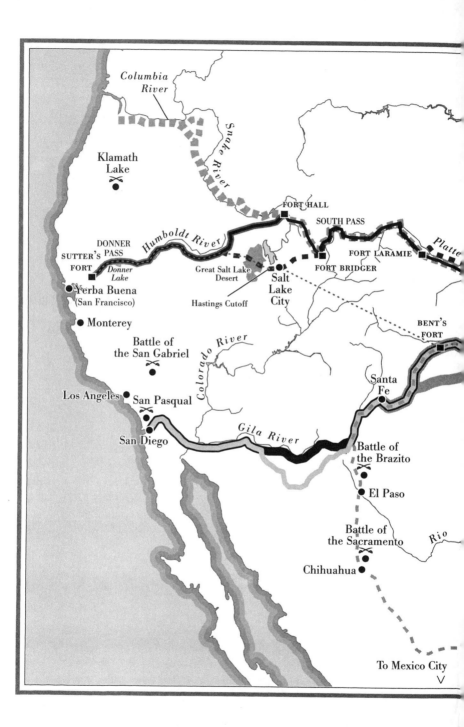

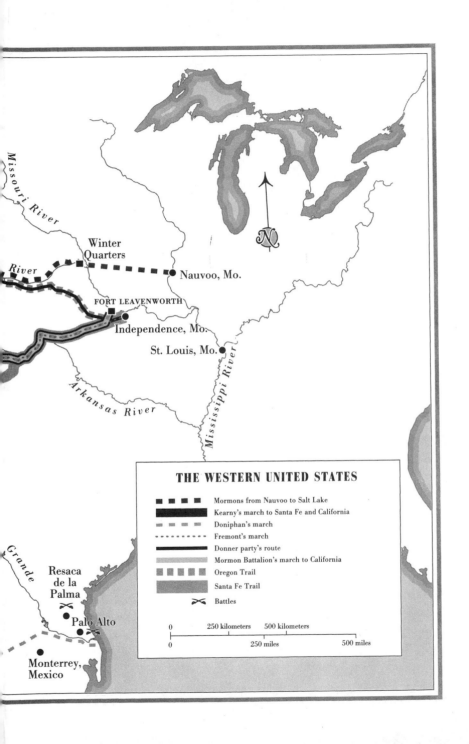

Missouri River

River

Winter
Quarters

Nauvoo, Mo.

FORT LEAVENWORTH

Independence, Mo.

Arkansas River

St. Louis, Mo.

Mississippi River

THE WESTERN UNITED STATES

- Mormons from Nauvoo to Salt Lake
- Kearny's march to Santa Fe and California
- Doniphan's march
- Fremont's march
- Donner party's route
- Mormon Battalion's march to California
- Oregon Trail
- Santa Fe Trail
- Battles

Grande

Resaca
de la
Palma

Palo Alto

Monterrey,
Mexico

| 0 | 250 kilometers | 500 kilometers |

| 0 | 250 miles | 500 miles |

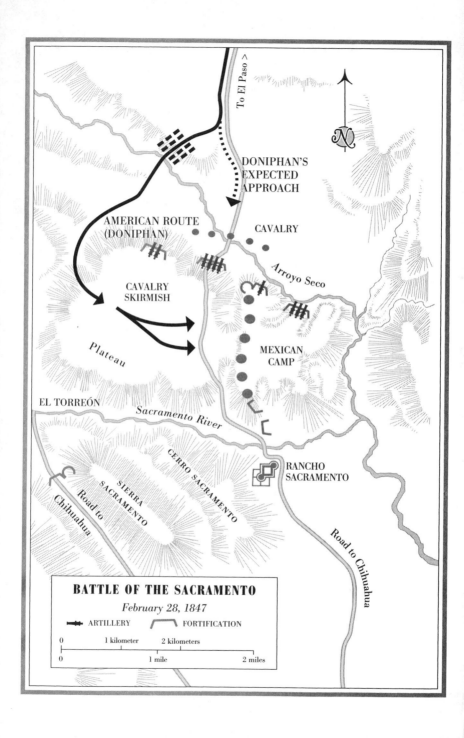

To El Paso >

DONIPHAN'S
EXPECTED
APPROACH

AMERICAN ROUTE
(DONIPHAN)

CAVALRY

Arroyo Seco

CAVALRY
SKIRMISH

Plateau

MEXICAN
CAMP

EL TORREÓN

Sacramento River

CERRO SACRAMENTO

SIERRA
SACRAMENTO

RANCHO
SACRAMENTO

Road to
Chihuahua

Road to Chihuahua

BATTLE OF THE SACRAMENTO

February 28, 1847

ARTILLERY   FORTIFICATION

0	1 kilometer	2 kilometers

0	1 mile	2 miles

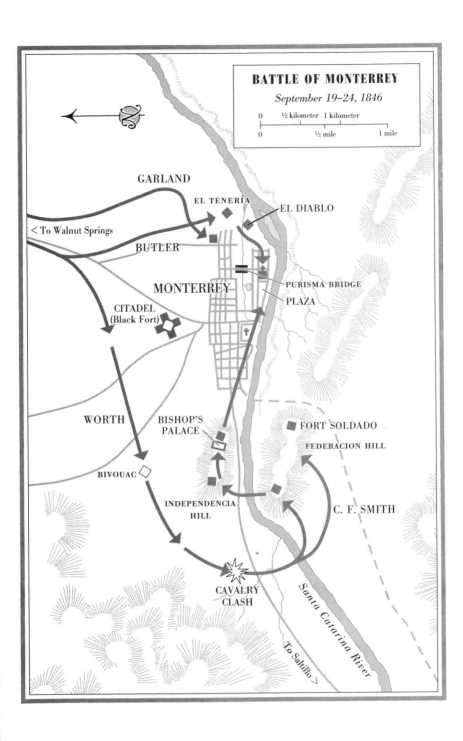

BATTLE OF MONTERREY

September 19–24, 1846

GARLAND

EL TENERÍA

EL DIABLO

< To Walnut Springs

BUTLER

MONTERREY

PURISMA BRIDGE

PLAZA

CITADEL
(Black Fort)

WORTH

BISHOP'S
PALACE

FORT SOLDADO

FEDERACION HILL

BIVOUAC

INDEPENDENCIA
HILL

C. F. SMITH

CAVALRY
CLASH

Santa Catarina River

To Saltillo >

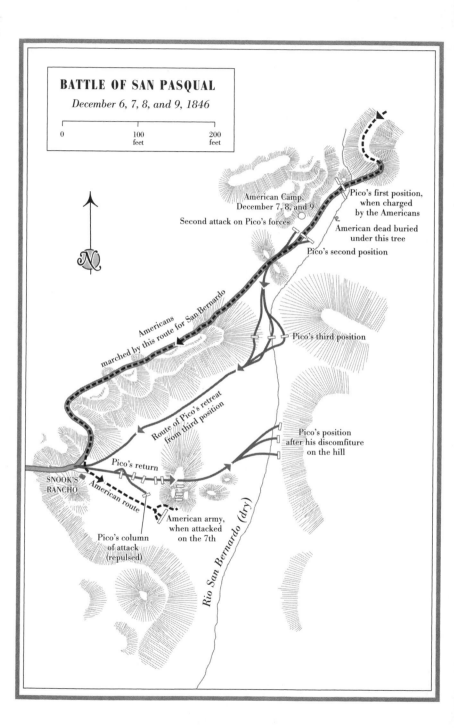

BATTLE OF SAN PASQUAL

December 6, 7, 8, and 9, 1846

0   100 feet   200 feet

N

American Camp,
December 7, 8, and 9

Second attack on Pico's forces

Pico's first position,
when charged
by the Americans

American dead buried
under this tree

Pico's second position

Americans
marched by this route for San Bernardo

Pico's third position

Route of Pico's retreat
from third position

Pico's position
after his discomfiture
on the hill

SNOOK'S
RANCHO

Pico's return

American route

American army,
when attacked
on the 7th

Pico's column
of attack
(repulsed)

Rio San Bernardo (dry)

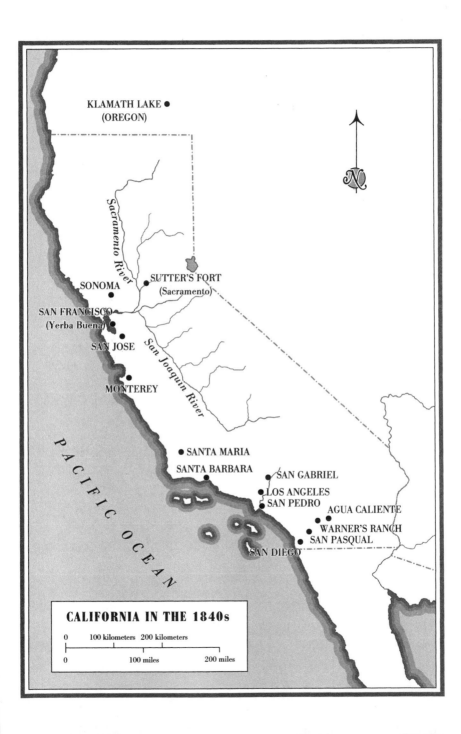

KLAMATH LAKE ●
(OREGON)

Sacramento River

SONOMA

SAN FRANCISCO
(Yerba Buena)

● SUTTER'S FORT
(Sacramento)

SAN JOSE

San Joaquin River

MONTEREY

PACIFIC OCEAN

● SANTA MARIA

SANTA BARBARA

● SAN GABRIEL
● LOS ANGELES
SAN PEDRO

AGUA CALIENTE

WARNER'S RANCH
SAN PASQUAL

SAN DIEGO

CALIFORNIA IN THE 1840s

0   100 kilometers   200 kilometers

0   100 miles   200 miles

KEARNY'S MARCH

A People in Motion

Late on an August afternoon in 1845, the most famous man in America, U.S. captain John Charles Frémont, departed Bent's Fort, the last outpost of American civilization, which lay in the foothills of Colorado's Rocky Mountains. With him were several score of the toughest, most experienced mountain men of the day—fur trappers and Indian fighters such as Kit Carson, Joseph Walker, and Bill Williams; the French-Canadians Basil Lajeunesse, Antoine Robideaux, Alexis Godey, and Auguste Archambault; a party of nine Delaware Indians; and an eighteen-year-old free black man who was Frémont's valet. Sixty-one of them in all, they made a formidable armed party, each man carrying a .50-caliber Hawken "buffalo rifle," two pistols, and any number of knives. They were headed west, into the setting sun, with instructions to chart the unknown.

Frémont's fame had reached him surprisingly early, at the age of thirty-two, after his first journey of exploration several years before, in which he disproved the widely held myth that the vast plains west of the Mississippi River were nothing more than a worthless, uninhabitable wasteland—the so-called Great American Desert. It was further enhanced by his second expedition, which "disclosed to multitudes a shining new land of flowers, sunshine, and wealth." American explorers in those days were accorded the sort of exultation once given to modern-day astronauts. Theirs was a difficult, often dangerous, but fascinating and useful world that let the common man see what lay beyond his antlike horizons.

Daniel Boone became a legend in his own time by pioneering the

Wilderness Road through the Cumberland Gap, and early in the century Lewis and Clark unveiled the secrets of the Northwest Territory. The U.S. Navy thrilled the nation with its report of the Exploring Expedition of 1838–1842 (the renowned "Ex.Ex."), which charted the Pacific from Alaska to the South Seas, including a detailed look at the American West Coast. But Frémont's revelations struck a note that set the country atremble, for by this time it was fairly bursting with European immigrants and others yearning for cheap, fertile land to sow and reap.

Aided in some measure by his wife's flair for literary composition, Frémont's published reports sent whole communities scurrying to acquire "prairie schooners," the great covered wagons that took Americans on their westward migration. It didn't hurt, by the way, that the wife, Jessie Benton Frémont, was the daughter of Thomas Hart Benton, at the time the most influential man in the U.S. Senate, who saw to it that his son-in-law's findings were distributed wholesale by the U.S. Government Printing Office.

Frémont's present mission was, ostensibly, a strictly scientific one, established to discover and chart the western expanse of the continent. To that end his expedition carried with it the most sophisticated instruments of the day: "a fine refracting telescope, two pocket chronometers, two sextants, a reflecting circle, a siphon barometer and cistern barometer, half a dozen thermometers and an assortment of compasses." And if the delicate barometers got broken, altitude would be determined by taking the temperature at which water boiled. A brilliant young artist and draftsman named Edward Kern was along to sketch flora, fauna, and topographical features. Also included were sacks of trinkets, clothing, and tools for the Indians they would inevitably encounter, as well as ample ammunition should the Indians prove hostile. The press had already branded Frémont the "Pathfinder," but in fact he found few paths that had not already been traveled by the Native Americans or indeed by the mountain men. The difference was that Frémont was able to map them and describe them in a way that only a trained engineer and scientist could.

Frémont was by now well versed in the rigors of such undertakings. The previous year he and his party got up the High Sierras too late, nearly froze and starved, and survived only by eating their pack animals and even the pet dogs that some of the men had acquired. Death could come in a flash in these fierce, uncharted climes—ambush by a war party; the sudden charge of a thousand-pound grizzly or the leap of a cougar; quicksand, desert thirst, prairie fire, flash floods, and heaven help the man who fell ill.

Now a new menace was in the air, the threat of war—war with Mexico, war with England. The U.S. Congress had just voted to grant the independent Republic of Texas statehood. Mexico immediately severed diplomatic relations and promised war if the Americans went through with it. Britain had begun making bellicose noises over U.S. claims to the immense Oregon Territory that included what are now the states of Oregon, Washington, and parts of Montana, Wyoming, and Idaho. Likewise, it was feared that the English, who possessed the world's most powerful navy, would come in on the part of Mexico if she went to war with the United States.

These problems were likely on Captain Frémont's mind as his little army plodded out of Bent's Fort toward the distant, snowcapped Rockies. Sixty men doesn't sound like much in the long scheme of things, but in the 1840s, in the sparseness of the western half of the continent, sixty well-armed, well-trained men were a force to be reckoned with, considering that in the entire province of California fewer than one thousand Mexicans could be counted on as a military force.

Frémont believed, or so he later said, that he was under secret instructions from the president himself, James K. Polk, to seize California from the Mexicans if war broke out. Navy Secretary George Bancroft had issued similar orders to Commodore John Drake Sloat, commander of the U.S. Pacific Squadron. At the time, there was a sizable community of American emigrants living there, most residing in towns along the coast or on farms in the Sacramento valley. It was anticipated that these sturdy people would rise up against the Mexican authorities in the event of war, or perhaps instigate a war themselves.

It was shaping up as an explosive adventure, but Frémont felt up to the task. If successful he knew he would come home covered in glory. Little did he dream that instead he would return under arrest and facing a court-martial for mutiny, a hanging offense.

.   .   .

The following year, 1846, the war with Mexico arrived. It broke out between a Mexican army on the Rio Grande and the U.S. Army under General Zachary Taylor, which President Polk had sent south to provoke hostilities. At least that's the way most people saw it. Polk's story was that the Mexicans had attacked American soldiers first, and on American soil, and he was sticking to it.

While the principal theater of the war remained along the Rio Grande, Polk also set into motion another event designed to fulfill his dream of an America "from sea to shining sea." He sent out urgent orders to Colonel (soon to be a general) Stephen Watts Kearny at Fort Leavenworth, Kansas—then considered the western "frontier" of the United States—to march his two-thousand-man Army of the West a thousand miles down the old Santa Fe Trail and capture the New Mexico Territory, a huge Mexican province consisting of Arizona, New Mexico, and parts of Colorado, which was presently being governed from Santa Fe. Kearny's further instructions were to march the army another thousand miles west to the California Territory, which also included what are presently the states of Utah and Nevada, and take that, too.

Polk's line of thinking was that the inhabitants of those far-flung provinces were being so ill served by their government down in Mexico City they would willingly submit to U.S. conquest. He wasn't far from wrong. In the New Mexico Territory, for example, the government seemed powerless to protect its farmers from the depredations of the wild Indians, at the same time taxing the citizens heavily for that exact purpose.

Still, Kearny's task was daunting. The Santa Fe Trail was tough and tricky. There had been trade up and down its course long enough that nobody was going to get lost, but weather, terrain, and hostile Indians were always challenging, and to get a whole army over it was a complicated project and logistical nightmare. Then there was the question of what lay in wait at the other end. Would the Mexican government send a large army up to defend the place? Would Kearny face insurmountable fortifications? Would the population be rebellious? And then, assuming success in Santa Fe, he would then have to move the California force another thousand miles, this time across some of the most inhospitable desert and mountain terrain on earth, which remained unmapped, unexplored, and all but unknown. It would be a dangerous enterprise, but danger was the business Kearny was in and Polk couldn't have picked a better man.

Kearny had entered the army nearly thirty years earlier, after graduating from Columbia College, and for the past decade he had commanded the First Cavalry Regiment. In fact, he had already come to be known in army circles as the Father of Cavalry. A newspaper reporter who had recently met him described him as "a man rising fifty years of age. His height is about five feet ten or eleven inches. His figure is all that is required by symmetry. His features are regular, almost Grecian; his eye is blue, and he has an eagle-like expression, when excited by stern or angry emotion, but in ordinary social intercourse, the whole expression of his countenance is mild and pleasing, and his manners and conversation are unaffected, urbane, and conciliatory, without the slightest exhibition of vanity or egotism. He appears the cool, brave, and energetic soldier." So it certainly appeared that Stephen Kearny was well equipped to lead the expedition the president had ordered—but there was something else. What Kearny didn't know, what he couldn't know, was that from the moment he marched the Army of the West out of Fort Leavenworth, on June 26, 1846, "the first phase, the political phase, of the American Civil War had begun."

By the 1840s a tense and immutable friction had begun to thrum across the American landscape, North and South. In the beginning the argument was largely political and, more specifically, economic. A decade earlier North and South had nearly come to blows as a result of a tariff passed over the objections of southern legislators, which put duties on foreign goods in such a way as to make them nearly unaffordable in the South. This legislation, known to southerners as the Tariff of Abominations, had been declared "null and void" by the state of South Carolina, forcing a showdown on the question of whether states must obey laws of Congress that they found obnoxious. The stalemate was broken when Andrew Jackson threatened to send federal forces to Charleston to enforce the law, but this left a bitter feeling among many southerners that only increased with time.

The immediate grievance in the North over war with Mexico was a fear that if the nation added Mexican territory in the Southwest it would mean loss of northern political power to the southern "slave power," which would move to occupy the new lands with their slaves. Up to now, a del-

icate balance in the U.S. Senate had been maintained between the two
sections of the country—eleven southern states and eleven northern—
so that a workable if uneasy balance had been achieved.

In 1821 Congress had forged a bitter settlement allowing Missouri
into the Union as a slaveholding state—the Missouri Compromise—
brokered by Henry Clay of Kentucky, in which slavery was henceforth
banned north of the southern Missouri boundary line. For twenty-five
years this had worked to keep the dangers of sectional politics at bay.
Until now—until Kearny's march, a quarter century later, which threatened to radically disturb the balance created by the compromise. By
this time the issue was further vexed by the growing abolitionist movement in the North, which had brought a moral dimension to the political
question of slavery. This tended to produce high passions, which were
inflamed when a relatively unknown congressman from Pennsylvania
inserted language into an appropriations bill that would have banned
slavery in any territory acquired by the United States from Mexico.
That legislation, known as the Wilmot Proviso, opened a Pandora's box
that neither laws nor common sense could ever close.

Kearny of course knew little or nothing of this. His immediate task
was to get to Santa Fe with his army and put the Mexican authorities
(namely one Governor-General Manuel Armijo) out of business.

Meanwhile, draped wretchedly along the banks of the Missouri River
from what is now Omaha to Council Bluffs, nearly seven thousand of
God's "chosen people" huddled starving and freezing and awaiting
their chance to move west. They were Mormons, of the Church of Jesus
Christ of Latter-Day Saints, whose unusual beliefs habitually caused
them to be driven away—often violently—from wherever they tried to
settle down. But now they were leaving the United States, or so they
thought, for what was identified on most maps as "Unorganized Indian
Lands" that had been portrayed so enticingly by the explorer John C.
Frémont in his recently published journals.

A significant hurdle, however, was that the Mormons had no money
to get there. Their leader, Brigham Young, had approached President
Polk for funds, on the basis that the government was responsible for
ensuring that such a large number of citizens could have a peace-

ful place to live without being attacked all the time. Polk responded that the U.S. government was not in the business of handing out travel money to religious sects but then, seeing as how war had just broken out with Mexico, he offered to provide good military pay to five hundred Mormon men if they would form a battalion and march to California with Kearny's army. This offer was accepted, and the Mormon men began to assemble themselves at Fort Leavenworth for the long trek ahead. For his part, Polk was glad the Mormons were clearing out—the farther west they moved, the better. If only somehow he could get the Irish to go with them.

Two hundred miles south, in mid-May of 1846, a different kind of emigrant party was poised at the jump-off point at Independence, Missouri, beyond which lurked hostile Indians, barren plains, searing deserts, insuperable mountains, and a thousand other dangers known and unknown. These were the families of George and Jacob Donner and James and Margaret Reed, who a month earlier had left their own prosperity behind in Abraham Lincoln's Springfield, Illinois, and saddled up for the long haul west. Most of the early pioneers were hardscrabble and had undertaken the treacherous journey because they could see no future at home, but the Donners and the Reeds were substantial folk, so the irony remains that if only they'd stayed put and tended to business, the horrors that overtook them would not have happened.*

Like many of the other emigrants, Reed and the Donner brothers had immersed themselves in Frémont's appealing recital of the golden West and concocted their own dreams, some of epic magnitude. They had also read a popular new book by a young adventurer named Lansford W. Hastings, who had made several trips to California and who was touting a new, shorter route south of the Great Salt Lake. It was said to take hundreds of miles off the old Oregon Trail, and would come to be known infamously as the Hastings Cutoff.

By publishing this handbook Hastings was thought to be an expert on California, but in fact he was more of a Babbitt-like booster, a salesman

---

*While it was true that the majority of emigrants were running away from poverty, 1846 was also the first year that a notable number of professional men—lawyers, doctors, clergymen, and writers—made the journey to the Pacific.

aspiring to attract settlers to the Golden Gate where—as Sam Houston had done in Texas but with none of Houston's cachet—he intended to provoke a revolution and turn California into a separate republic, with himself as president, king, dictator, or whatever. The fact was that while Hastings may have traveled his so-called cutoff he had done so on horseback with pack mules, not with the large, burdensome, ox-drawn wagon caravans that the settlers traveled in. It was dangerous—deadly, as it turned out—not to have drawn the distinction.

The people in this story, Frémont, Kearny, the Mormons, and the Donners, were all going places in 1846, which has been rightly memorialized as the Year of Decision. Departing the Kansas frontier, the farthest bastion of civilization, they plunged into the savage wilds in different directions and for different reasons, like the vast hordes of emigrants, American and foreign alike, who would follow them, but nevertheless they were all headed in the same way, which was westward.

Fifty years down the road a respected historian named Frederick Jackson Turner became famous by formulating a thesis about their migration, which he entitled "The Significance of the Frontier in American History." Turner attempted to quantify the pioneer expansion scientifically, in the manner of Darwin—a notion that now sounds quaint—to account for American exceptionalism.

If Turner had chosen to focus on the year 1846 he would have hit the jackpot. It had taken 250 years for the frontier to creep from the Atlantic colonies across the Alleghenies, and westward again across the Mississippi, about nine hundred miles in all. But by the 1840s a cyclone of events and conditions had whipped up a stupendous westward shift, fueled by the recent arrival of so many Europeans who were raised in places where land ownership was all but impossible. It was becoming that way, too, for many Americans: cotton, tobacco, sugar, hemp, and other cash crops had driven up the price of land while at the same time wearing out the soil, but word was out through Frémont and others that the West offered bountiful land for the taking—and with it the chance to begin a new life, free of persecutions and restrictions. The pioneers accepted the challenge. Some, like the Mormons, were fleeing from everyday Christian opinion that was pushing and threatening them. Others succumbed to population pressure; for still others, the new frontier drew them out of their old land to a new land with smiles and waves and endless promise.

And as the pioneers made this great leap, historian Turner postulated, they soon discarded many of the European characteristics and institutions that had been culturally ingrained since colonial society and developed for themselves a distinctly new American personality characterized by rugged individualism, tenacity, suspicion of authority, mistrust of government—to put it bluntly, they became less civilized. Much of this was doubtless true, considering the hostile and violent environment they had entered, and goes far in explaining why, for example, mountain men often scalped their slain enemies, same as the Indians did.

Whether Turner's thesis can be sustained is a matter of conjecture. By the turn of the nineteenth century the days of the frontier had passed, and other elements began to infiltrate and make an impact on the American psyche. But certainly today there are still important features of the national spirit that were driven by and molded from the frontier mentality.

Kearny's march is more than just a metaphor for the great western advance of 1846; it was an astonishingly difficult, daring, and heroic adventure within an overarching movement, led by Frémont and his fellow explorers and including the trek of the Mormons and the Donners and other wagon trains inexorably bound to cross the continent's last earthly frontier—a voyage that ultimately shaped the extent, affluence, and character of the United States of America.

CHAPTER TWO

Mr. Polk Gets His War

By the 1840s, America was writhing with energy and excitement propelled by two interlocking concepts that would tear the country apart twenty years on. The first was African slavery, which had reached American shores more than two hundred years earlier on a Dutch ship that arrived in Virginia with the first few of some 645,000 tribal Africans who were originally distributed throughout all thirteen colonies, and later, after the Revolution, in the various states. But by the early 1800s further importation of slaves was made illegal by an act of Congress, and northern states began to abolish the practice, freeing their slaves or selling them for servitude in the South.

This left the balance of the bondsmen, nearly three million of them by then, confined in the thirteen southern states, and mostly occupied in the cultivation and production of sugar, tobacco, rice, and foremostly cotton. By the 1840s a small but vocal organized abolition movement from the North was haranguing for their release; this, in turn, began to create a dangerous friction between the two sections of the country.

The second concept roiling in the minds of many Americans was what a New York journalist named John O'Sullivan had recently described as "manifest destiny." This notion embodied the belief—some even claimed it as a divine right—that U.S. citizens should accrete westward across the entire continent, spreading their culture, their economy, and their rule. Never mind that there remained a great number of Native Americans populating those vast regions since time immemorial, and also that the lands in question—from Oregon to Colorado, from New Mexico to California—were claimed by long-standing entitlements to the governments of Mexico and Great Britain. Nevertheless, according to the theory, manifest destiny trumped all.

Into these interesting and risky times, when U.S. congressmen were fighting duels over the slave question and ordinarily sane and sober citizens were running around shouting "Fifty-four Forty or fight!,"* stepped the newly elected U.S. president James K. Polk, who took office in March 1845. At forty-nine, Polk became the youngest president yet to assume office, an event that seemed to set off tremors reverberating to this day among historians who routinely describe him as a misanthrope who "didn't like people," or much of anything else except "politics." They saw "a tendency toward quick and rigid judgment" somehow reflected in his "probing blue eyes deep-set under dark brows" and a "narrowness of outlook" in his "powerful jaw that jutted from his countenance."

Just to show that the political climate then wasn't any better, and possibly worse, than today's unhappy partisanship, the opposition political party branded Polk in speeches and newspapers as "bland," "cold," "unimaginative," "strait-laced," "mediocre," "conniving," and "mendacious," and their electioneering slogan was a scoffing: "Who is James K. Polk?"

All right, just who *was* James K. Polk, the eleventh American president? The question is important because without him the citizens of Houston, Dallas, Los Angeles, San Francisco, Denver, Salt Lake City, Phoenix, Las Vegas, and points in between, would today quite possibly be governed by a regime in Mexico City, and the good residents of Seattle, Cheyenne, Boise, Butte, and Portland might likely be, well, Canadians. Those were the stakes, and stakes were high, even considering that many of these aforementioned place-names existed just barely or not at all when James Polk took office.

But the man Polk had a vision of America, as did his mentor, Andrew Jackson, that was as sweeping as the great prairies of the West. He saw the nation as a grand expanding panorama filled with appalling risks and soaring promise, and with wealth and happiness as its God-given design. For all the blandness and unimaginativeness his detractors laid

---

*An allusion to the degree of latitude, 54°40', in the Oregon Territory beyond which they would rather go to war with England than concede.

upon him, Polk saw an America from coast to coast, where many others saw only a vast uninhabitable wilderness, and his instincts told him that if he did not act it would likely be lost to the United States for the foreseeable future and possibly for all time. But the mere mention of attaining new lands from Mexico and creating new territories or states immediately caused trouble. Not only would such acquisitions be nothing less than outright thievery—"the biggest land-grab," in fact, said one, "since the czar took Siberia"—but, worse, they would lead to an expansion of slavery.

Polk was a transplanted North Carolinian whose fourth-generation Scots-Irish family in 1806 moved across the Appalachians to middle Tennessee—which was then considered to be the American "frontier"—when he was eleven. The Polks had come to America in the late 1700s, among the first great immigration since the landing of the Massachusetts Pilgrims and Virginia Cavaliers a century earlier, as one of the many British families who arrived in the mid-Atlantic states to escape the poverty brought on by imperial policies in the British Highland regions. These Borderers, as they were known, brought with them skills in farming or mechanics and the ethic of hard work, self-sufficiency, and independence and years later would form the core of soldiery in the War of 1812, the Mexican War, and, of course, the Civil War.

The Polks were farmers, like most southerners of the day, and once in the fertile bottomland of Tennessee soon went into the cotton-growing business along with their neighbors, among them Andrew Jackson. Since cotton required slaves, they began acquiring some. Over time the Polks—there were half a dozen families of Polks in and around Columbia, Tennessee—began to prosper and erect elegant plantation homes on or near the fertile Duck River. James's father prospered even more by engaging in land speculation, was elected a county judge, started a bank, and became close friends with the towering Jackson, who would soon be off on his own wild political ride.

Apparently Polk came by his political conservatism honestly; the Polk clan, James in particular, were committed Jeffersonians, opposing Alexander Hamilton's notion of a large central government, high tariffs, and the spending of citizens' tax money on "internal improvements," which were what government projects such as roads, canals, river clearing, and the like were then called.

At an early age, young James endured a life of ill health, which kept him frail and fraught with abdominal pains. These were eventually diagnosed as urinary stones, but the state of medicine being what it was a cure was risky and far from certain, and until the age of seventeen he endured his ailment at home, with little or no formal schooling. Finally, in 1812, the pain had grown so acute that his father sent him to Philadelphia to a well-known surgeon. It was an eight-hundred-mile trip in the back of a covered wagon over potted roads, but scarcely had his caravan entered Kentucky than James was seized by a "paroxysm" so terrible that it was decided to find a surgeon immediately rather than continue on to Pennsylvania.

The man they selected, Dr. Ephraim McDowell, was also a surgeon of some note, but the operation was daunting, nevertheless. First, anesthetics had not been invented, so the boy would have to undergo the procedure with only some brandy to help dull the pain. A description of the operation itself, though successful, is enough to make one blanch; suffice it to say that when it was over Polk recuperated but was apparently left either sterile or impotent since he fathered no children. This last result has been used by some of his detractors to explain various of Polk's less attractive character traits, including his mistrust and political vindictiveness.

He was, however, at last able to attend school and was enrolled in several private academies at which he excelled in Latin, Greek, mathematics, history, and the classics before finally crossing the mountains to the University of North Carolina, from which he graduated in 1818 with honors and as class valedictorian. From there he went to Nashville to study or "read" law under the wonderfully named Felix Grundy, a "giant of the criminal bar," former congressman, justice of the state supreme court, and future U.S. attorney general.

By 1820 Polk had completed his law studies and was admitted to the Tennessee bar, and Grundy had secured for him the job of chief clerk of the Tennessee Senate, which gave him a useful education in the parliamentary system. Those were heady days in Nashville legal circles, with not only Grundy and Andrew Jackson as associates, but

Sam Houston before he gained fame and fortune in Texas, as well as a young frontiersman named Davy Crockett who had recently been elected to the Tennessee legislature. Polk also joined the Tennessee state militia—the same organization that enabled Andrew Jackson's rise to fame at the Battle of New Orleans—attaining, in time, the rank of colonel.

The steps one takes that later bring great life-changing events are often imperceptible at the time, and so it was with Polk, in 1823, when he supported Andrew Jackson for the U.S. Senate. Though Polk probably could not have known it then, the national office soon gave the hero of the Battle of New Orleans and the Creek Indian wars widespread stature to sustain his eventual election to the U.S. presidency, and Polk as Jackson's friend, aide, protégé, and confidant went riding right along on Old Hickory's coattails.

The following year Jackson made his run against the dour John Quincy Adams of Massachusetts. He was leading in both the popular vote and the electoral college but then, in a move that infuriated many, the powerful senator Henry Clay of Kentucky persuaded his state's delegation to cast its electoral votes for Adams, even though the state legislature had instructed the delegates to vote for Jackson. Thus in 1825 Adams became president instead of Jackson and the furor was only exacerbated when, shortly afterward, Adams named Clay as his secretary of state in what was roundly condemned as "the corrupt bargain."

Meantime Polk had gotten himself elected to the U.S. Congress and soon became its Speaker of the House. By then Polk had acquired a wife, Sara, and considerable plantation lands in Mississippi and western Tennessee, complete with the slaves to man them. It is said that his policy toward his slaves was benign, and in various speeches in Congress he referred to slavery—as had Thomas Jefferson—as an "evil," though he never voted for any measure to ban the institution. In fact, when abolitionists began to bombard Congress with petitions, generating lengthy and acrimonious debates, Polk was institutional in imposing a gag rule on future petitions or debate, which naturally infuriated the abolitionists. As were practically all Americans of his period he was a racist, the present-day term for a concept that, in Polk's age, had not yet developed.

The following national election saw Andrew Jackson turn John Adams into a one-term president and set the stage for Polk to run himself for that highest of national offices, which he did, successfully, in 1844, beating out Jackson's old nemesis Henry Clay. What cinched it for the forty-nine-year-old Polk was that he came out for annexing the Republic of Texas as a U.S. state, while his opponents did not. America was clearly on the make at this point, and would not be denied, even though Mexico had threatened war if the United States granted Texas statehood.

Opposition to admitting Texas to the Union might have been a conscientious decision for Martin Van Buren and Clay, running again for president in 1844, but it was impolitic. Already, at that stage, the enemies of slavery had begun to suspect a secret ploy by crafty southerners to consolidate and expand their political power by adding Texas as a slave state, and at least one Senate opponent, Missouri's Thomas Hart Benton, believed it was "an intrigue . . . to get the Southern states out of the Union." But most Americans did not believe this; they were enthusiastic about the idea of having a territory so great as Texas as part of the United States. And most southerners especially so, because they assumed it would be a counterweight to the inclusion of more northern or midwestern free territories, which could tip the political balance of the Senate against them.

It is worth a brief digression here to trace a series of fateful events that conspired to pitchfork Texas into the Union, Polk into the White House, and a bountiful and seemingly boundless America to the edge of destruction by civil war.

By the early 1840s the once negligible American abolitionist movement had built up a considerable head of steam and was fraying nerves on both sides of the Mason-Dixon line. What had begun as an initiative to demonstrate the moral wrongness of slavery had developed into a multi-pronged political enterprise exerting pressure on all three branches of government as well as on the population as a whole, so that ordinary citizens were forced to choose sides, often against their wishes.

Into this fractious atmosphere came Captain Robert F. Stockton of Princeton, New Jersey, a forty-six-year-old naval officer, sometime politician, and abolitionist,* whose grandfather had been a signer of the Declaration of Independence. In 1841 Stockton convinced then U.S. president John Tyler to let him oversee construction and command of what he claimed would be the world's most powerful warship. Accordingly, two years later the USS *Princeton* was launched at the Philadelphia Navy Yard, a 164-foot, thousand-ton screw-sail steamship of the line sporting within her weapons' system two monster wrought-iron cannons named, respectively, Oregon and Peacemaker, each weighing more than 20,000 pounds and capable of throwing a 225-pound shot more than five miles.† The ship and one of its guns, the Oregon, had been designed by the brilliant Swede John Ericsson, famous later during the Civil War for building the USS *Monitor*; the Peacemaker gun, however, had been designed by Stockton himself, who, against all of Ericsson's good advice, had failed to strap metal bands, or hoops, around its breach, the weakest point of muzzle-loading cannon. Not only that, but while the Oregon had been proofed (fired) at least a hundred times, Stockton merely towed Peacemaker down the Delaware on a raft and discharged her five times before pronouncing her fit for duty. This did not bode well, considering the gun would have to withstand multiple firings of 50-pound charges of powder.

Meantime, efforts to bring Texas into the Union had been proceeding apace with President Tyler's new secretary of state Abel Upshur handling the delicate negotiations with the Texans, who had been leaning toward an alliance with Great Britain and/or France, neither of which was anxious to see a piece of property so large as Texas become a part of the United States and were offering inducements to prevent it. The American abolition movement was also trying to prevent it, for fear that acquisition of Texas would only make the southern slave empire stronger and harder to break up, and thus politicians were forced to walk an ever thinning line. Secretary Upshur, however, a courtly and diplomatic Virginian, had worked behind the scenes with Texas

---

*In the 1820s Stockton was instrumental in acquiring territorial rights to what became the country of Liberia on the west coast of Africa, to which the abolitionist American Colonization Society hoped to deport former slaves after they were emancipated.

†The steamboat had been invented a quarter century earlier, and the coal-burning oceangoing *Princeton* was a vast improvement, driven not by cumbersome side or rear paddlewheels but by a giant bronze propeller (screw) 14 feet in diameter, which was far more efficient.

representatives and key members of Congress on a transition he hoped would ruffle the fewest feathers over the slavery question.

Which made it all the more noteworthy when, on February 28, 1844, Upshur stepped aboard the USS *Princeton* along with several hundred other Washington dignitaries, socialites, and their ladies for an afternoon's cruise down the Potomac so that Captain Stockton could demonstrate the fighting prowess of his mighty battleship. Among the guests in addition to Upshur were President Tyler himself; his secretary of the navy, Thomas Gilmer; and Missouri's "Lion of the Senate," Thomas Hart Benton. Also aboard were seventy-six-year-old Dolley Madison, widow of the fourth U.S. president; Tyler's twenty-three-year-old fiancée, Julia Gardiner; and her father, Colonel David Gardiner of New York.

Right above Mount Vernon Stockton ordered Peacemaker fired and the crowd oohed and aahed when the big spherical shot smacked the river surface three miles down and skip-bounced out of sight. On the trip back upriver, Stockton ordered the gun fired again. Fortunately most of the passengers were below having lunch when, shortly after three p.m., the *Princeton* shuddered with a violent explosion—Peacemaker had blown up, just as Ericsson had feared, and the carnage was dreadful. A 2,000-pound iron chunk of the breech had swept the deck, leaving a bloody jumble of bodies and parts of bodies. Among the nine dead were Secretaries Upshur and Gilmer, the navy's chief of construction, the U.S. chargé d'affaires to Belgium, David Gardiner, and the president's own valet. A score of others were badly injured, including Stockton, who had severe powder burns on his face and all of his hair singed off. Nevertheless, the captain (of whom we shall hear much more later) ironically managed to deflect responsibility for the mishap onto Ericsson, who had warned him in the first place that the gun was not safe.

Among the consequences of the accident was that Tyler replaced his dead secretary of state with a fellow southerner, Senator John C. Calhoun of South Carolina, whose most immediate task was to finish out Upshur's negotiations for the incorporation of Texas into the United States.

Calhoun was one of the giants of the Senate, along with Benton, Daniel Webster, and Henry Clay. A graduate of Yale and a lawyer, he was once known as "Young Hercules" and later the "Cast-Iron Man" of the Senate, but as he grew older Calhoun also became something of a crank whose hard-line views on slavery kept abolitionists in an uproar all over the world.

In the years following the Revolutionary War, slavery—what the South called its "peculiar institution" and what Thomas Jefferson described as "a necessary evil"—appeared to be on the road toward extinction. It was basically a wasteful, costly, and inefficient system, in addition to the moral aspects, which were just then beginning to come into question. But then, in 1793, Eli Whitney invented the cotton gin, which meant that short-staple cotton, the variety capable of being grown over practically all of the South, could be proficiently cleaned (ginned) of its seeds and debris, which heretofore had consumed so much human labor that it wasn't worth the effort. In 1807 Congress had passed a law banning further importation of African slaves, and by 1810 most northern states had abolished the practice of slavery altogether. There were, however, by that time, already some one million slaves in the United States, and the newfound bonanza of cotton growing revived the practice and produced an extraordinary demand for their labor in the fields.

Thus Calhoun's home state of South Carolina went from producing fewer than a hundred thousand pounds of cotton in the year the Whitney gin was invented to exporting more than 30 million pounds twenty years later. Furthermore, this story was being repeated all over the South as "men whose fathers were pioneers or subsistence farmers were suddenly able to amass fortunes rivaling those of the wealthiest lowcountry rice barons." But because cotton growing was among the most labor intensive of agricultural crops, slavery, which had seemed to be on the way out, became very definitely in, a fact that was reflected in the sharp uptick in slave prices.

And as the abolitionists' cries predictably became more shrill, they were answered in the main by firebrands such as Calhoun, whose rhetoric became ever more bellicose.* Far from Jefferson's almost apologetic notion of slavery as a necessary evil, Calhoun actually began defending it as a "positive good," arguing that it raised blacks from their primitive

---

*At the height of the Nullification Crisis of 1832, when at Calhoun's behest South Carolina was threatening to secede from the Union over what it believed were unfair tariffs, President Jackson threatened severe repercussions, at which point Senator Benton chimed in, "When Andrew Jackson starts talking about hanging, men begin looking for ropes!"

natural state by giving them civilization, intelligence, and Christianity, as well as allowing them to serve a useful purpose.

Infuriating as these notions were to the abolitionists, it was nothing compared with the furor that erupted when Calhoun expressed them, and more, in an infamous and somewhat threatening letter to the British minister Sir Richard Pakenham, in which he accused England of trying to coerce Texas into abolishing slavery as a condition for aid or annexation by Great Britain and stated that an American acquisition of Texas was necessary to protect southern slavery from British meddling. In support of his argument that slavery was a "desirable" condition for blacks, Calhoun claimed that freed blacks in northern states had twice the ratio of deafness and dumbness, retardation, even insanity as those in the South.

When the contents of the letter got out reaction was swift and predictable. Where the late, unfortunate Upshur had tried diligently to sweep the matter of Texas slavery under the rug, Calhoun used the occasion to turn it into an inflammatory issue, not only in U.S. political circles but in international forums as well, since the abolitionist movement had in fact been born in Great Britain, which had only recently freed its slaves. And of course the news came as a direct affront to the Mexicans, who not only had also outlawed slavery but claimed their own proprietary interest in what the United States was calling Texas.

The upshot was that national support for Texas annexation evaporated, the treaty was rejected by an embarrassed Senate, and Calhoun was roundly denounced for his intemperate remarks and outlandish opinions. Nevertheless, the question of what to do about Texas hung over the nation like a pall, and soon worries reemerged that England or France or both might suddenly snatch her up with lies and promises. It wasn't a year from the election of Polk when both houses of Congress agreed to annex Texas by joint resolution, which might not have been the right protocol but it got the job done, even at the expense of Mexico's threat of war.

The abolitionists naturally put up a howl because Texas came in as a slave state, and the acrimony between the antislavers and the South had been irrevocably ratcheted up by Calhoun's fiery rhetoric. All of which leads us back to Captain Stockton's decision to ignore shipbuilder Ericsson's warnings about the megacannon Peacemaker that

killed Secretary Upshur and his nonconfrontational ways and gave us
the volatile Secretary Calhoun, who set the boiler to going with threats
and rumblings of secession from the Southland.

Southern secession certainly wasn't what Polk wanted, nor was war with
Mexico, but he would take it as it came, for he had a greater plan—what
Polk called his "great measures," which he shared with his new secre-
tary of the navy, the eminent historian George Bancroft.

There were four of them, constituting Polk's vision for America, he
told the startled Bancroft one afternoon, "striking his thigh for empha-
sis." The fact that he achieved them all during the single presidential
term he chose to serve is remarkable, for they were indeed significant,
even colossal, goals fraught with many dangers.

First, Polk told Bancroft, he would lower the so-called Tariff of
Abominations that had nearly caused South Carolina to secede from
the Union. This he hoped would defuse some of the hostility and antag-
onism that had been building between the two sections of the country.

Second, he would establish an independent treasury, instead of
re-creating Nicholas Biddle's National Bank in Philadelphia (the precursor to today's Federal Reserve), which had caused so much controversy and angst during Jackson's administrations; nor would he revert
to putting the government's funds in what were called "pet banks,"
which had stirred up endless troubles during the Tyler administration.

Third, Polk said, he would get the British out of the Oregon Territory, which comprised what are presently the states of Oregon, Washington, and parts of Idaho, Montana, and Wyoming, as well as a huge
slab of land in what the British thought was Canada. The British and
the United States had agreed to jointly hold this vast place, but Polk
was concerned that the mere presence of Englishmen in that part of
the country would prove not only unhealthy but permanent. In recent
memory Americans had fought two wars with the British, in 1776 and
in 1812, and feelings then toward the mother country were anything
but amiable.

Lastly, Polk informed Bancroft, he intended to acquire the California province from Mexico. This of course would be a tall order, for the
Mexicans would never give it up cheaply, but Polk's vision called for an

America stretching from the Atlantic to the Pacific. He could almost feel the nation growing, he told Bancroft, as immigrants poured in and babies were born. From a mere 4 million in 1790, the year of the first census, to 10 million in 1820, to nearly 20 million by the time of Polk's presidency, the American population was expanding, people were moving westward, and they needed room.

And California needed the United States, as well, Polk felt. There were barely five thousand whites living in the province, most of them men who were not taking much advantage of their bounteous territory. Here is the way Richard Henry Dana Jr. dismissed them in his adventure *Two Years Before the Mast* (first printed in 1840): "The Californians are an idle, thriftless people, and can make nothing for themselves. The country abounds in grapes, yet they buy, at a great price, bad wine made in Boston." They received little in the way of assistance from the government in Mexico City, which in any case was too far away to do much good. And ominously, it was known that both Great Britain and France had an eye on the province and were looking for some opportunity to acquire it.

In the summer of his first year in office Polk's world turned bellicose over the Mexican and Oregon questions. In July, he had his secretary of state, James Buchanan, send a note to British minister Pakenham offering to divide the Oregon Territory once and for all and settle on the 49th parallel as the borderline. It wasn't 54°40' but at least he wouldn't have to fight over it. Pakenham turned him down flat in a reply Polk found highly insulting, and without even sending the offer to the foreign office in London, which was then eight years into the reign of Queen Victoria.*

Polk's response was to order Buchanan to send another note to Pakenham withdrawing the offer, which brought the matter much closer to hostilities, since Pakenham had made no counteroffer, and thus the issue became a casus belli. Buchanan resisted such a course, espe-

---

*Pakenham's relations with the Americans were consistently less than cordial. Possibly this had to do with the fate of his favorite cousin, Major General Sir Edward Pakenham, who was slain by Andrew Jackson's troops in 1815 during the Battle of New Orleans.

cially since war with Mexico over Texas seemed imminent. But Polk ordered his secretary of state to deliver the note anyway and stop worrying about war with Britain, because the message in the note "is right in itself."

"Foreign powers do not seem to appreciate the true character of our government," he wrote in his diary.

It would not be the last time the timid Buchanan tried to thwart Polk. He can probably be forgiven on the grounds that the post of secretary of state is a diplomatic one and by its very nature seeks to avoid conflict through diplomacy rather than force of arms. But Polk was a stubborn customer, especially since he grew up under the wings of Andrew Jackson, who had a dedicated hatred for the British after they killed almost his entire family one way or the other during the Revolution, and then had the temerity to invade New Orleans in the War of 1812 when he was in charge there. British foreign policy then could most charitably be described as shifty, with a special talent in meddling and intrigue, and Polk, through his association with Jackson, had been made well aware of it.*

With their lust for colonies to exploit and the world's largest navy, the British were always looking for opportunity, and during this time they sensed several in the new world in addition to their stake in the Oregon Territory. The Republic of Texas, for instance, had been a possibility, until the Americans annexed it as a state. But the British were also very much aware of the fragile condition of Alta (upper) California and its tenuous ties to the government at Mexico City. Adding that rich and fertile land to their colonial string of pearls would be a coup of the first magnitude, or so it was thought by many Americans.

In the meantime, after consulting with his cabinet, in August of 1845 Polk had ordered Major General Zachary Taylor to move his 2,500-man army into Texas and station it at Corpus Christi. Taylor at first had seemed to Polk an ideal choice to lead the army. A descendant of *Mayflower* pilgrims, the sixty-one-year-old Kentuckian was a thirty-eight-year veteran of the army, having served in the War of 1812,

---

*For instance, Frémont's wife, Jessie, wrote that Rose Greenhow, whose husband was head of the Spanish department of the U.S. foreign service and who would later become an infamous Confederate spy, was in the employ of the British ambassador.

the Seminole War, and the Black Hawk War, in which he had captured Black Hawk himself. But most attractive of all to Polk was that the poker-faced Episcopalian was apolitical, or so it seemed. That would change, leading to a dramatic outbreak of bad feelings between the two men.

Six months later, in February 1846, Polk told Taylor to move his army 150 miles farther south, to the northwest bank of the Rio Grande, across from the city of Matamoros, and if anybody attacked him—or even *looked like* they were about to attack him—to repel them and press on into Mexico. This was of course deep into the disputed territory, and the Mexicans had already threatened war so many times it was beginning to sound hollow. Polk fully expected an attack, although he cautioned Taylor that "it is not designed, in our present relations with Mexico, that you should treat her as an enemy." To the Mexicans, the mere shift of Taylor's army was tantamount to war, since in their quasi-schizoid concept of diplomacy following their defeat in the Texas independence uprising, they continued to insist that they still owned *all* of Texas, while at the same time accepting that the border between Texas and the rest of Mexico was the Nueces River, some 150 miles *north* of the Rio Grande.

To mollify the Mexicans, Polk had earlier dispatched an emissary—the suave, urbane, Spanish-fluent former Louisiana congressman John Slidell—to Mexico City with instructions to offer Mexican president José Herrera up to $40 million for all the lands north of a line beginning where the mouth of the Rio Grande empties into the Gulf of Mexico, then westward to the present site of El Paso, Texas, and thence continuing westward to the Pacific.

President Polk thought he had a good shot. First, the New Mexico and California territories were wild, raw land, most of it uncharted, much even unknown, and inhabited mostly by savage tribes. That was about as much as they knew. Second, Mexico was almost beyond bankrupt, and Polk's $40 million was worth somewhere between $500 billion and a trillion dollars in today's money, depending on the calculation method. And third, in the brief twenty years since gaining independence from Spain, Mexico seemed reduced to a state of eternal war and instability, having fought half a dozen civil conflicts and changing governments no fewer than thirty-eight times in twenty-three years. In Polk's view, his was a fair offer: Mexico was broke and barely able to govern itself, let alone care for her far-flung northern territories.

It turned out he was wrong—at least about his offer having a good shot. By the time Slidell arrived in Mexico City in the autumn of 1845 the mood had changed. President Herrera was about to be ousted in favor of President Mariano Paredes, who was not only unsympathetic to the idea of parting with Mexican lands but was decidedly anti-gringo.* One good reason was that Slidell's mission somehow had been leaked to the Mexican press, which published stories complaining, as one paper did, that in "a few months more, we shall have no country at all."

So Slidell's reception was not exactly cordial. In fact he had little to do but wait around all day and write letters such as his final one to Polk on March 12, 1846, when he informed the U.S. president that "nothing is to be done with these people, until they have been chastised."

This was not long in coming. As Polk had surmised, Mexican soldiers could not resist the temptation to attack U.S. soldiers along the Rio Grande. They did this barely a month after Slidell departed Mexico, on April 24, when a thousand-man detachment of Mexican cavalry crossed the river and massacred a sixty-man U.S. patrol, killing eleven, wounding others, and taking twenty-six prisoners.

That was more than enough for "Old Rough and Ready" Taylor, who sent a dispatch to Washington on April 15, 1846, announcing, "Hostilities may now be considered as commenced," and straightaway pitched into the main Mexican army at Matamoros. Communications were still fairly primitive in those times, Taylor's dispatch being first sent by horse courier to Matamoros, then put aboard a steamboat bound for New Orleans, where it was relayed more than a thousand miles and, two weeks later on large sailing ships around the tip of Florida by what were called "fast mails," to President Polk at Washington City, which is what the District of Columbia was then called.

Polk had already decided to declare war on Mexico, even before Taylor's message arrived, but, unquestionably, at least in his own mind,

*Both Herrera and Paredes were generals in the Mexican army. In fact, most of the Mexican presidents of the era were or had been generals, and the transfer of power in Mexico, unlike that in the United States, more often than not was the result of a military coup.

it gave him the necessary casus belli that Navy Secretary Bancroft, the noted Harvard-educated historian, had told him he needed not only to fend off the inevitable European protests and remonstrations but also to be on the right side of history for posterity's sake.

With this in mind, on Sunday, May 10, 1846, Polk sat down at his desk in the White House to prepare his war message to Congress the following day. He had been in office scarcely fourteen months and until now his official duties had included primarily such mundane chores as receiving a platoon of aging veterans from the War of 1812 or a delegation of Potawatomi Indians in full paint and war bonnets.

But now, having just turned fifty years of age, President Polk found himself drawing up a document that would send tens of thousands of Americans into harm's way—some, many perhaps, never to return—a sobering consideration to be sure. Furthermore, as it happened to be a Sunday, in midmorning Polk put down his war message half finished and headed off to the Presbyterian church with Mrs. Polk and an entourage. It was apparently not something that went so far as to seem un-Christian to him, but Polk later regretted to his diary that the stern duty "made it necessary for me to spend the Sabbath in the manner I have."

News of the Mexican attack quickly spread and set the American public to seething, but not everyone was happy with Polk's decision to go to war. Among them was none other than John C. Calhoun, who had nearly started the Civil War several decades too early when he threatened to secede his state over an abominable tariff.

Because of Calhoun's august position within the Senate, Polk had summoned him to inform him of his intentions, but when the South Carolinian read the preamble to Polk's war message (he claimed to be scandalized that it placed the blame solely on the Mexicans, which he said offended his sense of honor) he failed to vote for it. In fact, what made Calhoun anxious was the distinct possibility of two intertwining results he envisioned growing out of a war of conquest with Mexico. The first was the "centralizing and consolidating tendencies in the [federal] government" that would further undermine states' rights and, even more perilous, the possibility that "a sectional struggle [would develop] over the conquered territory." A quick glance over Calhoun's illustrious career tells us that he could change his views as quickly and as often as a chameleon changes its colors, but it turned out in this case he was right on both counts.

Polk, meanwhile, was further vexed by the so-called Conscience Whigs, men who truly believed that the war was unnecessary and unjust because the issues might still have been negotiated peacefully. For their moralizations, Polk reserved his special scorn.

Next day in Congress Calhoun argued passionately against a war but wound up abstaining when it came time to vote. To his diary, Polk remarked, "There is more selfishness and less principle among members of Congress than I had any conception of, before I became president of the U.S."

Thomas Hart Benton, still clinging to his position that the Texas issue was merely a subterfuge to spread slavery, voted for the declaration anyway, as did Henry Clay, and it passed with only two nay votes. On Monday, May 11, 1846, Mr. Polk officially had his war.

CHAPTER THREE

The Pathfinder

Zachary Taylor wasted little time avenging the April massacre of his reconnaissance patrol. Nor did the newly arrived Mexican army commander, Mariano Arista, wait for the ceremony of a formal declaration of war; immediately he crossed his 4,000-man army over the Rio Grande and arrayed it for battle near the town of Palo Alto, on the road to Matamoros, near the present-day city of Brownsville, Texas.

On May 8, 1846, Taylor's 2,000 U.S. soldiers encountered this Mexican force astride the highway.

The Americans were a rough bunch, for the most part army regulars, with a large percentage of unruly Irish and German immigrants and a detachment of Texas Rangers, but they were officered by some of the best in the business, including West Pointers Braxton Bragg, Ulysses Grant, George Meade, Kirby Smith, John Sedgwick, and George Sykes—each of whom would rise to the rank of corps commander or higher during the Civil War.*

Taylor, Old Rough and Ready, was a no-nonsense commander, wealthy,† grizzled, aggrieved,‡ experienced, and incidentally against Texas annexation in the first place.

---

*Several hundred of these Irish deserted during the Mexican campaign, ostensibly on grounds that the Americans were prejudiced against Catholicism, which the Irish shared with the Mexicans. What befell them is the subject of an interesting footnote down the road.

†He grew up on a 10,000-acre plantation in Kentucky and also owned immense cotton plantations in Louisiana and Mississippi, one of which would be burned during the Civil War by Union troops after his son, General Richard Taylor, sided with the Confederacy.

‡Against his wishes, his daughter Sarah had married young Jefferson Davis, a West

Nevertheless, here he was, squared off against Arista, the hand-some, blond, aristocratic, American-educated Mexican commander, who had formed his superior-sized army into a line of battle a mile wide and a quarter mile away across a plain of dense chaparral. And there both sides remained as the sun crossed straight-up noon and began to sink into the hills, turning the situation into some sort of Mexican standoff, while each side sought to resolve its own dilemma.

Taylor had wanted to orchestrate a bayonet charge, confident that even though he was outnumbered two to one his tough, disciplined men would prevail. His problem was that Arista had spread out his larger force in a line so long Taylor's men simply couldn't contend with it; even if they crushed the center, the sides would close in on them.

Arista had also wanted to attack in strength, Alamo style, but when he looked at the thick chaparral, he realized he could never control his infantry over such terrain.* Ultimately he decided to wait for develop-ments, which were not long in coming.

Taylor had honed his twelve-pounder gunners into something called "flying artillery," a European invention in which the horse-drawn can-noneers would rush to a spot, quickly set up and get off a few rounds, then haul off again before the enemy guns could get a fix on them. Under the expert command of Brevet Major Samuel Ringgold (who was mortally wounded later that day) the flying artillery soon had hundreds of Mexicans falling all around General Arista. Frustrated, the Mexican general sent out a detachment of cavalry to silence them, but his horse-men soon encountered a "hollow square" of the Eighth U.S. Infantry Regiment (another European invention, of the Napoleonic era),[†] which unhorsed the majority of them.

Pointer now serving under Taylor on the Mexican border. Not long after the marriage in 1835 she died of yellow fever at Davis's plantation at Davis Bend on the Mississippi.

*For those unacquainted with southwestern chaparral, it is a combination of dense, fairly low scrub, often composed of dried prickly or thorny bushes and sage, small bent trees such as mesquite, cacti, and a host of smaller plants and flowers. Its favored resi-dents seem to be rattlesnakes, lizards, and coyotes.

†To form a "hollow square," an infantry regiment (usually 400 to 800 strong) would be given a series of officers' commands to move ranks in order that they formed, well, a hollow square, with rows of riflemen facing all four sides, so that it was theoretically impossible to surprise it, or to attack a weak point. It was especially effective against cavalry charges.

Meanwhile, U.S. riflemen were dropping Arista's men in their tracks, while the Mexicans were unable to avenge their tormentors because of faulty gunpowder.* Mercifully all the shooting set the chaparral on fire, which blanketed the battlefield with so much gun smoke that the fight was called off by both sides as though night had fallen. Before dawn the Mexicans withdrew a few miles back to a place called Resaca de la Palma. Unmercifully, a large number of Mexican wounded had been incinerated in the flames, and the once proud and exuberant Mexican Army of the North sat by its cooking fires that early morning contemplating the impending sunrise and not liking what it saw.

It is never an easy task to get soldiers to fight properly, and doubly hard when they have just been defeated. True, the Americans had not given Arista's men a thorough whipping at Palo Alto, but even the least experienced of them understood deep down that they had not won the day.

Thus it was with considerable apprehension, the following morning, that Arista's army, with the Rio Grande to its back and no bridge across, again looked north into the thick chaparral, and again beheld the blue-uniformed host of Taylor's American army marching toward them.

Likewise, Taylor noted that Arista's line was again intimidatingly long and the chaparral too thick for maneuvering an army across with any hope of organization. But this did not stop Old Rough and Ready. Against the best advice of nearly all his officers, he ordered a bayonet charge straight down the Matamoros highway.†

But first he ordered the artillery battery of the brave and unfortunate Major Ringgold, now commanded by Major Randolph Ridgely, to blow a hole through the Mexican center that rested on the roadway. No sooner had the cannons begun to fire than Ridgely and his men suddenly saw a troop of Mexican lancers bearing down upon them.‡ Ridgely managed to fire one gun point-blank into the head of the enemy

*The gunpowder was more volatile than they were used to, prone to explode, so they used less of it, thus putting themselves out of effective firing range.

†As the commanding general was holding an informal council of war that morning and advised by most of his officers to stay put and wait for reinforcements, some young subaltern walking past—nobody remembers who—sang out, "General, we whipped them yesterday, and we can whip them again." That settled it for Taylor.

‡While the Mexican infantry, composed mostly of illiterate Indians and mestizos, left much to be desired, the Mexican cavalry were arguably the best horsemen in the

column, then braced for the worst, but the leading Mexican horsemen went down like tenpins and the rest staggered off through the chaparral.

Taylor next ordered the Eighth Infantry Regiment to "Take those guns, and by God keep them!," which was done in short order with a bayonet charge down the road that also netted a Mexican general named La Vega, the news of which prompted Arista himself to come to the fighting front. He remained there but a short time, trying to rally his men before hightailing it south with the rest of his army and the Americans in hot pursuit. They did not stop at the Rio Grande but kept on going, drowning some three hundred in the process, until they reached Matamoros, minus approximately a hundred prisoners, a thousand killed and wounded, and twice that number of deserters.

For their part, the Americans had lost 34 killed and 113 wounded in the two days of fighting, and the Mexicans had been chased back across the Rio Grande. It was an auspicious beginning to a war that would only be formally declared three days later by Washington, but Taylor knew what all men know who rise to his military rank: it wouldn't always be this easy.

Nor was the "Oregon question" seeming to be easy for the Polk administration. As we recall, in July 1845, British ambassador Richard Pakenham had not only refused to accept Polk's offer to set the Oregon boundary at 49 degrees (roughly where it is today) instead of hundreds of miles farther north, as the American Fifty-four Forty or Fighters were demanding, but he declined even to submit the president's note to his superiors back in England.

Polk had then consulted his aging mentor, Andrew Jackson, who even on his deathbed continued to despise the British with a hatred that was almost indecent, receiving strong advice: "England with all her boast dare not go to war," roared Old Hickory. "No temporizing with Britain now!" However, during that long hot Washington summer of 1845 Buchanan, Polk's ever timorous secretary of state, began raising the issue of England's reaction to the declaration of war with

---

world, and their lancers, armed with razor-sharp eight-foot steel spears, were rightfully dreaded.

Mexico and wanted to know what he must say to the British and French ambassadors if they should ask if it was the United States' intention to annex California.

Polk replied that it was none of England's or France's business.

Buchanan countered that unless the United States made a pledge not to annex California, "You will have war with England as well as Mexico, and probably France also." To which the president replied that, before making any such pledge, "I would meet the war withEngland, France, or all of Christendom might wage, and stand and fight until the last man among us fell." Invoking the Monroe Doctrine, Polk further allowed that "neither as a citizen nor as President would I permit or tolerate any intermeddling of any European Powers on this continent."

It was a chancy situation, but throughout the year, and into early 1846, Polk hung tough, even after the British foreign minister ruminated that the president's intransigence could "finally lead to war itself" and well-founded reports began arriving of British warships headed for the North Pacific coast. Neither was Polk moved by a rumor that a Catholic priest had sailed from Ireland with 10,000 wretched British subjects escaping the potato famine, bound for settlement in California; nor by reports from the U.S. consul in San Francisco, Thomas O. Larkin, that British agents were urging Mexican authorities in California to subjugate American immigrants. In fact, these things seemed to solidify Polk's defiance. "If war comes with England," declared the president, "it will be their fault."

Since it is normally a national leader's worst nightmare to be fighting war on multiple fronts, Polk must have been pleasantly relieved when England finally blinked. The new Paredes government in Mexico in April 1846 had in fact offered the British the province of California in exchange for their financial assistance, but Lord Palmerston turned it down on grounds it would lead to war with the United States.

Apparently at some point it had become clear that Polk was no pushover, and British politicians, who were just beginning to enjoy the peace and prosperity of the Victorian age, concluded that owning *part* of something was better than the possibility of owning *all* of nothing, or than starting another expensive war halfway around the world, and so agreed to draw the partitioning lines for the Oregon Territory almost straight westward from what is now Lake of the Woods, Minnesota, to the San Juan Islands on the Pacific, so that Vancouver Island and everything north of there would be absorbed into British Canada.

Shortly thereafter, when the U.S. Senate ratified this by treaty, or agreement, with a vote of 41–14, Polk had fulfilled the first of his four Great Measures. He appeared to look upon it like filling in a giant jigsaw puzzle, suddenly and methodically adding to the United States what are now Oregon and Washington and more. Most of it was wild territory to be sure, and dangerous, but Polk had the vision to see it would not always be that way. So did another actor in this drama, the young army captain John Charles Frémont, who in the spring of 1846 was causing tremors in the West that would soon vibrate back to Washington and Mexico City.

It did not hurt that Frémont's wife, Benton's daughter Jessie, was a talented writer who undoubtedly tweaked his already enthralling story of life among strange and often hostile Indians, towering mountain majesties, mysterious alpine valleys, rushing rivers, and fertile purple plains, where the majority of citizens had been led to believe lay only what was called the Great American Desert. In any case, the adventures of Frémont were hailed far and wide.

It isn't hard to see why. Consider, for instance, this passage he wrote in the spring of 1844, traveling south again in California after his party had very nearly perished crossing the Sierra Nevada in the snows of winter.

"Our cavalcade made a strange and grotesque appearance, and it was impossible to avoid reflecting upon our position and composition in this remote solitude. Within two degrees of the Pacific Ocean; already far south of the latitude of Monterey; and still forced on south by a desert on one hand, and a mountain range on the other; guided by a civilized Indian, attended by two wild ones from the Sierra; a Chinook from the Columbia, and our own mixture of American, French, German—all armed; four or five languages heard at once; above a hundred horses and mules, half wild; American, Spanish, and Indian dresses and equipments intermingle—such was our composition. Our march was a sort of procession. Scouts ahead, and on the flanks; a front and rear division; the pack animals, baggage, and horned cattle in the centre; and the whole stretching a quarter of a mile along our dreary path. In this form we journey; looking more like we belonged to Asia than to the United States of America."

The public ate it up. His expeditions had earned Frémont the nickname Pathfinder, which various historians have pointed out was technically incorrect since he mostly followed western paths and trails already blazed by a handful of famed mountain men such as Jedediah Smith, Alexis Godey, and Kit Carson, who made their livings trapping and trading furs with Indians. This complaint might be valid if the sobriquet had been "Path*maker*." But it was not, and the fact is that Frémont did indeed find the paths others had made before him. His own fame rose, however, because of his abilities as a surveyor, botanist, geologist, zoologist, anthropologist, navigator, astronomer, and all-around jack-of-physical-sciences who could, and did, put to paper accurate longitudinal and latitudinal topographical maps, along with useful observations such as where to find water, firewood, and grassland for animals. This was what had never been done.

Until then, the vast spaces out to the Rocky Mountain basin and beyond were considered by most Americans the same way sailors viewed old nautical charts of distant oceans, where drawings of ferociously puffing winds were frequently accompanied with the inscription **Beyond here there be Dragons**. Because the report of Frémont's expeditions was issued by the Government Printing Office it was in the public domain and free for reprinting by U.S. newspapers—very many of which used the privilege—and ignited a virtual prairie fire of western migration into those heretofore mystical territories.

Frémont by then was in his early thirties, slender and strikingly handsome with piercing eyes, a lush dark beard, and a Gallic nose doubtless inherited from his father, a French wastrel who taught fencing, dancing, and languages and painted frescoes. In 1808 this Lothario had made off with Frémont's mother-to-be, an FFV from Richmond, after her elderly husband hired him to tutor her.* The couple fled to Savannah where in 1813 Frémont was born, and his father soon after died, leaving the family in reduced circumstances.

Frémont turned out to be a brilliant scholar but gross profligacy

*FFV is an abbreviation for First Families of Virginia, the southern equivalent to having arrived on the *Mayflower*.

led to his being kicked out of college before graduation. Still, he managed to land a job exploring and mapping former Cherokee lands in the Appalachian Mountains of Tennessee and Georgia with the famous topographer of the day Joseph Nicollet. It was the luckiest of happenstances for Frémont's glorious future; as he later recalled, "Here I found the path I was destined to walk" or, as one early writer put it, "He learned to pack a mule, and what to pack on it."

Appointed as a second lieutenant in the U.S. Topographical Corps, Frémont accompanied Nicollet on various mapping explorations in the North Carolina mountains and on tributaries of the Mississippi, and by 1840 his reputation was well enough established to propel him into the ranks of Washington society where he quickly found himself a favorite at the home of Senator Benton, the arch-expansionist, who also happened to be the father of the handsome, sixteen-year-old Jessie. This resulted in the sparking of an immediate friction between the young lieutenant and the senior senator from Missouri, who became irate when Frémont eloped with his daughter. However, once the deal was done Benton concluded there was nothing for it but to welcome Frémont into the family, which was a happy thing for Frémont's career, since Thomas Hart Benton was a world-class hater who had nearly killed Andrew Jackson in a disgraceful gunfight at Nashville in 1813.

In any case Frémont, in the late summer of 1845, with rumors of war with Mexico already brewing, departed the frontier at Westport (now part of Kansas City), the jumping-off point for western adventures, and headed down the Santa Fe Trail to Bent's Fort, Colorado, the last bastion of westward civilization until the Pacific coast. Ostensibly, the purpose of this expedition was to map the source of the Arkansas River, which lay along the eastern slope of the Rockies, but Frémont had in mind a grander plan he said had been conveyed to him through his father-in-law, Senator Benton, and which came from the highest authorities in government. It was necessarily vague, he said; there was, as yet, no war with Mexico, no Kearny's march. But Frémont felt reliably informed that his immediate future lay not across the Rockies but across the Sierras, in the Mexican province of California.

Traveling with him was a fascinating set of sixty-two armed mountain men, including Kit Carson, Frémont's chief scout and confidant, who needed no introduction to the American people since he was featured prominently in Frémont's published account of his exploits. Carson had come a-runnin' from his stock farm on the Cimarron River in New Mexico when a messenger informed him that Frémont was embarking on another journey of exploration.

Several years earlier Frémont had encountered Carson on a riverboat at the beginning of his second expedition and hired the wiry, bandy-legged, thirty-three-year-old mountain man and Indian fighter on the spot. It was the beginning of a long and prosperous friendship, and in the end Carson's fame eclipsed even that of Frémont when he became, in fact, a legend in his own time.

Christopher Carson had been born in Kentucky in 1809, but the family of ten children soon moved to a plot of land in Missouri that was home to the Daniel Boone family, and which was then the last outpost of the great frontier. When he was nine, Kit's father was killed by a falling tree, and soon Kit became apprenticed to a saddle maker where his job entailed stitching and repairing the saddles, gun covers, moccasins, and other leatherworks for the grizzly mountain men of the era, who even then were legendary in newspaper and pulp novels for traveling audaciously among the savages.

Kit didn't stay long in the leather shop, but ran away at age fourteen, and somehow he found his way five hundred miles southwest to Bent's Fort, then in the process of being built by the Bent brothers, who also became legends of the Southwest. The Bents took an interest in the tough young runaway, got him work with trading and trapping expeditions, and Carson soon became an old hand at mountainmanning, which is to say he did not hesitate to kill beavers, wolves, grizzly bears, Indians, or fellow mountain men if they gave him cause. One of these, an obnoxious loudmouthed French-Canadian, he shot in a duel because he was, well, obnoxious, which passed for cause in those times—and which is where the legend of Kit Carson began.

Although he had never learned to read or write, Carson was fluent in Spanish, French, and a dozen Indian tribal languages, including sign language and smoke signals. He had been in scores of close scrapes and seemed to have the nine lives of a cat, except that he had used them all up over and over again.

By the late 1830s the fur trade was in decline, victim of financial

panics and silk top hats,* and Carson decided to settle down as a stock
rancher. He took an Indian woman for a wife and a daughter was produced, but the wife died and it was on a trip back to St. Louis to find a
good Catholic education and home with relatives for his daughter that
Carson first encountered Frémont.

When Carson appeared at Bent's Fort in the Colorado Rocky Mountain foothills in August 1845, he brought with him for Frémont's third
expedition his partner in the stock ranch, Richard Owens, to join with
another of Frémont's old favorites, Alexis Godey, a rough-and-tumble
twenty-six-year-old French-Canadian fur trapper.

Frémont observed of this trio that "under Napoleon they might have
become Marshals, chosen as he chose men. Carson of great courage,
quick and complete perception . . . Godey insensible to danger, of perfect coolness and stubborn resolution; Owens equal in courage, and in
coolness equal to Godey, had the *coup-'ail* of a chess player, covering
the whole field with a glance that sees the best move. His dark-hazel
eye was the marked feature of his face, large and flat and far-sighted."

Also along was the trapper Basil Lajeunesse, who had accompanied Frémont on his previous expedition, and Edward Kern, a talented
Philadelphia nature artist, highly skilled at drawing and coloring birds,
animals, and plants. The party also included several dozen other men
who knew their way around the woods. Some would hunt for the expedition's food and scout for trails or hostile Indians, while others managed
and operated the surveying equipment and scientific gear.

At Bent's Fort, a large, fortified trading post on the Colorado plains
about a hundred fifty miles southeast of Denver, Frémont split his party
in two, sending half under two army lieutenants to explore and survey
the upper Arkansas River, while his half would push on over the Rockies and westward into Utah and Nevada and then across the High Sierras to California, where trouble was brewing.

By mid-September 1845 the expedition had reached the Great Salt
Lake and stopped to do some exploring. Over the years, a few old-timers
had made passing mention of the lake, and one or two tried to place it
on a map. No one, however, could explain why the lake was salty, way

---

*For a hundred years beaver fur had been the material of choice for top hats in Eu-
rope, but when the China trade opened up Chinese silk became the new choice; not only
was it shiny, it was cheaper and just as warm.

out here in the middle of nowhere. "It was generally supposed that it had no visible outlet," Frémont wrote, "but among the trappers, including those in my own camp, were many who believed that somewhere on the surface was a terrible whirlpool, through which its waters found their way to the ocean by some subterranean communication."

Frémont took note of a large island out in the lake that Indians told him could be reached on horseback because of the low water level. He, Carson, and a few others rode out to it and killed several antelope from herds they came upon. When they returned to camp an old Utah Indian was waiting for them, solemn as a stone, with news that he was owner of *all* the island's antelope and demanded to be compensated. "He was very serious with us," Frémont wrote, "and gravely reproached me for the wrong which we had done him. I had a bale unpacked and gave him a present—some red cloth, a knife, and tobacco, with which he declared himself abundantly satisfied for this trespass on his game preserve."

By then it was near the middle of October and Frémont knew all too well the hazards if the party did not get across the Sierras before the snows began. On his previous expedition they had nearly died to a man and he was anxious to move on. But which way? Last year's crossing had been south of what is now Lake Tahoe, but that had been approached from the north, coming off the Oregon Trail. Frémont reasoned that the fastest way would be straight ahead west from the Salt Lake, across the Great Basin.

Frémont had another, private reason to want to get across the mountains as soon as possible. Before departing from the capital, he had been given to believe that his mission, and his destiny, was to influence by whatever means the acquisition of California by the United States. This he had divined from meetings six months earlier with his father-in-law, Benton, and such diverse other luminaries as Daniel Webster, Secretary of the Navy Bancroft, and even President Polk himself, whom Frémont had met briefly at the White House.

"For me," he wrote later, "no distinct course or definite instruction could be laid down, but the probabilities were made known to me as well as what to do when they became facts. The distance was too great for timely communication; but failing this I was given discretion to act."

The fog of history has never entirely lifted upon Frémont's role in

this interesting installment of the acquisition of California, and soon
it would become even murkier with the West Coast arrival of a secret
messenger sent by the president himself. It appears that by this point
Frémont was under the distinct impression that if an opportunity presented itself in California his instructions were to act against the interests of the government of Mexico.

The problem now in Utah, however, was that every time he looked
westward all he saw was barren desert and, behind that, an endless
north–south chain of monstrous mountains, "looking like the teeth of
a saw . . . in winter-time a forbidding project." Far as the desert went,
none of Frémont's people knew anything about it. He inquired of Indians, but they "declared to us that no one had ever been known to cross
the plain, and so far out into it as any of them had ventured, no water
had been found."*

Frémont lingered several days contemplating the predicament,
studying the mountain wall with a telescope until he noted that "nearly
upon the line of our intended travel, and at the farther edge of the desert, apparently fifty to sixty miles away, was a towering peak-shaped
mountain that [looked to be] fertile."

Finally he sent Kit Carson and two other men, along with a mule
man with water and provisions, to leave that night to investigate, and he
would follow with the main exploring party next day. If Carson found
that the "peak-shaped" mountain was fertile, and contained water and
grass for the animals, they were to send up smoke signals. If the smoke
signals were negative, Frémont would return to the Salt Lake area and
consider what to do next.

Following a long, dry day's march, word came back to Frémont via
Carson's smoke signals that the mountain indeed had water, grass,
and firewood, and the next day the exploring party reached the place,
naming it Pilot Peak. After refreshing his party, he hurried westward
through the latening autumn of 1845, groping his way through valleys
and passes, examining, mapping, surveying, sketching, gathering fossils and geologic and botanic samples, measuring time and distances,
and naming things and places as he went.

---

*It is today known as the Great Salt Lake Desert.

CHAPTER FOUR

True West

Archibald Gillespie, a thirty-five-year-old lieutenant in the U.S. Marine Corps, was undoubtedly surprised, and probably shocked, when on October 30, 1845, he was ordered to the White House for a confidential nighttime meeting with the president. He was about to become a secret agent for the U.S. government.

What was said between Gillespie and Polk remains unknown, but a few weeks thereafter, when war with Mexico was looming, Gillespie found himself aboard a sailing vessel bound for California—via Vera-cruz, Mexico—disguised as a representative of William Appleton & Co. of Boston, Massachusetts, a shipping concern, in other words a government spy, part of whose job would be reporting on conditions, political and military, that he observed in Mexico.

Aside from Polk's personal instructions to Gillespie, if any, he was used as a clandestine courier carrying letters and directives from the president to Captain Frémont and others—including Commodore John D. Sloat, the U.S. Pacific Squadron commander—regarding what was expected of them in California considering the new turn of events with the Mexican government. Polk had timed Gillespie's arrival in California with the anticipated arrival there of Frémont, no mean feat allowing that these timings took six months or more to accomplish.

Gillespie, tall, freckled, and with a shock of red hair, who had been selected for the assignment partly because of his excellent command of the Spanish language, arrived in Veracruz on December 10, 1845, to behold a barren, filthy, lawless place, seething with anti-American sentiment and on the verge of yet another revolution.

It was also the birthplace and home base of the notorious one-legged general and perennial Mexican ruler Antonio López de Santa Anna, who had led the Mexican army in the butchery at the Alamo a decade earlier.* Since then, Santa Anna had been Mexico's president/dictator no fewer than seven times, by some ragged process of coup and countercoup, until his present exile in Havana, Cuba, which was under penalty of death. Unbeknownst to Lieutenant Gillespie, a few weeks after his own secretive nighttime encounter in the White House, an even more intriguing audience had been conducted between the president and a mysterious character named Colonel Alejandro Atocha, who said he was Santa Anna's close friend. For a "pecuniary consideration" of $30 million, Atocha informed a startled President Polk, the United States could have all the lands of California and New Mexico, and a treaty also ceding them Texas without quarrel, provided Polk would allow Santa Anna safe passage from Cuba to Veracruz, where he would regain control of Mexico and make arrangements for the sale.

When Polk asked how this could be, in light of the current high feelings in Mexico against giving up land to the Americans, Atocha told him the Americans would have to put the screws on the Mexican government. Santa Anna, Atocha said, was convinced that once he regained power it would be necessary for the United States to withdraw its emissary, Slidell, then march General Taylor's army from Corpus Christi down to the Rio Grande, and place a U.S. naval squadron to blockade Veracruz. Only then would the Mexican people believe the United States really meant business.

In addition, according to one report, the urbane, expensively dressed Atocha informed Polk that the sum of half a million dollars would be needed immediately for Santa Anna and himself "to sustain themselves," until the main balance could be paid.

Polk's reaction was that Atocha was untrustworthy; at least that's what he told his diary. "Col. Atocha is a person to whom I would not

*Santa Anna lost his leg in 1838 during the so-called French Pastry War and thereafter used an artificial leg made of corkwood, until he was surprised by an Illinois regiment while eating a lunch of baked chicken during the Battle of Cerro Gordo during the Mexican-American War. Santa Anna got away, but his leg did not, and it is presently on display at the Illinois National Guard Museum in Springfield. Over the years the Mexican government has sought to have the leg returned but, so far, no dice.

give my confidence," the president wrote. "He is evidently a man of talents and education, but his whole manner and conversation impressed me with the belief that he was not reliable. I therefore heard all he said but communicated nothing to him."

Maybe so, but within a few months Polk had withdrawn Slidell as ambassador, ordered Taylor's army from Corpus Christi to the Rio Grande, blockaded Veracruz with a U.S. naval squadron, and sent word to its commander that General Antonio López de Santa Anna be allowed to pass through safely on his way to Mexico from Cuba.

Polk did not, however, fall for the half a million in "walking around money" (i.e., bribe) that Atocha had angled for, and a good thing, too, since Santa Anna was possibly the most corrupt official in Mexican history, which is saying a lot. Wrote the historian Allan Nevins of Santa Anna, "In reality, he was a charlatan." He was also a master of the double cross, as Polk quickly found out after allowing him safe passage. Far from trying to sue for peace, Santa Anna had scarcely returned to Mexico and seized power when he exclaimed, "Every day that passes without fighting in the north is a century of disgrace for Mexico!" and proceeded to concentrate an army of 25,000 at San Luis Potosí to stop the American invasion.

All of this was in Lieutenant Gillespie's future, however, and he was overly anxious to get out of the sticky, fetid hellhole that was Veracruz. After dispatching a report to his superiors on the state of affairs he found in the town, Gillespie traveled four days by mule coach to Mexico City, a trip he described as delightful, passing through a rising country of citrus and other tropical fruit groves and roadsides with bright blossoms in wild profusion. When the coach reached the heights of the Mexican plateau, Gillespie and the others "looked down upon the Great Valley of Mexico . . . the innumerable spires of the distant city were faintly seen. The volcanoes were enveloped in clouds, all but their snowy summits, which seemed like marble domes towering in the sky."

Alas, the marine officer's arrival at the national capital coincided with the outbreak of the umpteenth (thirty-second) revolution during the tumultuous quarter century since Mexico gained independence from Spain. With Santa Anna still exiled in Cuba, this time the army of General Mariano Paredes had deposed the current *presidente*, General José Herrera, who had fallen from grace merely by hinting that he might consider treating with the Americans for the purchase of Texas or any other Mexican property. During his stay in Mexico City, Gillespie observed Mexican army battalions marching north toward the Rio Grande, and he found the press and people in the capital, if anything, even more vitriolic against the United States than he had the citizens of Veracruz.

The very presence of Polk's envoy Slidell—though he was never officially received by the Mexican government—"they declared an insufferable insult to the City—and a degradation of the national honor." In Gillespie's opinion, war loomed right over the horizon.

Heading out of the city for the West Coast port city of Mazatlán, Gillespie disguised himself as a Mexican, complete with serape, sombrero, sash, and a pistol stuck in his belt, and boarded a stagecoach for the two-week trip to the Pacific coast. When he arrived there, waiting for him was the American sloop of war USS *Cyane*, which would carry him first to the Sandwich Islands (Hawaii), then eastward to Monterey, the capital of California.

There he finally arrived on April 17, 1846, one week before General Arista's massacre of the American cavalry patrol along the Rio Grande, which touched off the Mexican war. His first contact was with the U.S. consul general for California, Thomas Larkin. For him Gillespie had special instructions, which he delivered orally, since even before entering Mexico he had committed to memory and then destroyed the documents of instruction he had received in Washington, as a precaution against their falling into the wrong hands.

The message basically—and here is what has become clouded over the years—was that the president, the secretary of state, and the secretary of war wanted Larkin to become a secret agent of the U.S. government to try and pry California away from Mexico. Like the territory of New Mexico, the California province was too far away for the government in Mexico City to administer, and it had been that way for years (even since the fictional time of Zorro, when lawlessness and corruption prevailed and rich dons abused the people). In fact, in the whole enormous province only a few hundred *caballeros* and their families (known as *Californios*) presided over rich estates from San Diego to San Francisco, raising cattle, horses, and generally living the good life without very much direction from anybody.*

These colonists from Spain had arrived in increasing numbers with the official Spanish establishment in 1769 of the Alta California mission system, which over the next sixty years built a chain of twenty-one Catholic missions all along El Camino Real (the king's road) that ran near the Pacific Ocean from San Diego to San Francisco. The object of these missions—subsidized by the then Church-influenced Spanish government—was to attempt to civilize the various tribes of Indians who lived in the distant province and turn them into useful, Christian, and—most important—tax-paying citizens.

Administered by the Franciscan order, and backed by government troops, the missions controlled huge sections of land—tens of thousands of acres—and at one point were estimated to have had perhaps a hundred thousand Indians under their sway.†

By the late 1820s the missions had large agricultural and livestock operations and seemed to be accomplishing their goals. But then the successful Mexican revolution against Spain convulsed their world, and the newly independent Mexicans passed a law of "secularization," on grounds it couldn't afford to subsidize the missions anymore.‡ This action has also been characterized as "a polite term for robbery," since the mission properties were quickly confiscated by corrupt bureaucrats, broken up, and auctioned off for pittances, often to the relatives and cronies of Californio authorities or Mexico City politicians. At the same time, the government began encouraging Mexicans to immigrate to California and colonize it, but this did not occur. The Indians, of

---

*Aside from the Indians, California had at this point a population of about 5,000 living there, 4,000 of them Mexicans; of the rest about half were Americans and the others were mostly Europeans.

†Many of these missions have been at least partially restored, and the most famous is probably the one at San Juan Capistrano, now a tourist attraction immortalized in the song "When the Swallows Come Back to Capistrano," recorded first by the Ink Spots in 1940. Stretching along some 650 miles of coastal California, the missions were located so as to be roughly a day's donkey travel from each other.

‡Moreover, it was also because the government was trying to extricate itself from the grip of the Catholic Church, which had become too intertwined in Mexican culture for the new nation's liking.

course, got little or nothing for their sixty-odd years of devotion, and those who didn't drift back to the wild tribes began hanging around and begging or took up horse stealing and other disagreeable pursuits.

By the time of Frémont and Gillespie's arrival, California had been divided by the Mexican government into four military districts, each with its *comandante,* and a governor, Pío de Jesús Pico IV, part Indian, part black, part Mexican, part European, and a self-made California aristocrat, who lived much of the time in Los Angeles, a thriving town of about 250 souls. In recent years, the Mexicans in this territory* had watched with growing alarm as scores of American settlers began to push in from Oregon and take up farming and ranching in the rich valleys between the Sierras and the Coast Range.

At first, when they were just a handful, the Americans' presence seemed harmless enough, but soon the reality of what had happened in Texas began to dawn on the Californios. This was no idle supposition; *Niles' Register,* a weekly journal, had recently observed that "There will soon be more Yankees than Mexicans there, and they will, most likely, establish a government of their own, entirely independent of Mexico."

Governor Pico, who had boot-strapped himself from a two-bit dram shop proprietor to owner of a half-million-acre ranching enterprise, probably best summed up the Californios' viewpoint when he said, "What are we to do then? Shall we remain supine, while these daring strangers are overrunning our fertile plains, and gradually outnumbering and displacing us? Shall these incursions go on unchecked, until we shall become strangers in our own land?"

The answer to these questions came soon enough, when Pico—who favored breaking California away from Mexico and aligning her not with the United States but with England—issued an edict banning further American immigration from the Oregon Trail. Furthermore, after a tour of inspection of the northern valleys, General José Castro, the military *comandante,* published an additional decree that reduced the presence of those Americans already farming or ranching there to

---

*Being ports of call, all of California's cities had healthy populations of foreigners as well—Americans, British, continental Europeans, Russians, and Asians—who had arrived by ship and for one reason or another stayed on.

"provisional" status, meaning he could kick them out anytime he saw fit. Naturally, this created more fear and ill will between the two sides.

And so it was upon this dicey state of affairs that Captain Frémont, of the United States Army, dropped in with his large posse of heavily armed frontiersmen.

Frémont and his party had descended the California side of the Sierra Nevadas through the crest of a 7,200-foot pass on December 3, 1845, an eyelash ahead of the snows that nearly did him in at that altitude during the previous expedition.

After clawing across the Great Salt Lake Desert, Frémont had divided the expedition at Pilot Peak, sending part of it to explore along the Humboldt River while he and the rest crossed over the mountains to Sutter's Fort, a large trading post and ranch in the California Valley that he'd visited the year before.

Nearing the mountains, the explorers began finding signs of human life, notably that of miserable "Digger" Indians, who inhabited this part of America. It was generally agreed among the trappers, mountain men, Mexicans, and even other Indian tribes that the Diggers represented a sort of low bar on the scale of human development, as they appeared squalid and were essentially limited to gathering roots and acorns or occasionally killing small game—a far cry from the ideal of the "noble savage" concept that had gained popularity in European art and literature. Even slaves, or ex-slaves, disdained the Diggers. A woman pioneer on her way to Oregon described them in a letter to her sister: "Their food consists of bugs, crickets, ants and worms. In winter they live in the ground, and in summer they wander from place to place."

Frémont came upon a Paiute, "naked as a worm," in the foothills as he searched for the pass through the mountains: "We found a single Indian standing before a little sage-brush fire over which was hanging a small earthen pot, filled with sage-brush squirrels. He was deep in brown study, and did not hear or see us until we were upon him. Escape was not possible, and he tried to seem pleased, but his convulsive start and wild look around showed that he thought his end had come. As so it would—abruptly—had the Delawares been alone. With a deprecating smile he offered us a part of his *pot-au-feu* and his bunch of squirrels. I reassured him with a friendly shake of the hand and a trifling gift. The Delawares lingered as we turned away, but I would not let them remain. They regarded our journey as a kind of war-path, and no matter what kind of path he is on the Delaware is always ready to take a scalp when he is in a country where there are strange Indians."

And that wasn't all. A day or two later Frémont and his companions found a good camp by a spring where they had cooked and eaten a freshly killed antelope, and were now lounging by the fireside, smoking and enjoying themselves.

"[Kit] Carson who was lying on his back with his pipe in his mouth, his hands under his head, and his feet to the fire, suddenly exclaimed, half rising and pointing to the other side of the fire, 'Good God! Look there!' In the blaze of the fire, peering over her skinny, crooked hands, which shaded her eyes from the glare, was standing an old woman, apparently eighty years of age, nearly naked, her grizzly hair hanging down over her face and shoulders."

She had assumed the fire was a group of her own tribe, ran away in fright, but was brought back, where it was quickly ascertained that she was starving. "She had been left by her people at the spring to die, because she was very old and could gather no more seeds and was no longer good for anything," Frémont wrote.

They gave her a quarter of the antelope, "but no sooner did she get it into her hand than she again darted off into the darkness." Some of the men went after her but the woman had vanished. Before they departed next morning, Frémont's men left her "a little supply from what food we had."

The Indians, it seems, had figured out a system or way of life that was practical, if unforgiving.

The party crossed over the Sierras and arrived at Sutter's Fort on December 10, 1845. Sutter's was a large, self-contained adobe stockade that had been constructed a decade earlier by John Augustus Sutter—a Swiss national fleeing financial reverses—at the confluence of the Sacramento and American rivers, at what is now the city of Sacramento. Sutter named it New Helvetia (New Switzerland). It contained a saddlery and a blacksmithy and offered fresh horses, cattle, and feed for sale.*

With his party united once again, Frémont set out to pay his respects at the province capital, Monterey. They had been four months in the wilderness since departing Bent's Fort. Accompanied by the U.S. vice consul William A. Leidesdorff, Frémont sought out Governor Pico, only to find he had gone to Los Angeles, but he did meet with the commanding general, Don José Castro. To this officer Frémont asked permission to continue exploring and described his expedition as a party of geographical surveyors looking to find the nearest route from the United States to the Pacific Ocean. The men composing it, he said, were private citizens and not soldiers.

"The permission asked for was readily granted," Frémont recorded, "and during the two days I stayed I was treated with every courtesy by the general and the other officers."

Procuring supplies and fresh horses in San Francisco and Monterey, Frémont's band was reunited by mid-February in the San José valley. After telling General Castro that he intended to leave California once his party was refitted, Frémont instead proceeded to head south for his explorations, having run-ins first with a grizzly bear, which, smelling breakfast, burst into camp one morning and "treed even the Delawares,"† and, second, a band of so-called Horse-Thief Indians, which ended in death for at least one Indian.‡

The reason Frémont later gives us for his detour south was his curiosity about the giant redwood trees he had heard about and to take in the seascape of the Pacific Ocean. Secretly, also, it was to pick out a future home site, or so he said.

"Always, too, I had before my mind the home I wished to make in

---

*Sutter's Fort became famous for its connection with the Donner expedition, and even more so shortly thereafter with the discovery of gold at Sutter's Mill and the consequent California gold rush.

†Before being shot dead by somebody. Frémont estimated that the beast weighed at least a thousand pounds.

‡The "Horse-Thief Indians" were tribes or bands composed at least partly of former "mission Indians" gone wild again, who preyed on ranchers' livestock, mostly horses, some of which they rode or traded but most of which they ate. Rustled cattle proved too slow for fast getaways from Mexican posses, but also it was said these Indians actually preferred horseflesh to beef.

this country," he wrote, "and first one and then another place charmed me. But none seemed perfect where the sea was wanting, and so far I had not stood by the open waves of the Pacific. This I wanted for my mother. For me, the shore of 'the sounding sea' was a pleasure of which I never wearied."

So Frémont had headed southwest toward Santa Cruz and Monterey Bay, over the towering Coast Range where gigantic redwood forests formed a colossal, sun-dappled cathedral down to the blue expanse of ocean—and it was there that trouble found him.

Having granted Frémont permission to refit his party so as to depart the province, General Castro prudently ordered his people to keep an eye on this outlandish, heavily armed congregation. When they turned back south, passing only twenty miles in fact from Monterey, he flew into a rage.

"In the afternoon [of March 3, 1846] the quiet of the camp was disturbed by the appearance of a cavalry officer and two men," Frémont wrote. "The cavalry officer proved to be a Lieutenant Chavez, with a communication from the commanding general."

Castro had ordered Frémont out of California forthwith, and in no uncertain terms he promised that force would be used in the event of noncompliance.

Taken aback by this inhospitable reception, Frémont began by dressing down Chavez, for General Castro's "breach of good faith and the rudeness with which he committed it," and in the end "refused compliance to an order insulting to my government."

With that, Lieutenant Chavez departed to report to Castro, and Frémont marched his company to the summit of a nearby mountain called Gavilan Peak "and proceeded immediately to build a rough but solid fort of strong logs." Not only that, but "while this was being built a tall sapling was prepared, and on it, when all was ready, the American flag was raised amidst the cheers of the men."

There Frémont remained for three days, ensconced beneath Old Glory, on Mexican soil, defying General Castro, who had assembled a force of several hundred men below, including a band of Indians who, Frémont asserted, "were being kept excited by drink."

Late in the afternoon on the second day, Frémont continued, "We discovered a body of cavalry coming up the wood road, which led from the Monterey road to our camp."

Frémont took forty men and set up an ambush but the cavalry "halted, and after some consultation, turned back."

By the end of the third day the thing had turned into a deadlock that appeared unsolvable, when Frémont's flagpole fortuitously toppled to the ground, allowing him "to take advantage of the accident" by telling the men this was an omen that they should move camp, "having given General Castro three days to execute his threat."

This seemed to have relieved tensions for all concerned, as Frémont now turned the expedition north toward Oregon. Right after he left, an Englishman arrived with a proposition from General Castro, which Frémont said was an offer to "unite my force with his [Castro's] and jointly march against Governor Don Pio Pico."

This was typical, Frémont said, "of the Mexican revolutionary habit," but instead he marched on northward toward Oregon, to survey the area and shoreline around the great Klamath Lake.

For his part General Castro nailed up a proclamation in the billiard room of army headquarters ("Not the usual place," according to the U.S. consul Larkin) informing California's citizens that a gang of American *bandoleros* (highwaymen, robbers) was on the loose in California, and that he and "two hundred patriots had driven them out." Some of Castro's officers further bragged to the newspapers that they drove Frémont's party "into the bulrushes of the Sacramento River, and that in their haste, they had left some of their best horses behind."

This turned out to be untrue, at least according to Larkin, who wrote to Secretary of State Buchanan of the incident: "The horses proved to be those belonging to the Californians themselves, and had strayed into Captain Fremont's band, and on raising camp they were turned out and left behind."

Frémont's route took him up into the Sacramento valley, carpeted in the early springtime with vast fields of blue nemophila and the California golden poppy. It was the time of the salmon run, and every river they crossed was teeming with salmon "three or four feet in length." They observed a footrace between Indians who "were *entirely* naked," and passed by 14,000-foot Mount Shasta ("Shastl," in Frémont's language). At one point they inadvertently made their camp "in a bear garden, where the rough denizens resented our intrusion and made a lively time for the hunters, who succeeded in killing four of them." During this fracas Charley, one of the company's Delawares, got his nose broken, but Frémont managed to set it himself, "and it healed without a trace of injury. I was always proud of this surgical operation," Frémont wrote, "and the Delaware was especially pleased. He was a fine looking young man and naively vain of his handsome face, which now had a nose unusual among his people; the aquiline arch had been broken to knit into a clear, straight line, of which he became very vain."

At one point Frémont had a fright when the big, jovial French-Canadian Archambault failed to return from a hunting expedition. They were worried that he'd fallen prey to Indians, but on the third day he and his horse turned up, exhausted and half-starved, and indeed he had encountered Indians but had made his escape in a series of close calls.

When they reached the dark, pine forests of the Klamath Lake ("Tlamath" is Frémont's spelling) they encountered a tribe of Klamath Indians of whom Frémont said, "Though they received us in apparent friendship, there was no warmth in it, but a shyness which came naturally from their habit of hostility." He had met these Indians in the winter of 1844 on his first trip to the Klamath region, and though his experience was friendly he had his suspicions, since the Klamath were a warlike people.

One night in camp Frémont's ear caught the faint sound of horses' hooves and, when he went to investigate, two men on horseback emerged from the darkness and into the firelight. They turned out to be an advance party sent by Lieutenant Gillespie, who had made the hazardous six-hundred-mile journey from Monterey with only a handful of men in order to overtake Frémont and deliver his secret messages. One of the party, to Frémont's surprise, was Samuel Neal, who had been a member of his previous exploring expedition and who had stayed in California in the ranching business. The other was one of Neal's associates.

Gillespie, they told him, was in grave danger, as their group, which had been composed of only six, was being trailed by a band of Indians. Neal, in fact, confided to Frémont that he didn't think Gillespie could be reached in time to save him, but Frémont was determined to try. As he tried to sleep that night, Frémont "lay speculating far into the night on what could be the urgency of [t]he message which had brought an officer of the Government to search so far after me into these mountains?"

Before dawn the party of relief set out, ten of Frémont's handpicked men including himself, Alexis Godey, Kit Carson, Basil Lajeunesse, Richard Owens, Joseph Stepp, and a half-breed (or métis) named Denny and four Delaware Indians, as well as Neal and his associate.

A late snow and fallen timber made the ride "hard and slow," some forty-five miles back to a spot where Frémont calculated he would intersect Gillespie in an open meadow in the forest, with a stream, "if no harm befell him on the way." Though they had seen no Indians thus far, they did find tracks indicating that Indians had followed behind Neal's advance party. To Frémont's relief, "The sun was about going down when [Gillespie] was seen issuing from the wood, accompanied by three men. All were glad to see him," Frémont said, "whites and Indians. It was now eleven months since any tidings had reached me."

That night by the fireside, as the little relief group camped on the edge of the meadow, Gillespie shared his letters and messages from Washington.

"I now became acquainted with the actual state of affairs and the purposes of the Government," Frémont recalled later. Gillespie's information "absolved me from my duty as an explorer, and I was left to my duty as an officer of the American Army with the further knowledge that the Government intended to take California. I was warned by my Government of the new danger against which I was bound to defend myself, and it had been made known to me on the authority of the Secretary of the Navy [Bancroft] that to obtain possession of California was the chief objective of the President." There was also a personal letter to Frémont from his father-in-law, Senator Benton, which, he said, contained some sort of code reinforcing Frémont's interpretation of his new duties.

Furthermore, Frémont recorded, "Now it was officially made known to me that my country was at war . . . I had learned with certainty from the Secretary of the Navy that the President's plan of war included the taking possession of California, and under his confidential instructions I had my warrant."

Here was where Frémont ignited a controversial firestorm that has vexed historians from that day to this, since it would have been impossible for him then, on May 9, 1846, to have known that war with Mexico had broken out, because the Mexican massacre of General Taylor's cavalry patrol had only occurred April 26, word of which did not reach Washington until May 9, and the official declaration of war was not passed by Congress until May 13. What's more, Frémont made matters worse by stating a bit later in his memoirs: "I saw the way opening clear before me. War with Mexico was inevitable; and a grand opportunity now presented itself to realize in their fullest extent the far-sighted views of Senator Benton, and make the Pacific Ocean the western boundary of the United States."

In light of what happened later, of Frémont's central role in wresting California away from Mexican authority, many historians have seized on these apparently contradictory statements—that it had been "made known" the country was at war versus "war was inevitable"—to condemn Frémont as a sinister provocateur, a brigand, a flagrant violator of orders, a bullying land grabber, even an out-and-out liar.

What can be known is that Frémont's knowledge of any war with Mexico had to have been brought to him by Lieutenant Gillespie. And since Gillespie could not have known there was in fact a declaration of war, it might be helpful to reexamine what exactly he did know.

For one thing, as he traveled through Mexico he had seen all the warning signs, the newspaper headlines, the mood of the people, the Mexican army troops marching north toward the Rio Grande, a consensus that "war was in the air." For another, rumors of war abounded in every California settlement, as news drifted slowly northward. Then, very soon before Gillespie left San Francisco to search for Frémont, he was made aware by the U.S. consul Thomas Larkin himself that "Commodore Sloat may, by the next mail, which should be within six or eight days, have a declaration on the part of the United States against Mexico, in which case we should see him in a few days to take the country."

What seems likely is that, given this information, Frémont concluded the United States was either at war or terribly close to being at war, and that given the huge gaps in communication over such wide spaces he had sufficient latitude to justify a military takeover of the province of California. None of the communications has survived, but we do know that Polk's instructions to Commodore Sloat had been to seize the California ports with his naval squadron the moment war broke out. And we also know, or should know, that young company grade officers, when left on their own, often do impetuous, even inexplicable, things.

In fact, since his arrival in early December of 1845, Frémont remained, for the next twelve months, the only U.S. Army officer in California. And it appears that he acted in accordance with what he thought he was supposed to do.

In any case he went to sleep that night beneath the cold, hard stars above the Oregon meadow filled with thoughts and aspirations of what this exciting news would bring on the morrow. His reveries, however, did not last for long; he had scarcely closed his eyes, in fact, when a sort of "thunk" resonated in the camp. Kit Carson, famous as a light sleeper, was the first to awaken; he called out to Basil Lajeunesse, "What's the matter over there?"

There was no answer. Then, suddenly, Carson and Owens leaped to their feet shouting, "Indians!" The "thunk" that had awoken Carson, Frémont wrote, "was the sound of an axe being driven into Basil's head." What caused Carson to shout "Indians!" had been the dying groans of the métis Denny, who had been axed and riddled with arrows as well.

Suddenly with shouts and whoops the party of Klamaths charged into the campsite, barely lit by the flickers of the campfires. They first met a Delaware named Crane, who was "jumping from side to side in Indian fashion, and defending himself with the butt of his gun." Five arrows struck Crane and he went down; then Carson or one of the others shot and killed the leader, who was their chief, and the others fled, but from the darkness of the woods they kept up a deadly rain of arrows into the camp until nearly dawn. Frémont and the others hung blankets from the low boughs of cedar trees to deflect the arrows. Every so often several of the Klamaths would rush in, trying to recover the body of their chief, but they were driven off by gunfire.

At one point Godey, one of the great mountain men, stepped over to one of the campfires to look at something wrong with his gun and made himself a target. Carson shouted out, "Look at the fool! Look at him, will you!" At this uncivil rebuke, Godey "turned resentfully toward Carson for the epithet bestowed upon him," Frémont later wrote, noting that Godey was "the most thoroughly insensible to danger of all the brave men I have known."

By sunrise the Indians had departed, their tracks indicating fifteen to twenty had been involved in the attack. The cold gray morning light revealed, in Frémont's words, "a sorrowful sight" of the bodies of Lajeunesse, Crane, and Denny. One of the Delawares scalped the dead Klamath chief, and Carson seized an English-made hand axe that was tied to the Indian's wrist and "knocked his head to pieces with it."*

The men packed the bodies of their dead onto mules and set out for Frémont's main encampment. They'd intended to bring their comrades back and bury them properly in some nice spot by the lake, but after about ten miles, as Kit Carson tells it, the narrowness of the trail resulted in the bodies' being "much knocked against the trees, and becoming much bruised," and it was decided to bury them then and there. They held a brief service in a laurel thicket, digging the graves with their knives, as they had no shovels, and burying the men wrapped in their blankets beneath the laurels. "There are men above whom the laurels bloom who did not better deserve them than my brave Delaware and Basil," Frémont recorded bitterly. "I left Denny's name on the creek where he died."†

As they reached Lake Klamath Frémont reported "many canoes" coming from different directions, an intended ambush, but he put his men in defensive posture and nothing materialized. The reunion with the others was anything but happy. The Delawares were especially anguished and went into mourning, blackening their faces with campfire soot, Frémont said, then "sat around brooding and waiting for revenge."

This was not long in coming. Frémont, too, was outraged. "I determined to square accounts with these people before I left them," he said. "It was only a few days back that some of these same Indians had come

---

*There was additional bitterness attached to this because all of them knew the Indians were being supplied with processed metals for axes, arrowheads, spear tips, etc., by the British at the Hudson Bay Company outposts in the Oregon country, and there was suspicion that the Englishmen were suggesting to the natives that they use these more sophisticated weapons on Americans.

†It remains Denny's Creek today, just off Oregon's Highway 140, close by the Rogue River National Forest.

into our camp, and I had divided with them what little meat we had, and unpacked a mule to give them tobacco and knives."

That evening Frémont held a powwow with the Delawares about the best way to avenge Crane's death. The two chiefs, Swonok and Sagundai, consulted and told Frémont that if he would take all the other men out of the camp, but leave the Delawares behind, the Klamaths would soon come to scavenge and the Delawares would kill them.

This was done and "it was not long before the morning stillness was broken by a volley," Frémont said, noting that the Delawares now carried additional scalps on their belts. Carson was particularly aggrieved because Lajeunesse had been a friend for years and thousands of wilderness miles. "The Indians had commenced the war with us without cause," he said. "I thought they should be chastised in a summary manner, and they were severely punished."

Next day the expedition continued on toward the main Klamath village beside the lake, which contained about fifty lodges. Frémont sent Carson and a party of ten ahead to reconnoiter but they were discovered and fighting broke out. When Frémont and the others came up, he said, "I saw a dead Indian sitting in the stern of a canoe. On his feet were shoes which I think Basil wore when he was killed."[*]

The Klamaths had come out of their village into a field of sage and were shooting arrows, but the rifles of the mountain men took an awful toll and forced the Indians to retreat into a stand of pine, with fourteen killed. Frémont's men then marched on the village and burned it to the ground.

Frémont then moved about a mile away and was making a secure camp when reports came that a number of Indians were moving on them through the forest. He decided to investigate, taking along Carson, two Delawares, and Archambault. Suddenly they came upon an Indian scout, Frémont said, who had drawn an arrow in his bow aimed

---

[*]A few modern historians have suggested that it was not Klamaths who attacked Frémont but a band of Modocs, with whom the Klamaths were at war, and so Frémont and his people wrongly murdered the Klamaths. But there is no reputable evidence of this, and one is disposed to believe that Frémont, Carson, and the other mountain men, who had encountered the Klamaths on previous expeditions as well as this one, could easily tell the difference.

right at Kit Carson. Carson raised his rifle but it misfired. Then Frémont shot and missed, but he managed to drive his magnificent horse,
Sacramento, directly into the brave, knocking him down just in time for
the Delaware chief Sagundai, who was following right behind, to leap
from his horse onto the Klamath and split his skull with his war club.
"It was the work of a moment," Frémont recalled, "but it was a narrow
chance for Carson. The poisoned arrow would have gone through his
body." For the rest of his days Carson was grateful to Frémont for his
life-saving gesture and retold the story at every opportunity.

The avenging having been accomplished, Frémont now turned his
thoughts south to California and the next day, May 10, 1846, set the
party out for the upper valley of the Sacramento. They had not traveled
far when he came across a macabre sort of tableau. Along the trail was
a tree with an arrow stuck into it. From the arrow hung a fresh, bloody
human scalp.

Later Frémont learned that the scalp originated with Lucien Maxwell, one of two scouts he had sent ahead. Earlier that morning Maxwell and his companion had come across an Indian and challenged
him. The Indian responded but chose unwisely to bring a bow and
arrow to a gunfight, the result of which Maxwell had "put up in the trail
to tell the story."

Be that as it may, Frémont led his band past the grisly object, back
into the Mexican territory, his mind probably racing with prospects.
What he would find there was beyond even his wildest imaginings.

CHAPTER FIVE

Kearny's March

On May 14, 1846, the day after Congress passed the declaration of war against Mexico, President Polk had orders sent to Colonel Stephen W. Kearny at Fort Leavenworth, Kansas, to march his Army of the West—numbering all told no more than two thousand—down the Santa Fe Trail to New Mexico and capture that vast Mexican province in the name of the United States of America.

This was a grave decision for the administration, since New Mexico actually consisted of what is now the heart of America, running all the way up from New Mexico and Arizona to Utah and Colorado. Furthermore, once that was accomplished, Kearny's orders were to push on across uncharted territory to California and capture it, too, so long as war between the two powers existed. It was a tall order with colossal implications. There are times in history when things can be done, and there are times when, for one reason or another, they simply cannot be done. Here was where history collided with chance.

On that same day, the president became embroiled in another row with his timorous secretary of state. James Buchanan had been a Pennsylvania lawyer and senator with presidential aspirations when Polk tapped him for the post, though he must have regretted it almost from the outset, as Buchanan turned out to be a contrarian and a quibbler. As noted, Buchanan had engineered disputes with the president in 1845 over his handling of the Oregon question for fear the British would declare war. This time the argument was over language Buchanan proposed to send U.S. ambassadors abroad about the administration's war aims.

In Buchanan's view, specific wording needed to be included that denounced any notion that the United States intended to acquire California, New Mexico, "or any other Mexican lands." Polk was appalled, telling Buchanan he thought such declarations would be "unnecessary and improper." In fact the acquisition of those Mexican territories was exactly what the president had in mind.

Buchanan countered by warning that if the American ambassador to Great Britain did not formally deny that the United States had any territorial aims with respect to Mexico, "he thought it almost certain that both England and France would join with Mexico in a war against us."

At this, Polk went into a rare fit of pique. He told Buchanan, somewhat disingenuously, that while his administration had not entered the war for conquest, the taking of California was probably going to be the result since Mexico was broke and had no other way of indemnifying the United States for the costs of the war, nor for paying the large number of claims against her held by American citizens.

Here was where he further informed the by now startled secretary of state that the U.S. war with Mexico was none of the business "of England, France, or any other power," and, for that matter, that he was not afraid of "war with all the powers of Christendom."

At this point the rest of the cabinet weighed in loudly on the side of the president, including his secretaries of the treasury and navy and the postmaster and attorney generals, and a chastened Buchanan stalked out without another word. Next day he sent over a new draft of ambassadors' instructions minus the language Polk felt was offensive.

Just as this uproar was winding down, Polk also became embroiled in an unseemly to-do with Winfield Scott, general in chief of the army.

Scott was a larger-than-life figure in every sense of the word. For one thing, as a young man he was a gigantic six-foot-five weighing 230 pounds, but by the time of the Mexican War he had become enormously corpulent. He was a genuine hero of the War of 1812 and gained in rank through the Black Hawk and Seminole wars, and he had supervised the removal of the Cherokee Indian nation from the South until, in 1841, he finally attained the nation's top military post. Known by then as "Old Fuss and Feathers," for his gaudy uniforms and insistence on elaborate martial ceremonies, Scott was tremendously vain and easily angered and was among those with strong aspirations to become president. He was also a shrewd military scholar and tactician with an excellent grasp of strategy.

On the same day that Polk got into his argument with Buchanan over the wording of the ambassadors' instructions, he placed Winfield Scott in charge of army operations in Mexico. The government would provide as soon as possible some 20,000 volunteers from the southern and western states,* with a further 30,000 men from northern states if circumstances demanded it.

Yet even then a tension had already developed between the two men based primarily on the mutual political distrust between Polk, the committed Democrat, and Scott, who was a dedicated Whig. To his diary that night Polk confided, "Though I did not consider him in all respects suited to such an important command, yet being commander-in-chief of the army, his position entitled him to it if he desired it."

So it was with surprise and annoyance when, less than a week later, Polk learned that Scott did not intend to go to Mexico and take command until September, which was nearly five months distant. The president, anxious to get on with defeating the Mexicans, told his secretary of war, William Marcy, to order General Scott down to Mexico forthwith or relieve him of command. This brusque send-off unleashed a firestorm of vituperation from the oversensitive general in chief, who set the tone of his response to Marcy by this sentence: "My explicit meaning is, that I do not desire to place myself in the most perilous of all positions, a fire on my rear from Washington, and the fire in front from the Mexicans." Scott further went on, in the opinion of Nevins, the editor of Polk's diary, "in a highly offensive and egotistical letter," fraught with "extraordinary indiscretions," which accused the Polk administration of "ill-will" and "pre-condemnation" as well as the almost treasonous charge of doling out military officers' commissions to Democrats as political payback.[†]

---

*Because they were closer and had more direct transportation to the scene of the action; many of these men were members of so-called state militias, which corresponded roughly to today's National Guard.

[†]Although General George McClellan's open hostility to Abraham Lincoln during the Civil War runs perhaps a close second, Scott's outburst in fact may have been the most insubordinate act by an American military chief until Douglas MacArthur's contemptuous behavior toward President Harry Truman during the Korean conflict.

Polk, Marcy, and others in the cabinet were astonished and incensed by Scott's outburst, and Polk himself sat down with Marcy to craft a response, which condemned the general in chief in what one historian of the period called "a masterpiece of pained condescension." It charged Scott with "bad faith" toward the president, the government, and himself, as well as "a reckless disregard for the interests of the country," and concluded by rescinding the president's offer that Scott lead the American armies in Mexico.

This put a severe quietus on Winfield Scott's presidential aspirations, which would have been a shoo-in had he returned victorious from the Mexican War. The sobering reality of his predicament caused Scott to embarrass himself yet again in responding to the secretary and the president, opening his letter with a remark that would hold him up to ridicule for the remainder of his political life. He complained that he had digested Secretary Marcy's rebuke "as I sat down to a hasty plate of soup," and went on to explain that the "fire in his rear" was ignited not by the president but instead by certain congressmen, as well as by the secretary of war himself, which of course only made matters worse. The press had a field day. In May of 1846, as Frémont made his way back from Oregon to California, and Kearny prepared to start down the Santa Fe Trail, Polk nominated Zachary Taylor to command the armies fighting in Mexico, while Scott remained in Washington, floundering furiously in his hasty plate of soup.

It took Kearny less than six weeks to organize, train, equip, and provision his Army of the West, and on June 26, 1846, its leading elements marched out of Fort Leavenworth and turned southwestward onto the vast plains of Kansas toward the New Mexican capital, traveling 962 miles. The trick was to reach Santa Fe quickly, and occupy it in the name of the United States of America, before the government in Mexico City could send an army to reinforce its garrison.

The 620 men of the First U.S. Dragoons, the nation's first cavalry regiment, formed the core of Kearny's command. They would be accompanied by a 220-man battalion of artillery, commanded by Major Meriwether Lewis Clark, a West Point graduate and son of William Clark, of Lewis and Clark fame; a 200-man battalion of foot infantry; 800 Missouri volunteer mounted infantry, many of them riding on Missouri mules, commanded by Colonel Alexander W. Doniphan, the St. Louis attorney who had saved the Mormon elders from execution in 1838; a detachment of topographical engineers; and, finally, a wagonload of presents for any Indians who might be encountered.

There was also a caravan of a hundred covered wagons led by long-time Santa Fe trader James Wiley Magoffin, another of the administration's covert emissaries, who had presented himself to Kearny following a long and secretive conference in the White House a month earlier with President Polk himself and a letter of introduction from Secretary of War Marcy for Kearny, stating that Magoffin might well be able to offer the expedition "important services" in its mission of capturing New Mexico. Just how important will be revealed farther along in the story. In addition, a 600-man regiment of New York volunteers would make the trip to California aboard ships that left from Hoboken, New Jersey, timed to meet Kearny's planned expedition to the coast by land. The 500 men of the Mormon Battalion would follow down the trail after several weeks of crash military training at Fort Leavenworth and link up with, it was hoped, Kearny and his command.

These men were mostly young and hardy, the volunteers having been long warned of the hardships of the trail: the forced marches, sometimes without water or firewood; the dangers of crossing so many rivers; and the menace of wolves, rattlesnakes, grizzlies, and wild Indians. But few of them were prepared for what they saw as Leavenworth, the last outpost of the frontier, faded into the distance and finally out of sight and they were on their own.

"The march of the Army of the West as it entered upon the great prairies, presented a scene of the most intense and thrilling interest," wrote Private John W. Hughes of the Missouri Volunteers, a schoolteacher. "The boundless plains, lying in ridges of wavy green not unlike the ocean, seemed to unite with the heavens in the distant horizon. As far as vision could penetrate, the long files of cavalry, the gay fluttering of their banners, and the canvas-covered wagons of the merchant train glistening like banks of snow in the distance, might be seen winding their tortuous way over the undulating surface of the prairies."

The Santa Fe Trail itself has become the stuff of legend, celebrated in story, song, and motion pictures, often quite incorrectly.* By the time of Kearny's march, the trail had been in use for a quarter century as a trading route from the Midwest to Santa Fe, whose population, because of distance, was practically isolated from Mexican commodities, even such as they were. In fact, although it took about six weeks for a Missouri wagon train to reach Santa Fe, it took much longer for one to arrive from the interior of Mexico, and then it was usually filled with inferior goods that were much more expensive.

By the mid-1840s a typical American trading caravan might consist of a hundred or more wagons owned by a dozen or so proprietors, carrying $100,000 to $200,000 worth of goods ($2 million to $4 million in today's money). The load typically consisted of various finished cloth, ribbon, and thread from New England mills; pots, pans, pottery, and utensils from Pennsylvania and elsewhere; glassware; medicines; hardware such as nails, needles, screws, brass, iron, chisels, files, hatchets, saws, and locks and chains; coffee grinders; guns, knives, swords; items of clothing such as caps and hats, aprons, shoes; finished dry goods and assortments of groceries: rum, gin, brandy, port, Madeira, whiskey, bourbon, moonshine, syrup, sugar, candies, peppers and spices; cigars and chewing tobacco; soap; tinned oysters, sardines, mackerel; and playing cards.

The New Mexicans flocked to buy the American wares. In the beginning, traders reported making profits of up to 2,000 percent, returning to Missouri with leather thongs of Mexican silver and gold coins and herds of Mexican mules and donkeys.† They brought back huge bundles of buffalo skin robes, which they bought for twenty-five cents apiece and could sell in St. Louis for $6 to $8.‡ During these early years of the trail Mexican gold and silver were the coins of the realm

---

*The illustrious 1940 film *Santa Fe Trail*, for instance, starring Errol Flynn, Olivia de Havilland, and Ronald Reagan, has little to do with the Santa Fe Trail, other than a brief reference to abolitionist John Brown's activities in Kansas. But the arbitrary use of the name as a title for the picture is an indication of just how famous the trail had become.

†These the ancestors of today's renowned Missouri mule, which is the envy of mule men—such of them as remain—everywhere.

‡Alas, even by the 1840s some of the more "civilized" Indian tribes were complaining that the Cheyenne were killing off buffalo for their hides at such a rate as to litter the prairies with heaps of rotting meat, dangerously depleting the herds.

in Missouri, and the frontier towns prospered as more traders made it to Santa Fe.

In time, however, especially after the revolution deposed the rule of Spain in 1821, the Mexican authorities began imposing tariffs on imported American goods, making them more expensive, and profits fell—first they settled around 30 to 100 percent and then they dropped below that as tariffs increased. They declined further over time as Santa Fe's citizens acquired more of the American goods and needed fewer of them.

So trade slowed. The thousand-mile trek was not only arduous and expensive but naturally could be extremely dangerous.* Sometimes trading caravans were wiped out almost to a man by unexpected blizzards or by marauding Indians. There were Pawnee, Apache, Cheyenne, and Arapaho, but the most dreaded of all were the Comanche, who, in the words of the historian Bernard De Voto, "were not only professional marauders and murderers, they were also practicing sadists. . . . They did a profitable business in white captives, whom they brought back by the score from their raids. No one has ever exaggerated the Comanche tortures. The authenticated accounts fill thousands of pages, and some are altogether unreadable for men with normal nerves. They had great skill in pain and cruelty was their catharsis. In short the Comanche killed and tortured more whites than any other Indians in the West, stole more horses and cattle, and were a greater danger." Gang rape of women was de rigueur, "and the many captive children could be entertainingly dismembered."

Now that was the righteous view of a highly educated and celebrated white historian of the mid-twentieth century.† De Voto's sentiments tend to beg a conversation over what might be termed the "temporal fallacy," which is to say an assignment of present-day ethics, values, and morals upon people, tribal or otherwise, who lived in centuries past.‡ In other words, it is tempting to conclude that since the Indians grew up

---

*In fact the trail split near the southern Colorado border; one route, known as the Cimarron Cutoff, was nearly a hundred miles shorter but it crossed a desert, while the other was longer as it crossed many streams and rivers.

†Bernard De Voto was a brilliant, if eccentric, scholar of western history, who will be cited from time to time in this story.

‡Some historians refer to this as "presentism."

as savages they didn't know any better, and thus it is wrong to condemn them for brutality. However, by the same token it follows that it would be equally wrong to denounce behavior of the whites, who often reacted to Indian raids and depredations by wiping out whole villages in retaliation, since it had been ingrained in the culture for hundreds of years that Indians were more or less a subhuman species who understood only brutality.

There is plenty of room for rubs in all this philosophizing but it is also beyond the scope of this book to conduct a moralizing seminar on nineteenth-century standards of behavior; suffice it to point out how treacherous the Santa Fe Trail could be. Consider, for example, the fate of Jedediah Smith, one of the most famous of the storied mountain men, who, after a short lifetime of spectacular western exploits and discoveries, at last met his end at the hands of a band of Comanche.

Smith, then only twenty-five, had been one of the early fur trappers along with such characters as Jim Bridger, Kit Carson, and John "Liver-eatin'" Johnson, blazing trails from the Missouri frontier to California and Oregon, facing down grizzly bears, blizzards, starvation, and thirst, when in 1831 he decided to give up trapping and enter the Santa Fe trading business and got up a caravan with his brother, Austin, and fellow trappers William Sublette and Thomas Fitzpatrick. It went well until they reached the Cimarron Cutoff, when Indians killed a member of the party who had been hunting antelope.

A few days later Jedediah and Fitzpatrick went ahead of the party to look for a watering hole. They reached a spot that looked promising and Fitzpatrick began to dig, but Smith continued ahead to see if he could locate a better source. He never returned and a search turned up nothing. When the cavalcade reached Santa Fe a few weeks later, Austin Smith was shocked to discover his brother's rifle and pistols offered for sale by Mexicans. Confronted, the Mexicans said they had purchased the weapons from some Comanche who claimed they obtained them from a white man they had killed on the Santa Fe Trail.

The Comanche apparently went on at some length about what happened on the fateful afternoon, which Austin related in a letter to their father shortly afterward and which was later released for publication by a nephew. Among the ways a man could die on the Santa Fe Trail was something as simple as going to look for water.

"He [Jedediah] had dismounted while his horse was drinking, to quench his own thirst, and then remounted. Twenty Comanche, who were in hiding, waiting for buffalo to come to the water, came out."

Smith tried to get them to go back to the wagon train and trade, but the medicine man suddenly approached Smith and was warned away. Then the Indians managed to frighten Smith's horse, and when it turned they fired arrows at Smith, one wounding him in the arm.

"He instantly turned and shot the chief dead, and, drawing his pistols, killed an Indian with each.* Then, grasping his ax, he dashed in among them, dealing death at every blow. Slashed with knife cuts and pierced with a lance thrust, he sank down from loss of blood. The Indians approached to scalp him, when he suddenly rose and stabbed three with his knife, and dropped dead. But he was not alone; there were thirteen of his enemies stretched dead on the ground. The Comanche concluded that he had been more than mortal, and that it would be better to propitiate his spirit, so they did not mutilate his body, but later gave it the same funeral rites they gave its chief."

So said Jedediah Smith's nephew, presumably relying on Jedediah's brother's account to his father. Fanciful or not, horrifying things could happen, very quickly, out on the plains.

Most of the time, of course, things didn't turn out that way, but it was always a good idea to travel in as large a caravan as possible—and if trail travel ever had an ideal model, certainly linking up with an entire United States Army expedition was as close to it as could be got. At least that's the way eighteen-year-old Susan Magoffin saw it as the big prairie schooners prepared to roll out of Leavenworth down the rough and rutted track toward God knew what.

She was a member of an old and wealthy Kentucky family, and the lively and intelligent newly wedded bride of Samuel Magoffin, twenty-seven years her senior and, with his brother James, an old hand at Santa Fe trading. She was also pregnant. This was meant to be a sort of honeymoon trip, an American safari, as it were, complete with all the dangers. The Magoffins had wanted to get a last haul of goods down

*These would have been single-shot percussion cap pistols.

the trail before the much rumored war with Mexico broke out, and now that it *had* broken out the matter was all the more urgent. Magoffin had fitted out his caravansary in expansive style, including a large conical tent "made in Philadelphia by a regular tent maker," dressing table, carpet, folding chairs, and a "fully equipped bed."

And so it was with a hopeful air that Susan Magoffin set out from Fort Leavenworth that bright summer morning in a fancy carriage pulled by mules, along with fourteen big wagons* of goods, each pulled by twelve oxen, an assortment of supply wagons, another carriage for Susan's maid and attendant, twenty teamsters, drivers, outriders, a dozen horses and mules, two hundred spare oxen, and "last but not least our dog, Ring," a thoroughbred greyhound.

Everything was exciting and fresh to the young beauty raised in the sophistication of My Old Kentucky Home—the stark prairie skies, the "bracing weather, cool and fine."

She exulted, "Oh, this is a life I would not exchange for a good deal. There is such independence, so much free, uncontaminated air, which impregnates the mind with purity."

Just as she was absorbing all of this purity, the teamsters began their job of hitching up the hundred or so mules and oxen, another novel sight, accompanied by "the cracking of whips, the lowing of cattle, braying of mules, and hallowing of the men," simultaneously the clear wholesome atmosphere of the Kansas plains suddenly erupted in a blue cloudburst of horrible profanity, which is the lingua franca of muleskinners everywhere but certainly not anything the refined Mrs. Magoffin might have heard back in antebellum Kentucky. Neither history nor her diary record the depths of her scandalization, other than that she found the swearing "disagreeable."

"The animals are unruly, tis true," she wrote, "and worries the drivers' patience, but I scarcely think they need to be so profane." And with that pronouncement, amid the marching columns of General Kearny's

---

*Most of these freight wagons were known as Conestoga wagons, which had been introduced some one hundred years earlier by German Mennonites in the Conestoga Valley near Lancaster, Pennsylvania. They were from sixteen to twenty-one feet long and four feet wide (to fit on bridges and ferries) and had long bows like a boat—thus the name "prairie schooner."

Army of the West, the Magoffin party saddled up and lurched westward onto the undulating prairies.

Kearny's march, in fact, was strung out over nearly a hundred miles, with various elements released several days apart, for the simple reason that so many men and animals on the trail back to back would create a nightmare of logistics and backups. At many places there would be bodies of water to cross and mountains to navigate, and it would have been foolish to allow the entire army to get bunched up waiting behind a few stalled wagons trying to negotiate some obstruction.

It didn't take long for the voyagers to discover the stark strangeness and beauty of the Great Plains, which until recently, as noted, was referred to as the Great American Desert and was so recorded on most maps, believed by most to consist of an empty wasteland.

Along a branch of the Kansas River, reported Lieutenant William H. Emory, a topographical engineer, "a seam of bituminous coal crops out; this is worked by the Indians, one of whom we saw coming towards us, driving an oxcart loaded with coal. For the most part the soil is sandy loam, covered with rich vegetable deposits, the whole based upon a stratum of clay and limestone."

Emory was an explorer and skilled cartographer. It was his duty, as Senator Benton had put it, "to ascertain whether or not the Southwest was worth taking by force and, if so, whether or not it was worth keeping!" A thirty-five-year-old Maryland aristocrat raised on an Eastern Shore plantation, Emory had married a great-granddaughter of Benjamin Franklin and considered himself more a warrior than a scientist or geographer.

Nevertheless, he made careful observations: "Trees are to be seen only along the margins of the streams, and the general appearance of the country is that of vast, rolling fields, enclosed with colossal hedges." For the first few weeks of the journey, he wrote, the grass was "luxuriant," and the trees were mainly "ash, burnt oak, black walnut, chestnut oak, black oak, long-leaved willow, sycamore, buckeye, American elm, pig-nut hickory, hack-berry, and sumack." But, he said, "towards the west, as you approach the 99th meridian of longitude, the growth is almost exclusively cottonwood, and westward past that point, "the country changes almost imperceptibly, until it merges into the arid, barren wastes . . . with the occurrence of cacti and other spinose plants."

The barometric readings he took each day showed they were on an almost indiscernible but steady climb, as their height above sea level rose from a thousand feet, to two thousand, to three, until they were traveling along barren plains three-quarters of a mile in the air. It was there that they saw their first buffalo.

At first only a small band of the beasts appeared, and they killed two of them for food, "at the expense of a couple of fine horses, which never recovered from the chase.* The next day," Emory reported, "immense herds of the buffalo were seen. Except for the buffalo, game is very scarce, and cannot be depended upon to support a party of men, however small their number." The buffalo, however, "where they range, may be relied upon to support a column of many thousand men, but their range is very uncertain."†

The emptiness of the plains posed another problem, as Lieutenant Emory noted in his diary—the newfound absence of trees—in which "not one of these is seen in an entire day's journey," which in turn left buffalo dung (more palatably known to French explorers as *bois de vache*) as the only remaining fuel for cooking and warmth.

While this inspired a certain amount of gratitude among some—as opposed to having nothing whatsoever to cook with—it did not sit well with many, including George Rutledge Gibson, an erstwhile lawyer and newspaper publisher in Independence, who had been elected second lieutenant after volunteering in the Missouri regiment under Colonel Doniphan.

"Tonight we had to cook with buffalo manure for the first time," he recorded, adding that "the smell of the smoke is not agreeable, and

---

*Emory blamed the horses' deaths on the switch from a grain-fed diet to grass, which he said caused them to become "very weak." However, he might also have considered the extra strain on a horse's heart, unaccustomed to such exertions at that altitude.

†On such long marches the army supplied a limited amount of food that could be carried—usually salt pork and flour for bread and biscuits—as well as herds of beef cattle, but when these were consumed the soldiers were expected to forage for meat, water, and whatever fruits and vegetables they might stumble on. Buffalo would have been a godsend.

some, rather than use it, went without cooking." But after some days, he said, "we became used to it, except our cook, who preferred wood."

For Gibson, and most of the others, it was not all some holiday excursion. Mile after mile they trudged, often covering twenty-five miles a day and more, as Kearny relentlessly pushed them to reach Santa Fe before it was reinforced by the authorities in Mexico City. One evening after a twenty-seven-mile forced march, Gibson's feet were so swollen he had to cut his boots off. Many times they went without water for long periods, and their tongues swelled, and lips cracked, and mouths became "slimy."

Men began dying. Some drowned crossing streams or from other mishaps, but most from illnesses that today would be routinely treated and easily cured. They were buried in their uniforms, most of them, wrapped in a winding sheet and left on the prairies with crude wood crosses carved with their names to mark the spot, their graves often covered by their friends with such stones as could be found to discourage digging by wolves and other creatures.

They were often plagued by swarms of gnats and grasshoppers—the former maddening with their singing whine, the latter repulsive as they were crunched and squashed under tramping feet—but the mosquitoes arrived as a biblical scourge.

One night, as darkness came, Susan Magoffin reported the mules and horses first became restive, then edgy, then frantic, as a perfect cloud of mosquitoes descended upon the caravan. The animals tore at their harnesses and many bolted. Susan herself recorded: "I found my feet covered with stings, and my dress full where they had gotten on me . . . millions upon millions were swarming around me, and their knocking against the carriage reminded me of a hard rain. It was equal to any of the plagues of Egypt."

As she lay "in a stupor," sick from the stings, her husband, who had tied up his head and neck with handkerchiefs, told her to "run if I could, with my shawl, bonnet and shoes on (and without opening my mouth—so as not to inhale them) . . . into the tent." Once inside "they pushed me straight in under the mosquito bar" and "There I sat in my cage, like an imprisoned creature frightened half to death."

By this time the summer heat was often close to a hundred degrees. Horses died by the scores. Jacob S. Robinson was a Portsmouth, New

Hampshire, journalist who had found himself in St. Louis when war broke out and, apparently having nothing better to do, volunteered as a foot soldier in Doniphan's regiment. About five weeks out, on the fourth of August, he reported that his company had traveled thirty miles from dawn to dusk. "This has been a trying day," he wrote, "heat intense. A water mirage appears, but no water, and worst the dreaded Sirocco or hot wind blows, which burns us even through our clothes. Five horses died." And two days later: "No grass was to be had; and eleven horses died."

Practically everyone reported the mirages. Susan Magoffin tried to describe the sensation in her charming, schoolgirlish prose: "And for the first time I have seen the 'Mirages' or false-ponds. It is so deceiving to the eye, that the thirsty traveler often breaks from his party with anxious eyes to gain the long wished for luxury, but ere he reaches the brink it vanishes from his sight." She was under the impression that the mirages were caused by "a surcharge of carbonic acid precipitated upon the flats and sinks of the plains, by the action of the sun."

Lieutenant J. Henry Carleton, riding these same prairies, had a different theory: "The day being very hot and there not being a breath of wind, a mirage rose from the dry and sterile prairie which produced a crinkling motion of the air near the surface of the ground, similar in appearance to that arising from a heated stove. The line of sight being tremendously refracted by it," he wrote, "every far off object had neither definite place or certain proportion. Every remote depression of the surface of the ground . . . seems to be covered with water . . . and the intervening elevations rising out of them like islands . . . a positive Polynesia in miniature—and not an illusion which the first shower or high wind might dissipate in a moment, and leave in its stead nothing but an arid and uneven waste."

The men found Kearny a stern taskmaster but, in his favor, as a creature of the regular army, the general was sometimes nonplussed by the cavalier military bearing of the Missouri Volunteers. On one scorching July afternoon he confronted Private Robinson's commanding officer, a Captain John Reid, while riding inspection.

"Captain, have your men no jackets?"

"Some have, some have not," Reid said.

"Make your men put their jackets on, or I will dismiss them from the service," Kearny rejoined.

"My men," said the captain, loftily, "came here not to dress but to fight."

Faced with this sensible response, Kearny wisely backed off. Still, his discipline could be harsh, as Robinson recorded: "Five men were tried by court-martial for insubordination, and sentenced each to carry forty pounds of sand every two alternate hours during the day."

There was one thing everyone agreed on, however—the snakes. Once the wagons had gotten down the trail a few hundred miles from Fort Leavenworth, somewhere in the vicinity of Pawnee Rock, where the terrain became arid and the prairie dog towns began to appear, the countryside was crawling with rattlesnakes. Practically everyone who kept a journal mentions an encounter. Jacob Robinson, for instance, had found a beehive and he and his companions "were furnishing ourselves with honey," when "one of our company, named Ferguson, was bitten by a rattle-snake."

Robinson and the others "gave him rattle-snake's master [apparently some kind of antidote, or perhaps a totem] and a quart of whiskey, which seemed to have little or no effect as to producing inebriation but soon relieved the pain of the bite and—'amazingly'—the man quickly recovered."

As they passed through prairie dog country, Robinson noted that most of the prairie dog burrows were occupied by an owl and a rattlesnake in addition to the prairie dog. How and why these unlikely creatures kept house together was anybody's guess.

Lieutenant Gibson reported on July 9: "After we got up this morning, we found a rattlesnake in our blankets. It had slept between the first lieutenant and myself, and near the captain's face."

On July 20: "We passed two large rattlesnakes in the road, killed by some person who preceded us."

And on July 23: "We killed several rattlesnakes in our camp this evening, but none were found in our blankets this morning as anticipated."

Susan Magoffin had taken "a little stroll" around camp with her maid one evening after dinner when she almost stepped on a large snake. She screamed and both took off, one from the other, the snake

apparently frightened by being screamed at. Later she came back, tim-
idly curious, to look for it, "but it had gone. I can't tell where." (Which
probably made it worse.)

Aside from snakes, mosquitoes, hostile Indians, and drought, the
trail was fraught with other perils. As the caravan approached Pawnee
Rock, a little less than halfway to Santa Fe, they found themselves
in what was—then as now—the tornado capital of the world. Pawnee
Rock is (and likely was) statistically 158 percent more likely to see a
tornado than the rest of the country. More than one of those keeping journals recorded that on the banks of the Arkansas River, where
trees grew, a great many were knocked down and others had their tops
blown out.

It was also nearby here that yet another travel hazard was discovered—a company of Missouri Volunteers on the march had been
attacked, and routed, by a herd of buffalo.

Pawnee Rock was then a large, blufflike promontory where it was
said that Indians, principally Pawnee, would gather to look out across
the plains for buffalo herds (or encroaching enemy tribes or other
trouble).* There was also a legend that a meager band of Pawnee had
once fought to the last man there against an entire tribe of Comanche,
in much the same fashion as a handful of Greek Spartans had conducted one of history's most famous last stands during the Persian wars.

In any event, Private Robinson and some of his comrades climbed
the heights of Pawnee Rock to see what they could see, and "in this
vicinity we saw the first great herd of buffaloes that we had met with.
From the top I witnessed one of the grandest sights ever beheld. Far
over the plain to the west and north was one vast herd of buffaloes;
some in column, marching in their trails, others carelessly grazing.
Every acre was covered, until in the dim distance the prairie became
one black mass, from which there was no opening, and extended to the
horizon.

"Every man was astonished," Robinson wrote. "We had heard of the

---

*From nineteenth-century photos it appears that Pawnee Rock has been dramati-
cally altered, probably by a combination of erosion and human tinkering. Today the
Rock is far less precipitous and craggy, as if someone had worked it over with earthmov-
ing equipment. A large stone monument placed there in the early part of the twentieth
century was toppled by a storm and remade shorter.

large numbers frequently seen, but had no idea such an innumerable herd could be gathered together. Most of them were traveling south, (probably for water) so as to come across our path.

"Their front ranks," Robinson recounted, "very obligingly made way for us for about two miles," and the men assumed the buffalo would behave like a herd of cattle. But instead: "As the main body moved on they could be kept off no longer. They rushed through our ranks, throwing us into complete confusion; stopped further progress of our wagons; and though an hundred shots were fired at them, we could not drive them away until the crowd passed."

Thoroughly shaken, the soldiers called it a day and sat down to supper. "We killed 40 of them—cooking our meat with buffalo-dung, which burns as well as charcoal."

In the meanwhile, Kearny had taken ill, from what we do not know, as was so frequently the case in those times. We do know that on July 20 he was able to ride only eight miles before having to dismount. Next day he requisitioned a ride in Lieutenant Emory's wagon, which had been equipped with springs to protect his delicate scientific instruments; this allowed him to proceed with his army. They were then halfway to Santa Fe and whatever lay in store for them there.

CHAPTER SIX

The Santa Fe Trail

About six weeks after departing Fort Leavenworth, following blazes, old ruts, abandoned vehicles, the bones of livestock, and other markings along the Santa Fe Trail, leading elements of the caravan reached Bent's Fort, an imposing stockade that reared up out of the Rocky Mountain foothills like a great medieval citadel. Built in the previous decade as a trading station by three wealthy fur traders—the Bent brothers, Charles and William, and Ceran St. Vrain—the fort was the lone outpost of western civilization along the thousand miles of trail between Missouri and New Mexico.

The establishment was located in a nook on the headwaters of the Arkansas River, on ground nearly a mile high, where travelers could view the snowcapped 14,000-foot eminence of Pike's Peak, about eighty miles to the northwest, where behind it rose "the dim outline of the great spine of the Rocky Mountain chain."*

The post's accommodations were spartan but positively elegant compared with what the *voyageurs* had been through on the trail. The main enclosure, several hundred feet square, was built of adobe, or sun-cured bricks, about four times larger than common bricks, with walls six feet thick and fifteen feet high, guarded at opposite ends by two large round bastions upon which lookouts were posted round-the-clock to spot for Indian trouble. The entrance was protected with stout gates and, like

*Half a century later a Colorado schoolteacher named Katharine Bates penned the words to "America the Beautiful" after a mule-wagon visit to the "purple mountain majesties" of Pike's Peak's crest.

the Alamo, there was no back door. The walls were built with loopholes for shooting and there was also a small cannon for defense. To discourage sneak attacks, the tops of the walls were planted with cacti, precursor to modern-day razor wire.

Outside was a corral for horses, mules, and oxen, which could be herded in at night or in case of danger, and beside the river was an icehouse for the storage of meat, perishables, and the luxury of ice in the often scorching summer heat. Inside the hollow square of the fort were a blacksmith's, barber's, tailor's, and carpentry shops, a kitchen, dining hall, armory, storeroom, an all-important trading room, and numerous private "apartments" or hotel rooms, with packed-earth floors, rude beds and mattresses, and a few bathtubs. The second floor contained a saloon with billiard tables and outside there was also a racetrack and cockfighting ring, everything—or almost everything—a jaded mountain man might want.

Susan Magoffin had been a tremendously good sport through all the hardships of the trail, even though for the past few days she had been unwell with problems associated with her pregnancy, which was entering its third term. Various "doctors" had prescribed so-called medicines for her, some of which seemed to help temporarily, but she, above all, understood that "mine is a case to be treated gently, and slowly, a complication of diseases. The idea of being sick on the Plains is not at all pleasant to me; it is rather terrifying."

Thus it is easy to tell from her diary how relieved she was to get off the plains and into the comparative refinement of Bent's Fort. "The outside exactly fills my idea of an ancient castle," she wrote. "There is but one entrance, and that is to the east.

"Our room has a dirt floor, which I keep sprinkling constantly," she wrote. "We have two windows looking out on the plain. We have our own furniture and we eat in our own room.* It is like keeping house regularly." With her husband off periodically to see to the wagon train, Susan made friends with one of the dragoons, a Captain Benjamin Moore, also of Kentucky, who it turned out seems to have been a some-

---

*Travelers at Bent's and other outposts often furnished their rooms with gear from their own wagons.

what distant kinfolk. "Both yesterday and this evening," she said, "we have taken a little walk up the River, such as we used to take last winter in N.Y., from Spring Street to Wall Street."

But amid this tide of youthful enthusiasm there encroached too soon a terrible undertow of sadness.

On Thursday, July 30, Susan wrote, "Well, this is my nineteenth birthday! And what? I feel rather strange, not surprised at its coming, nor to think that I am growing rather older . . . but this is it—I am sick!"

As she lay there, day after day, with "strange sensations in my hips, my head, my back," unable to rise, she all the while took time to set down in her diary the noises she heard through her window, "the shoeing of horses, neighing, and braying of mules, crying of children, scolding and fighting of men," their own servants, "gambling off their own cloths till some of them are next to nudity," and coming to her husband for loans, and "the arrival of a warrior band of Arapaho Indians." All this for a solid week she dutifully recorded, until on August 6, 1846— she deliberately fixes the date and the year—"the mysteries of a new world have been shown me since last Thursday. In a few short months I should have been a happy mother and made the heart of a father glad, but the ruling hand of a mighty Providence has interposed."

Susan's baby had had to be aborted or she would have died as well. Throughout the ordeal she clung to her faith like a bat to a cliff—"To come unto Him when our burden is grievous and heavy to be borne"; that's how she got through it, but it was a cruel experience for a girl who'd just turned nineteen on the Santa Fe Trail.

Captain Philip St. George Cooke was a slim, six-foot-four-inch, thirty-seven-year-old Virginia gentleman who had graduated from West Point a decade earlier and spent most of his time on the frontier. When Cooke's troop of First Dragoons arrived at Bent's Fort, he was surprised to be summoned immediately into the presence of Kearny, who informed him that he was being detached and sent on a secret mission.

Under cover of a white flag of truce, Kearny told him, Cooke was to organize a detail and proceed to Santa Fe, escorting two men to the Mexican territorial governor, General Manuel Armijo, the corrupt, greedy functionary who presided over the province. The purpose of their mission, Kearny told him vaguely, was to "plant an olive branch" with the Mexican *comandante*, in hopes of securing a peaceful conquest of the territory. The two men whom Cooke was to accompany were one Señor Gonzáles, of Chihuahua, and James Magoffin, the longtime Santa Fe trader and Susan Magoffin's brother-in-law. At play here were those "important services" previously alluded to by Secretary of War Marcy in the letter of introduction he gave to Magoffin.

Cooke's journey, for which he picked a dozen of the best cavalrymen from his troop, as well as the two "emissaries," took several weeks to reach Santa Fe, passing through some smaller Mexican villages as he neared the capital, which of course gave General Armijo fair warning of his coming. The closer to Santa Fe they got, the more spectacular was the mountain terrain, as Cooke describes in his memoirs: "The scenery of my piedmont route—from Raton [pass] to Santa Fe—is greatly improved; wooded hills, many bright streams, some natural parks. The buffalo grass under the stately pines and cedars looked fresh swept and washed; the air was exhilarating, but the charm over all was the almost dazzling sky."

Like so many men of his class in those times Cooke was an accomplished writer, as well as a scientist, linguist, equestrian, and cold-blooded killer when necessary. He often sprinkled his prose with Dickensian references and other contemporary allusions, and as they approached Santa Fe many of his sentences seem to have been written with a wink and a smile.

"I was struck on the road, with the number of people passing, and their lively mood. We fell in with one very merry party; chiefly the family of an old man, as lively as a monkey, and not much larger; perhaps it was a wedding party—a very pretty girl rode on an ass . . ."

Also along the route they would frequently spot large detachments of Mexican cavalry, which appeared to be watching them in a quasi-threatening manner. And when they finally reached Santa Fe his entrance was blocked by a fierce-looking guard of horsemen, "who howled out their 'alarm' with so hideous intonation that I mistook it for a menace."

For the first time, Cooke took out his white handkerchief and placed it on the point of his saber (a gesture he leads us to understand was distasteful for him), whereupon the commander of the Mexican guard escorted the party into the town plaza in which, "thousands of soldiers and countrymen called out en masse to meet our army [meaning his party]."

They were ushered into the governor's "palace," which Cooke described as a "large and lofty apartment with a carpeted earth floor," in which they found General Armijo "seated at a table, with six or eight military or civilian officials standing."

"There was no mistaking the governor," Cooke said. "He was a large man." In fact, he was once described by the English traveler George F. A. Ruxton as "a mountain of fat"! A former sheep thief and grafter, Armijo had risen to become *alcalde* (mayor), and then customs collector, before being appointed governor-general of the province. The governor, Cooke said, "wore a blue frock coat, with a rolling collar and a general's shoulder straps, blue striped trowsers with gold lace, and a red sash."

Cooke informed Armijo that he had a letter from General Kearny to give him "at his convenience," and upon its delivery Cooke was given more or less the run of the town, as well as sleeping quarters, while Messrs. Magoffin and Gonzáles conversed in private, late into the night, with their longtime acquaintance—if not longtime friend—Governor Armijo, presumably dispatching their aforesaid "important services."

If any American was equipped to treat with Armijo it was James Magoffin, who, unlike his brother—Susan's husband, Sam—had gone to Mexico in 1828, after college, and lived there for nearly two decades, marrying into a wealthy and influential Mexican family. James Magoffin was active in Mexico as a trader and had held U.S. consul posts in two towns, including Magoffinville, which is present-day El Paso.

Tall and handsome, Magoffin was known to be charming, well mannered, an excellent host, and a stimulating conversationalist, fluent in Spanish and French. And if that was not enough, Magoffin was a frequent visitor in Santa Fe and enjoyed good relations not only with Armijo but with his regular army commander Colonel Diego Archuleta.

Kearny had made no bones about his intentions in the letter Cooke delivered to Armijo. The general informed the Mexican governor that while he came "as a friend," his intention was "to take possession of the country over which you are now presiding." This, Kearny said, he hoped could be done peaceably, but if not, "I have more troops than I need to overcome any opposition you may be able to make against us." Advising Armijo to "submit to your fate," Kearny warned the Mexican that "the blood which may be shed, the sufferings and miseries that may follow [armed resistance] shall fall upon your head, and instead of the blessings of your countrymen you will receive their curses."

Next day, "soon after the sun rose," Cooke's party took its leave of Santa Fe, but not before the captain was feted by General Armijo with a morning breakfast of chocolates ["Chocolates such as only Spanish and Mexicans can make—served on a silver tray—it is an article of my culinary creed!"] and a promise from Armijo that upon the morrow he would march out of Santa Fe "with six thousand men" to meet General Kearny on the field of battle.

Exactly what had transpired between Armijo, Magoffin, and Don Gonzáles is, like the question of Lieutenant Gillespie's alleged instructions from Polk to Frémont, shrouded in the fog of history-without-documentation. We shall meet the issue head-on farther along in the story, but in point of fact Armijo did turn out, presently, with his six thousand—or thereabouts—armed men to threaten General Kearny's undertaking.

As he rode out of Santa Fe, Captain Cooke ruminated over Armijo, whom he saw as "distrustful of the population he has habitually fleeced" and "halting between his loyalty to his army commission, which has been lately bestowed [pride], and a desire to escape the dangers of war [cowardice] upon terms of personal advantage [stealing]." As Cooke passed through the gate out of town he could not resist a temptation.

"Rising in my stirrup I turn and with a defiant gesture, call out, in good English, 'I'll call again in a week.'"

Meantime, Kearny's army had departed Bent's Fort and was making its way to Santa Fe, on August 5 crossing the Purgatory River, otherwise known as the "River of Souls," in Mexican territory.* Kearny had issued a proclamation and saw to it that Captain Cooke's party

---

*Also known as the Purgatoire, a name given it by French explorers, but the soldiers called it the "Picket Wire."

and others distributed copies as they rode down the trail. Addressed to the general populace (excluding the Indians), Kearny decreed that he was entering Mexico "with a great military force, with the object of seeking union and to ameliorate the condition of its inhabitants." His statement ordered all residents to "remain tranquil," with the assurance that "they will not be molested by the American army, but on the contrary, they will be respected and protected in all their rights, both civil and religious," and warned that those who resisted or took up arms "will be looked upon as enemies and treated accordingly."

On the seventh they encamped near the entrance to the Ratón, a difficult fifteen-mile pass where Susan Magoffin took a "ramble" through the scenery. "On all sides are stupendous mountains," she wrote, "forming an entire breast work to our little camp," as she took in her surroundings, with her faithful dog, Ring, all the while keeping "strict watch for Indians, bear, panther, wolves, &c., and [who] would not even leave my side as if conscious I had no other protector at hand."

Travel down the valley of the Purgatory was anything but comfortable, Susan reported, owing to numbers of large stones strewn along the trail, "just the thing to bounce a wagon's wheels [off], unless there is the most careful driving." One of her companions wrote of the river, "We emerged from the gloomy solitude of its valley with a feeling somewhat akin to that which attends escape from a place of punishment."

Emerging from gloomy solitude or not, once the expedition got into the 7,000-foot pass, the progress became fairly excruciating, with advance measured in yards per day instead of miles. The road was frequently so steep that the men had to unharness the mules and push or pull the wagons themselves. Susan Magoffin remembered: "And it takes a dozen men to steady a wagon with all its wheels locked—and for one who is some distance off to hear the crash it makes over the stones is truly alarming."

Meantime, Kearny's army had been capturing all sorts of "spies," who had been sent out by Armijo to ascertain the strength of his forces. Most of these characters were policed up by the detachment of Charles Bent, of Bent's Fort notoriety, who was acting as guide for the expedition. By now it was August 11 and the spies, who had been captured in bunches and who numbered all told about a dozen, were "mounted on diminutive asses, and cut a ridiculous figure alongside the thumping big dragoons," wrote Lieutenant Emory, who also seemed dumb-founded that the Mexicans guided their donkeys by "beating them with clubs" instead of using a bridle and reins. A search revealed that the Mexicans were carrying a proclamation from Armijo's government that called all men aged between fifteen and fifty to arms "to repel the Americans who were coming to invade their soil and destroy their property and liberties."

All in all, according to Emory, the Mexicans offered a "pathetic appearance," with grinning faces "almost of idiocy," and instead of hanging them, which under military law he had every right to do, Kearny remarked to Emory, "If I have to fire a round of grape into such men, I will live with remorse the rest of my life." He made the Mexicans sit and watch his army pass by, including the artillery, then, after informing them that much more was to follow, turned the spies loose to make their report to General Armijo.

On August 14, as they neared the town of Las Vegas, according to Lieutenant Emory, a "queer cavalcade" rode into camp in the form of a messenger detail from Armijo, consisting of a lieutenant, a sergeant, and two privates of Mexican lancers "dressed in their best bib and tucker."

These men produced a letter from Armijo, the gist of which was that his citizens had risen to the danger of American conquest, and the only thing left was for the two sides to have it out. He suggested that Kearny halt his army at the Sapillo River, while Armijo would march his people to the Vegas, and the two of them could "meet and negotiate on the plains between them." The meaning of "negotiate" was unclear, and Kearny kept his forces moving until they themselves reached the banks of the Vegas, with no Armijo in sight. Kearny summoned the Mexican lieutenant and told him to go back to his commander and say to him that "I shall soon meet him, and I hope it will be as friends."

With that, Kearny entered the town of Las Vegas, the largest settlement yet seen on the trail, which was surrounded by cornfields and great flocks of sheep and goats. Emory thought the place resembled "an extensive brick-kiln." The soldiers found the Mexicans eager to trade, and bargains were soon struck for pigs, chickens, butter, sweets, and other items unobtainable on the trail. Meantime, Kearny had issued strict orders for the men to treat the citizens in a civil fashion, and "pay for every turnip, every ear of corn," and that army livestock would be kept out of Mexican fields—a rough precursor to the notion of "winning hearts and minds."

"From white men who reside here, we learn that the Governor exercises the most despotic sway over the common people, aided by the priests," Lieutenant Gibson, of Doniphan's regiment, reported. "All were much disappointed at the poor appearance of the people, and began to realize fully the stories we had heard of the low condition, ignorance, and want of spirit which was characteristic of the country."

What Gibson had actually come face-to-face with was the curse of Mexico, peonage, which, Lieutenant Emory had earlier remarked, "has all the disadvantages of slavery without any of the advantages."

Emory, a patrician Marylander from a slaveholding family, would have known what he was talking about in 1846, and his allusion here is from the peon's point of view rather than the master, or *patrón*.

The system of peonage had begun long before, during Spanish rule, as a scheme under which millions of impoverished and uneducated Indians, and later mestizos, or mixed races, were enslaved in a kind of permanent indentured servitude. At an early age, or even from birth, the peon, having been induced or forced to borrow some sum of money from the *patrón*, found himself legally indebted until the loan was paid off. The *patrón* would in turn pay the peon a pittance each month for his labor, but never quite enough to care for his own needs, let alone to repay the loan, and thus the peon borrowed more and more, further ensnaring himself in debt.

Like American slavery, the peonage system was enshrined in Mexican law; the main difference between the two was that peons could not legally be sold from master to master and therefore did not have capital value. The *patrón*, however, unlike the slaveholder, had no legal obligations to the peon, so when the peon became infirm or too old to work, he or she was simply cast aside to starve, suffer, or die—a decided disadvantage for the peon. In the American South, that was against the law, which is what Emory was referring to. If Gibson—who was something of an aristocrat himself, Virginia born and with both grandfathers having fought in the Revolution—knew or cared about any of this he didn't show it. He considered the Mexicans filthy, and he observed somewhat snobbishly that "they lack that neatness, that taste and refinement we left in the States, a few only having a genteel appearance."

Next morning things got off to a rousing start when word came in that six hundred Mexicans were formed in the pass two miles away to meet Kearny's army. No sooner had that been digested than a party of officers who had ridden all the way from Fort Leavenworth caught up with the van and dashed into camp bearing a dispatch from Washington containing the commission for Kearny as brigadier general. It was soon revealed, however, that the reason the officers—a major, a captain, and a lieutenant—had hastened down the trail was to get in on the fighting, which they were relieved to find had not yet occurred.*

After ordering a substantial portion of his force to see about the six hundred Mexicans, Kearny strode into the town square, overflowing with citizens who had been told an important announcement was forthcoming. With the *alcalde* and other town officials in tow, Kearny ascended upon the roof of one of the houses facing the square and made the following pronouncement: "Mr. Alcalde and people of New Mexico, I have come amongst you by the orders of my government to take possession of your country, and extend over it the laws of the United States."

He explained that his army came as "friends" and "protectors," not as "enemies" and "conquerors." He absolved them from allegiance to Armijo, or the government in Mexico City, and told them that *he* was governor now. He said that while he did not expect them to take up arms and fight against their own people, he likewise did not expect them to take up arms and fight his people. Or, put more bluntly, Kearny said, "He who promises to be quiet but is found in arms against me, I will hang!"

Kearny recited the abuses of the Armijo government—the high taxes and lack of services, mainly the lack of personal protection.

"The Apaches and Navajoes come down from the mountains and

*Included in the dispatches was a promotion for Lieutenant Emory to captain; he will be so recognized from here on.

carry off your sheep, and even your women, whenever they please. My government will correct all this. And, I repeat again, will protect your religion. I know you are all great Catholics." (Here he was countering rumors that had emanated from the Armijo government that the Americans would persecute the Catholics, even, some said, to brand them on the cheek, like livestock.)

Kearny then informed the startled *alcalde* and his officials that "the laws of my country require that all men who hold office shall take the oath of allegiance," and that, if they did so, they could keep their jobs. There was hesitation and some uncomfortable shuffling. The captain of the local Mexican militia began studying his shoes. As Emory described it, "This was a bitter pill, but it was swallowed, and closely watched by the crowd of expectant faces below, the oath was duly taken." Afterward, "the citizens grinned, and exchanged looks of satisfaction," and even though there was no spontaneous outburst of cheering, "their burdens, if not relieved, were at least shifted to some ungalled part of the body."

That ceremony concluded, Kearny and the rest of the party "descended by the same rickety ladder from the rooftop, mounted our horses, and rode briskly forward to encounter the 600 Mexicans in the gorge of the mountains, two miles distant."

Captain Emory, leading his small detachment of topographical engineers, sums it up from here: "The sun shone with dazzling brightness, the guidons and colors of each squadron, regiment and battalion were for the first time unfurled. The drooping horses seemed to take courage from the gay array. The trumpeters sounded 'to horse,' with spirit, and the hills multiplied and re-echoed the call. All wore the aspect of a gala day, and as we approached the gorge where we expected to meet the enemy, we broke into a brisk trot, then into a full gallop, preceded by a squadron of horse [cavalry]. The gorge was passed, but no person was seen.

"One by one the guidons were furled; the men looked disappointed and a few minutes found us dragging out slow lengths along, with the usual indifference in regard to every subject except that of overcoming space."

In another two miles they came to another pass but it, too, was deserted. Nine miles later they reached another town, "where General

Kearny assembled the people and harangued them much in the same manner as at the Vegas." Still no Armijo but "reports now reached us at every step that the people were rising and that Armijo was collecting a formidable force to oppose our march at the celebrated pass of the [Apache] cañon, 15 miles from Santa Fe."

What had occurred behind the scenes at Santa Fe had all the trappings of an opéra bouffe. On the one hand, Armijo was smart enough to realize that nothing less than the entire 250,000 square miles of the New Mexico province was at stake here, including the 250-year-old capital, which he had taken a solemn oath to defend. On the other hand, his defense was, to his mind, wholly inadequate and might very well expose him, personally, to real danger.

Armijo had at his disposal about 250 trained regulars, infantry, dragoons, and lancers, and enough artillerymen to man the seven cannons in his possession. As well, there were approximately 7,000 military-age men in the province, most of whom were familiar with firearms. On the other hand, he had no money to maintain any of these people with pay, supplies, or provisions, for the simple reason that he had stolen it all.

For nearly twenty years the authorities in Mexico City had been content to let the New Mexico province exist financially solely on the revenues from import duties claimed against goods brought through the customs offices at Santa Fe and Taos by American wagon trains coming down the Santa Fe Trail. This had worked out fairly well until Armijo took over, first as customs collector, then governor, after which the treasury strangely began to run deficits.

As Kearny's army approached, Armijo asked the province assembly to appropriate an emergency $1,000 loan (about $50,000 today) to activate his military force. The assembly agreed, but reconsidered next day, possibly after taking into account what had become of the customs revenues.

Nevertheless, Armijo was prompted to issue another in a series of his proclamations, this one vowing to "sacrifice [his] life and interests for [his] beloved country." With that in mind he began at once to assemble a military force in New Mexico at the narrow pass at Apache Canyon. The pass itself presented one of the most formidable military obstacles in the territory. Armijo set up his main defenses about fifteen miles from Santa Fe, at a place where the walls of the narrow canyon "rise 1,000 to 2,000 feet—a gateway," according to Emory, "which in the hands of a skillful engineer and a hundred resolute men, would have been perfectly impregnable."

Armijo had positioned his artillery pieces among the rocks and bottoms of this natural fortress and had his army—estimated at about 2,000 to 3,000 men, including the veteran dragoons—set up behind an abatis, or breastworks of felled trees with sharpened ends. From there, Kearny's army would have found itself in the dangerous predicament of being at the wrong end of an artillery funnel, and with any skill and determination at all the New Mexicans might have held off the American advance indefinitely.

Except that as soon as it was apparent that Kearny's army was fast approaching, Armijo hightailed it out of there, leaving the remainder of his men to fend for themselves.

Kearny had received advance word of this disgraceful departure from a prisoner who had been captured by one of Bent's patrols, an officer named Salazar, who was the son of a high official in Santa Fe. This man told of an argument between Armijo and his subordinates, which ended with the governor's decision to depart the province in utmost haste. One of Kearny's officers wrote of this informant, "The Gen. told him he would keep him a prisoner, and if he found that he had told him falsely, he would hang him."

Actually, it appears Armijo's decision to desert his post had been made several days previous, at which time he had appointed his lieutenant governor to act with power of attorney over all of Armijo's lands and other nonmovable property. In any case, the governor rode back to Santa Fe from Apache Canyon, escorted by about fifty of his dragoons, and piled all his belongings and portable wealth onto a wagon train in preparation for leaving the province. It was said that when word got out the citizens "became panicky" and an angry crowd descended on the governor's palace. As Armijo prepared to leave, this crowd began to threaten him as he mounted his horse. But the governor, "always a resourceful man," reached into his coat, whose pockets he had filled with gold and silver coins, pulled out some coins, and flung them at the mob, and while they scrambled to pick them up he got upon his horse and made his getaway.

Meantime, General Kearny had named Captain Cooke's troop as his advance guard to enter Apache Canyon. When he reached the dangerous part of the pass Cooke reported finding "only a rude breastwork of felled trees across it." Following Armijo's departure, the rest of the Mexican defenders had run away, leaving the Army of the West free to enter Santa Fe, which it did around sundown, August 18, 1846, not quite two months after its leading elements departed Fort Leavenworth, Kansas.

For the first time in its history the United States had taken by military conquest a territory belonging to a foreign nation—and, remarkably, without firing a shot.*

What had persuaded Armijo to give up New Mexico without a fight has been the subject of much historical speculation through the years. It has been said he was simply a coward, or that he wanted to escape with his ill-gotten gains rather than face the possibility of being taken prisoner, but the most tantalizing suggestion is that he had been bought off by Uncle Sam. In this version, James Magoffin's visit prior to Kearny's arrival was the occasion for a bribery offer in exchange for Armijo's compliance with the U.S. takeover.

Captain Cooke's family lore certainly seems to have it so. Cooke's great-grandson Philip St. George Cooke III, writing in 1964, referred to Cooke's 1878 chronicle of the expedition in which Cooke escorted Magoffin, stating: "What he did not tell was that he was the only officer on the frontier that the government would trust with the large sum of gold used to bribe Armijo to leave Santa Fe and New Mexico, without fighting the forces of the United States Army."

Moreover, after the Mexican-American War had ended Magoffin presented the U.S. government with a claim for $50,000 (about $1.5 million today) for services rendered. Although there is no direct mention of a bribe in connection with Armijo and the acquisition of New

*One might argue that Andrew Jackson's conquest of Spanish West Florida during his 1818 expedition to suppress a revolt of Seminole Indians and runaway slaves represented a U.S. military coup, but Jackson's action was quickly disavowed by Washington as being unauthorized and the territory returned to Spain.

Mexico, it is easy to see why such a matter might have been omitted from a public document. Despite objections and arguments from officials in the War Department, the government in fact paid Magoffin the sum of around $30,000, presumably at the direction of Secretary of War Marcy, who had originally vouched for Magoffin in his letter to Kearny, and in which he referred to the important services that the savvy Santa Fe trader might render to the general's expedition.

While the subject has drawn considerable interest from historians, the fact is that in 1848 the United States government wound up paying Mexico handsomely for all the territories it acquired during the war, and even if Armijo *was* bribed it wouldn't be the first time in U.S. history—and one way or another it likely won't be the last.

When most of the army had finally gotten into the city plaza the U.S flag was run up and a thirteen-gun salute fired from Kearny's artillery, which had been posted on an overlook. Then the troops encamped for the night. There was no trouble from civilians or from the former Mexican belligerents, who it was said had taken to the mountains. Captain Cooke, acting as provost, reported that he "took charge of the city with a guard of only fifty men."

Apparently many residents, fearing they knew not what, had fled in advance of Kearny's approach. A prominent Mexican political leader posted a notice trying to calm the "dread" of the people, and decrying the fact that "many families are leaving their homes in order to hide in the deserts, as if [Kearny's] forces were composed of cruel and sanguinary savages."

That night General Kearny slept on the floor of the governor's palace, while Cooke noted that "the taverns and saloons were overrun by the hungry and thirsty volunteers, and at last I had to drive them all out. After midnight I lay down on my cloak in the main hall of the 'palace,' and there, with my saddle for a pillow, slept soundly."

Next morning Kearny repeated his public change-of-allegiance ceremony, receiving indifferent if not reluctant pledges from province officials, whom he left in place to perform their duties so long as they took the oath, once more explaining that the consequences of violation lay at the end of a rope. He met with Colonel Doniphan, the lawyer, to create some kind of territorial legal framework for the citizens. The result, which Doniphan modeled on Mexican statutes, the U.S. Constitution, Missouri statutes, and the Livingston Code of Louisiana, was so brilliantly constructed that much of it—known as the Kearny Code—remains today as a principal basis of law in the Southwest.*

A few days later the chiefs of the many Pueblo tribes in the area arrived at the Governor's Palace and not only pledged submission but "expressed great satisfaction" at the American conquest. According to Captain Emory, the chiefs informed General Kearny that Pueblo lore was steeped in a tradition that "a white man would come from the far east and release them from the bonds and shackles which the Spaniards had imposed, not in the name of, but in a worse form, than slavery."

Kearny ordered Emory and several of his engineers to start building a fort that would guard against both any attempt by the Mexicans to recapture their province capital as well as depredations by the Indians.

Then he began preparing for a greater ordeal, the long march west, another thousand miles across terra incognita, to California and the Pacific Ocean.

*In writing the code, Colonel Doniphan welcomed the assistance of the volunteer private Willard P. Hall. Doniphan and Hall, also a lawyer, were then opposing candidates for Congress in Missouri—the colonel as a Whig and Private Hall as a Democrat. When news arrived that Hall was the victor, Doniphan congratulated him and offered to discharge him from the army so he could serve his term. But Hall declined the offer and went on to California with the Kearny party, earning accolades for his service. He later was elected governor of Missouri.

CHAPTER SEVEN

Some Days You Eat the Bear; Some Days the Bear Eats You

When Zachary Taylor was fighting and winning the Battle of Resaca de la Palma, John C. Frémont was tending to business in California. When he reappeared in the Central Valley at the end of May 1846, following the tempestuous tour of Oregon's Klamath Lake, Frémont found the forlorn province in a political and civil uproar.

Word of war with the United States still had not reached California authorities, but there was trouble enough as it was. Governance of California had always been fragile. It was too far removed and too large to be effectively governed by Mexico City, which remained consumed by political turmoil and seemingly eternal war. Mexico was not only bankrupt but indebted to many nations of the western world. Moreover, the Californians and the Mexicans were frequently at odds with each other, and there was often talk of breaking away from Mexican rule. Then there was the fractious struggle for control between the southern Californians and northern Californians, with "general this" and "general that" (almost everyone who could ride a horse, it seemed, called himself a general) perpetually threatening to attack each other. Meantime, the Indians—who had been out of hand since the dissolution of the Franciscan missions—continued to prey on farmers, ranchers, and travelers. And now the American settlers had become the new focus of strife.

The once jovial General José Castro, military commander in the north, had not been the same since his disagreeable run-in with Frémont at Gavilan Peak. He insisted that California was becoming "Texasized," meaning that the influx of American settlers would someday take over, as they had in Texas.

Meantime, in Los Angeles, Governor Pico concluded that California would be better off independent and had refused to recognize or obey the authority of President Herrera in Mexico City. To reimpose his supremacy, Herrera appropriated funds for General Mariano Paredes to equip a sizable punitive expedition to bring Pico back into line. Instead, Paredes used the money to finance a coup against Herrera and made himself president of Mexico. This was typical of the sort of political chaos that prevailed in Mexico City.

Just about the time Frémont was descending the valley from his Oregon expedition, Castro began making bellicose preparations, including the purchase of several hundred horses in Sonoma, which was quickly distorted by an American settler to "a force of 250 *men* on horseback" moving toward the Sacramento valley. By then California was in the full spring dry season as Frémont's expedition picked its way southward. Wheat fields, wild oats, and other crops were brown and brittle. Trailside foliage was dusty and limp and the streams low and sluggish. But with each passing day it seemed a new report or rumor came in of impending danger to the American settlers.

Alarmed ranchers and farmers told that during the past few weeks Indians in their employ had begun sneaking off to join their wild brethren in the mountains in preparation for a general uprising. Other reports said that agents of Castro were inciting the Indians and offering rewards for burning the Americans' wheat fields, which were just then dried to the point of being combustible.

One story was that Castro was building a fort in the High Sierras that would turn back any new immigrants. Another account had it that Castro was in the process of acquiring Sutter's Fort, which was the core support system for American settlers in the Sacramento valley. In fact, there was truth in this story, and had the acquisition gone through it would have made the Americans' position in the valley untenable, since Sutter's was the sole source of sustenance, civilization, and safe haven in case the Indians went on the warpath. Sutter, who had long ago become a Mexican citizen and was in fact an officer of the government, at first resisted Castro's overtures to purchase his operation, but later he relented, apparently on the theory that, if the Mexican commander wished, he could simply seize the fort and pay him nothing. Castro never sought to occupy the fort, however, which rendered his acquisition moot, and in fact Frémont occupied it himself and in the name of the American government commissioned Sutter a lieutenant in the U.S. Army.

Meantime, Kearny and his soldiers were still floundering around in the Arizona desert, but ever since Frémont's standoff at Gavilan Peak in March 1846, settlers had begun looking to him for security and protection of their interests. Now they implored Frémont to defend them against Castro. By May, the Americans had become even more jumpy after word got around about the government edicts (or proclamations) forbidding foreigners from owning land in California and subjecting them to arbitrary expulsion at the whim of the authorities. They were not afraid of Castro, the settlers said, but they needed someone to take charge and organize them and lead them in a fight against his Californio forces.

But Frémont, still unaware that the United States and Mexico had gone to war a few weeks earlier, demurred. He told the settlers he held no authority to attack the Californios, but that if *they* wished to do so on their own he would not stand in the way—and as a matter of fact he would give them tacit assistance in planning their operations. Clearly Frémont was stalling, hoping for news of war to legitimize his actions.

In the coming days more groups of settlers gathered around Frémont's camp with further disturbing rumors. Others began packing up to leave California, certain they would be attacked. Meantime, Frémont sent Lieutenant Gillespie to San Francisco to obtain much needed supplies from a U.S. warship anchored there. His request included such necessities as flour, soap, and tobacco, but also "a keg of gunpowder, three hundred pounds of musket-ball lead, and eight thousand percussion caps."*

---

*Much has been made of this requisition of munitions by historians seeking to prove that Frémont deliberately exceeded his authority in California and that he had already determined at this point—war or no war—to join or lead an uprising of the settlers to take over the province. Since there is no documentary or testimonial proof of this, it is noted here for what it is worth. Moreover, Frémont had reached the extent of his exploratory range, and his party would have been preparing at some point to head back across two thousand miles of treacherous territory. It might simply have been that he wanted to equip them with ample ammunition for their weapons.

An event that was presently riling the Americans was the Californio acquisition of the aforementioned herd of horses from Sonoma. The horses were being driven by a military detachment toward General Castro's headquarters in Santa Clara, about forty miles south of San Francisco at the southern end of San Francisco Bay. A rumor had leaked out that these animals were mounts for a newly recruited army, which would soon march against the settlers.

With Frémont's blessing, at dawn on June 7 a posse of settlers made a surprise attack on the Californios' camp, netting the Americans both weapons and the horse herd. Emboldened by their achievement, they next set out for Sonoma, residence of General Mariano Vallejo, who had sold the Californios their horses and commanded the garrison there. It was the settlers' conviction that control of Sonoma, about forty miles northeast of San Francisco, would give them control of the Sacramento valley and at least temporarily stymie whatever plans Castro had in mind.

On June 12 a band of heavily armed settlers, led by a tall, nail-tough American named Ezekiel Merritt, closed in on Sonoma at dawn—in particular on the military barracks—and easily captured the place without a shot being fired. In the process they took into custody General Vallejo and his staff, as well as nine old brass cannons, two hundred fifty muskets, and a hundred pounds of gunpowder. For better or worse, the cat, or cat's-paw, of insurrection was now out of the bag.

General Vallejo, who in fact considered himself a friend of American annexation of California, had donned his best uniform to greet his captors, expecting, as was customary with men of his rank, to be released on parole, or upon his personal recognizance. Instead, the settlers began talking about making him a prisoner. At some point during the discussion Don Vallejo—known to be an excellent host—broke out the brandy, and by midday a full barrel had apparently been ordered up from his cellar reserve. With no clear leadership, the "negotiations" broke down into an orgy of conviviality until, said one of the settlers, the brandy "had well nigh vanquished the victors."

At last it was decided to hold Vallejo, his American brother-in-law (and translator) Jacob Leese, and half a dozen other officials as a kind of ransom, or insurance, and incarcerate them in Sutter's Fort. But beyond that no clear plan had emerged and it seemed the revolt was falling apart for lack of purpose. Then a man named William B. Ide entered the picture and rallied the crumbling morale. Ide, a fifty-year-old teacher, carpenter, and farmer from New England, set just the right tone for the reeling American rebels, crying out, "Saddle no horse for me—I will leave my bones here!" in reference to waverers who were talking about packing up and leaving California.

Ide wrote a "proclamation" of the overthrow of the California government by the settlers, filled with blustery denunciations of "despotism" and other maltreatment by the authorities. The document announced that California was now a "republic" and that democratic elections would soon be held.

Then, in the Sonoma plaza, the Mexican flag was summarily hauled down and in its place was hoisted the famous "Bear Flag."

Hastily cut and sewn from materials found at hand, this rude banner became the emblem of what became known as the Bear Flag revolt, a source of immense pride for some Californians and a cause of shame and reproach for others.

So the story goes, the flag was designed by William Todd, a cousin of Mary Todd Lincoln, wife of the future president. One of the settlers' wives was said to have donated some red flannel for a single stripe at the bottom, and a lone star was drawn and colored in, using a paint of brick dust and blackberry juice. Prominent on the face of the flag was the silhouette of a grizzly bear, symbolizing strength and ferocity. Missourians in the party insisted it looked more like a full-grown hog, but in any case this was the height of Manifest Destiny.*

In the meanwhile Frémont, while still refusing material help to the settlers on grounds it could be construed as interfering in another nation's affairs, had decided to deal with the growing Indian threat, which he justified by noting that a large Indian war party theoretically could cut off his rear echelon as he tried to return to the United States.

Throughout his career Frémont had been exposed to and connected with a wide variety of Indians and developed an opinion of them fairly common with the times. He had seen firsthand their depreda-

---

*The original Bear Flag remained on display in San Francisco until April 1906, when it was destroyed in the fire that followed the great San Francisco earthquake.

tions and their capacity for cruelty, lying, thievery, killing, and other un-Christian, un-American, and uncivilized behavior—including the recent murder of his friend Basil Lajeunesse—and was therefore not disposed in general to think kindly of Native Americans.

Thus, while the settlers were moving against Sonoma, Frémont set out with most of his party of exploration to inflict a "rude but necessary" preemptive strike against the presumed Indian uprising. At dawn his party pitched into a camp along the Sacramento River, surprising the inhabitants, killing a few, scattering the rest, and firing or ripping down their shelters and food bins. A number of the natives, Frémont's scouts reported, were wearing black paint (war paint) and some had been conducting war ceremonies. He repeated the procedure at villages up and down the river until by the end of the day the natives in that area of the valley had been sufficiently chastised—dispersed and defeated—so that Frémont now felt no threat or pressure to his rear.

Meantime, General Castro and Governor Pico had been doing an odd kind of Mexican hat dance with each other while they should have been organizing to put down the Bear Flag rebellion. Castro, convinced that Pico was out to get him, started recruiting an army, ostensibly to deal with recalcitrant American settlers but in fact had headed it south to Los Angeles to remove Pico from power. That's what Consul Larkin believed the herd of 250 horses had been intended for. At the same time, Pico suspected as much and began raising his own army on the false pretense of riding north to assist General Castro against the settlers, when he actually intended to use it to oust Castro from power. It was in the midst of this mazy whipsaw that word arrived of the Bear Flag revolt, and the incarceration of General Vallejo and his companions at Sutter's Fort, which rendered the question of power and control moot, and both Castro and Pico adjusted their focus to the problem of revolution in their country.

Castro immediately issued his own proclamation, which denounced the settlers as "adventurers" and called on the population to "arise en masse, divine providence will guide us to glory." The general didn't have much to work with, but he managed to raise 160 men, soon joined by a band of 25 more led by a barber. On June 23 they moved north toward Sonoma. On the way, a detachment of this force captured two

American couriers and, it was said, butchered them with knives. As word of the atrocity spread, settler families began fleeing their farms into Sonoma.

For the next several days there was some desultory fighting all around San Rafael, which finally became too much for Frémont to bear. He decided to play his hand.

When messengers from Ide arrived and pleaded for Frémont to join and lead the settlers' revolt, Frémont concluded that a crisis was at hand and it was "unsafe to leave events to mature under unfriendly, or mistaken, direction," or so he wrote later. He ordered his party, now consisting of 180 men, including some settlers, to saddle up and head for San Rafael, where the fighting was.*

Castro's forces had gone, however, and nothing remained but bitter talk about the mutilation of the two American couriers, who apparently had been well known and well liked. About that time a small boat, which had crossed San Francisco Bay, put in at San Pedro Point and landed three Californios right under Frémont's nose. Kit Carson rode down with a party and apprehended these people, two youthful twins and an elderly man, then galloped back to Frémont for further instructions. The confusion over what happened next is yet another result of the contradictory evidence from this somewhat obscure period in U.S. history.

It is a fact that the three men who debarked from the boat were shot by Kit Carson and his crew. How and why remain murky; various testimony after the fact says they were shot trying to escape, killed by Frémont's Delaware Indians, shot when they resisted, or murdered in cold blood on Frémont's instructions. No one will ever know the truth, but the fact that Carson shot these men should surprise no one; among his most enduring traits was that he was a steely-eyed killer. Still, the incident remains a stain on Frémont's record.

Castro's forces managed to escape a confrontation with Frémont's band entirely by means of a trick. They sent out a courier, knowing he would be captured, with a letter saying Castro was on his way to

---

*Here Frémont took the rather dubious precaution of writing out his resignation from the army, in order to avoid any political embarrassment to the U.S. government should the adventure turn sour. He ordered it sent by the next post to his father-in-law, Senator Benton, to be used at his discretion as the situation developed.

attack Sonoma. Frémont took the bait while the Californios rode off in the opposite direction. Finding Sonoma safe, Frémont went looking for a fight and wound up tracking his adversary all the way to Sausalito, only to find that the enemy had escaped in boats to the other side of San Francisco Bay.

Looking across the narrow neck of the bay Frémont could see an enemy fort guarding the entrance on the opposite shore. He determined that it needed to be reduced so American ships could safely enter the estuary with munitions and supplies. William D. Phelps, the salty captain of the *Moscow,* an American merchant ship, offered to ferry a detachment across the strait in one of the ship's boats to attack the fort, and a spiking party was organized, consisting of Frémont, Carson, Lieutenant Gillespie, and a dozen others, "men singled out as the best shots," including a gunsmith. Daybreak found them just off the southern "gate," or entrance to the San Francisco Bay, now bathed in the first rays of sun, which Frémont promptly dubbed the "Golden Gate," a name that has stuck through the years. Just as they landed, several Californios fled the fort on horseback. Once inside the crumbling fortification they spiked fourteen long brass Spanish cannons with the aid of some rat-tail files procured from the *Moscow.**

Afterward, Captain Phelps, an inveterate man of the sea, set down his impression upon first meeting Frémont, the famous landlubber, whom he had previously known only by reputation. "My imagination had pictured him out somehow as I thought he ought to look. . . . I suppose[ed] I should see a full-whiskered military man, towering in size above all his command, stiff with uniforms and straps, looking blood, bullets and grizzly bears." Instead, Phelps said, someone "pointed out to me as Capt. Fremont, a slender, well-proportioned man of sedate but pleasing countenance, sitting in front of a tent. His dress, near as I remember, was a blue flannel shirt, after the naval style, open at the collar, which was turned over; over this a deerskin hunting shirt, figured and trimmed in hunter's style, blue cloth pantaloons and neat moccasins, all of which had very evidently seen hard service. His head was not cumbered by a hat or cap, but a light cotton handkerchief,

---

*"Spiking" renders a cannon useless by clogging the firing touch hole. It cannot be easily undone and usually requires drilling or even retooling at a factory.

bound tightly round his head, [and] surmounted a suit which might not appear very fashionable at the White House or be presentable at the Queen's levee, but to my eye it was an admirable rig to scud under or fight in."

With the enemy fort silenced, and San Francisco Bay now open, on the Fourth of July, 1846, Frémont returned to Sonoma, which was by then teeming with settlers engaged in wild excitement at the prospect of ending Mexican rule. It had been almost exactly a year since he had crossed the Missouri with his Party of Exploration, and they'd made it two thousand miles across the continent to what might well have seemed the other side of the world. With Castro's forces now on the run and northern California secure, at least for the moment, Frémont held an Independence Day celebration that included artillery salutes and speeches and concluded with a military ball. Next day he got down to more serious business.

All of the men who were fit to fight, including Frémont's desperados, were organized into what he styled the California Battalion—now 234 men organized into four companies and officered by leaders selected for their proven field merit. What they looked like is anybody's guess, and there was probably no better guesser than Frémont's most prominent second-generation biographer, Allan Nevins, who conjured a picturesque apparition of the men most responsible for delivering California into the United States.

"The California Battalion, a motley array of voyageurs, trappers, scouts, former sailors, frontier farmers, and ranchmen, was a body unlike any other that has ever fought on American soil, and yet with close affinities to our pioneer fighters in all generations. Miles Standish, Robert Rogers, Daniel Boone and Davy Crockett would have recognized the breed at once. Most of the men wore broad-brimmed hats pulled low over the eyes, shirts of buckskin or blue flannel, and buckskin trousers and moccasins, all much the worse for wear and smeared with dirt, blood and gunpowder. From a leather girdle about every man's waist hung an ugly-looking bowie or hunter's knife, and sometimes a brace of pistols. Most of the recruits were bearded and long-haired; all were sunburnt and fierce of visage. A single sorry-looking bugle sounded the calls." And, he might have added, they were pound for pound among the most ferocious fighters on the planet.

Nevins was correct, of course, except that America *had* seen their ilk before—that bizarre mix of lawyers, merchants, freed blacks, Louisiana planters, pirates, and Tennessee and Kentucky backwoodsmen who threw back the mighty British army at the Battle of New Orleans in the War of 1812; or, at the height of the American Revolutionary War, the eclectic 200-man crew of John Paul Jones's *Bonhomme Richard,* its decks awash in blood, who took the HMS *Serapis* in plain view of the British Admiralty off Yorkshire. Indeed, America had seen the likes of these men before and would see their likes again into the future. General Castro and his lieutenants had seen them, too, and wanted no part of them; he marched his army back to Santa Clara to await developments.

Meanwhile, Frémont took the California Battalion to his old camp on the American Fork, near Sutter's Fort, and began whipping them in shape with drill and rifle practice. He'd only been at it a few days when on July 10 joyous news arrived from the coast. Three days earlier, Commodore Sloat, of the U.S. Pacific Fleet, had hoisted the American flag over Monterey and San Francisco. The war between Mexico and the United States had been declared nearly two months ago. California, according to a proclamation by Sloat, was now U.S. territory. Frémont celebrated the occasion by running up the American flag next morning to a twenty-one-gun salute, a symbolic gesture that ended the short-lived Bear Flag Republic. They were all Americans now.

The messenger who brought this news also brought a U.S. flag for Sonoma, as well as one to be run up at Sutter's Fort, and a message for Frémont saying that Sloat desired him to march his California Battalion to Monterey as soon as possible. It took a little over a week to get the men equipped and across the Coast Range to Monterey, which they reached on the nineteenth of July. As they marched along the harbor road, Frémont's men were agog to see, amidst several smaller American warships, a massive British battleship of the line riding at anchor just offshore, its Union Jack floating on the ocean breeze. "Many of my men," Frémont explained, "had never seen the ocean, or the English flag."

This vessel was the eighty-gun HMS *Collingwood,* flagship of Rear Admiral Sir George Seymour, commander of the British Pacific Fleet, which caused some tense moments when it appeared outside the Monterey bight three days earlier. Almost everyone from Sloat, to Frémont, to Larkin—let alone Polk, Bancroft, and the government in Washington— was convinced the British had designs on California, especially if war broke out, which might provide England the opportunity to take the province "under the protection of Her Majesty's crown."

As the British behemoth entered the harbor, Sloat had immediately sent word to recall all the sailors and marines who were ashore and ordered his ships readied for action, but he needn't have worried. To everyone's relief, the 200-foot *Collingwood* eased her sail, rounded up, and dropped anchor in the harbor, peaceful as a tycoon's yacht.

Sloat's conquest of Monterey (and by proxy all of California, according to his proclamation) had been almost too easy. When his flagship *Savannah* drew up in the harbor, Sloat as a courtesy had offered to honor the Mexican flag with a twenty-one-gun salute, but the *alcalde* declined on grounds there was no gunpowder to return it. When, after several days he finally got around to demanding a formal surrender, Sloat was informed by the *alcalde* that there was no Mexican flag to be hauled down during the ceremonies, since none had been flown at Monterey for many months, and none could be found.

The conquest, however, had been accomplished in a hairbreadth nick of time. As if to confirm the worst fears of the American officials at the *Collingwood*'s arrival, the first thing Admiral Sir George Seymour said to the American naval commander was, "Sloat, if your flag was not flying on shore, I should have hoisted mine there."*

That would of course have posed interesting dilemmas, as the British Pacific Fleet was as fully armed as the American one, if not more so, and any military conflict might have touched off another world war of Napoleonic magnitude. The problem was that Sloat was preposterously tardy in reacting to events and to his orders. But he was sixty-five years old, a martinet, apparently something of a nervous Nellie, and was not about to rock any boats.

Secretary of the Navy Bancroft's instructions, delivered to Sloat by

*This quotation is contained in a lengthy statement by Rodman M. Price, an officer under Sloat and the future governor of New Jersey. Written many years after the fact, the statement purports to chronicle the various international intrigues and other machinations attendant to the capture of California.

Lieutenant Gillespie, had ordered the Pacific Squadron to capture the major California ports and hold the country *immediately* upon word that war with Mexico had commenced. That word was received by Sloat at Mazatlán on May 17, when the U.S. consul in Mexico reported that hostilities had broken out on the Rio Grande between the Mexican army and General Zachary Taylor's forces. But instead of moving at once to shift the fleet north to California, Sloat dawdled, waiting for more exact reports—in particular, he said later, word that a "declaration of war" had been issued.

Fresh in Sloat's mind, or so he reportedly said later, was an awkward affair initiated four years earlier by a previous commander of the U.S. Pacific Fleet. In 1842 Commodore Thomas ap Catesby Jones had also captured Monterey to keep it out of British hands, based on rumors that the United States and Mexico had gone to war. When the rumors proved unfounded Jones, a hero of the Battle of New Orleans in the War of 1812, did everything in his power to smooth over the mistake with the Mexicans, but when word of the blunder finally got back to Washington he was court-martialed and "censured," which for officers in the navy is a fate next to death.

As weeks passed by, Sloat continued to procrastinate, causing younger and more eager officers to shake their heads, wring their hands, and talk in whispers, but it was not until more than a month had passed and news arrived confirming that the U.S. Navy had blockaded Mexico's eastern seaboard that Commodore Sloat finally acted, sailing the squadron north to capture the California coast.

Sloat got his censure anyway. To justify his indolence, Sloat wrote a letter to Navy Secretary Bancroft explaining that while he had word of fighting, he had no knowledge of any declaration of war, and therefore he was being careful "to avoid any act of aggression." Bancroft replied that "your anxiety not to do wrong has led you into a most unfortunate and unwarranted inactivity . . . you remained in a state of inactivity and did not carry out the instructions."

The town of Monterey was busy as a hive when Frémont's army rode through on the way to its encampment. British and American sailors and marines mingled in the streets with Mexicans and seamen from whalers and assorted traders, residents, and visitors. But if there was lingering doubt by the British as to whether to stay out of the California affair, it was apparently laid to rest by this martial procession. An awestruck lieutenant in the Royal Navy gave his description of the battalion as it arrived in the city: "They naturally excited curiosity. Here were true trappers, the class that produced the heroes of Fennimore Cooper's best works. The men had passed years in the wilds, living upon their own resources; they were a curious set. A vast cloud of dust appeared first, and thence in long file emerged this wildest, wild party.

"Fremont rode ahead, a spare, active-looking man. He was dressed in a blouse and leggings, and wore a felt hat. After him came five Delaware Indians, who were his body-guard, and have been with him through all his wanderings; they had charge of the baggage-horses. The rest, many of them blacker than the Indians, rode two and two, the rifle held by one hand across the pommel of the saddle.

"His original men are principally backwoodsmen from the State of Tennessee and the banks of the upper waters of the Missouri. He has one or two with him who enjoy a high reputation in the prairies. Kit Carson is as well known there as the Duke is in Europe.* The dress of these men was principally a long loose coat of deerskin, tied with thongs in front; trowsers of the same, of their own manufacture. They are allowed no liquor, tea and sugar only; this no doubt has much to do with their good conduct; and the discipline, too, is very strict.†

"They were marched up to an open space on the hills near the town, under some long firs, and there took up their quarters, in messes of six or seven, in the open air. The Indians lay beside their leader. In justice to the Americans I must say they seemed to treat the natives well, and their authority extended every protection to them. The butts of the trapper's rifles resemble a Turkish musket, therefore fit light to the shoulder; they are very long and very heavy, carry ball thirty-eight to the pound."

During the next days there was much visiting of Frémont's camp by officers and sailors from the *Collingwood* and from the American fleet, and a great deal of conversation about shooting and marksmanship,

---

*The reference is to Wellington.
†He cites no reference or proof for this last assertion, and it is probably false.

which led to marks being put up against trees, which, as with soldiers and sailors everywhere, led to serious wagering.

For his part Frémont, accompanied by Lieutenant Gillespie, went straightaway to Sloat's headquarters aboard the *Savannah*. At first, Frémont said, the commodore "seemed glad to see me," but soon he became "excited over the gravity of the situation in which he was the chief figure; and now, wholly responsible for its consequences." Sloat demanded to know under whose instructions Frémont had taken up arms against the Mexicans.

"I do not know by what authority you are acting," Sloat huffed. "I know nothing. Mr. Gillespie . . . came to Mazatlan, and I sent him to Monterey, but I know nothing. I want to know by what authority you are acting."

Frémont replied that he had acted on his own authority at Sonoma and elsewhere, when the situation seemed to be coming apart. At this information, Sloat "appeared much disturbed," and he told Frémont he had raised the flag at Monterey only because he assumed that Frémont had been acting on *written* orders from Washington to overthrow the Mexicans in California. Before Frémont could explain, he said, the commodore became "so discouraged that the interview terminated abruptly . . . [and] he did not ask me for another."

Frémont returned to shore in shock that Sloat had somehow relied on authority conferred on *him* to justify raising the American flag in a country that was at war with the United States, adding that "the situation now had something in it so grand that hesitation was incomprehensible. I knew that the men who understood the future of our country and who at this time ruled its destinies, and were the government, regarded the California coast as the boundary fixed by nature to round off our national domain."* Frémont had left Washington the previous year "with full knowledge of their wishes, and also of their purposes so far as these could be settled in the existing circumstances."†

---

*He is referring, of course, to Messrs. Polk, Benton, Marcy, and Bancroft.

†These recollections are from Frémont's memoirs published forty years later. Controversy remains over what exactly were his charges from the various officials. Here Frémont seems to be saying that there was a kind of tacit understanding between him and the Washington authorities that he was to act to secure California if the opportunity presented itself.

Walking beside the ocean, Frémont said he went out on the Point of Pines, a craggy promontory that juts into the sea, dotted with the well-known stunted Pacific pines. From there, he said, he could see warships at anchor in Monterey Bay—the massive *Collingwood* surrounded by smaller U.S. vessels. "There lay the pieces on the great chess-board before me," he waxed metaphorically, "with which the game for an empire had been played. I was but a pawn, and like a pawn had been pushed forward to the front at the opening of the game."

In the face of what he again believed was lack of definitive authority from Washington, Commodore Sloat once more become intransigent and idle, loitering his command at Monterey for the next several weeks, much to the consternation of Frémont, who wanted to get on with the total conquest of California before the Californios could regroup or the Mexicans sent an army to retake the province.

In the meantime, Sloat's replacement arrived in the USS *Congress*. He turned out to be none other than Commodore Robert Stockton, who had presided over the tragedy of the *Princeton* explosion on the Potomac and the skulduggery down in Texas just prior to the outbreak of war.

Stockton was made of wholly different cloth than Sloat and seemed just as anxious as Frémont to consolidate American gains in California; however, as he explained to Frémont, his orders did not call for him to take over for Sloat for some days. Frémont then threatened—though that is probably too strong a word for it—to take his party back to the United States. At least he told Stockton that he would make that decision overnight, whereupon Stockton prevailed on him to stay, saying he would have command of the Pacific Fleet in a few more days.

Next morning Stockton sent a message to Sloat emphasizing the importance of either capturing General Castro and his army or driving him out of the province. "Until either one or the other is done, I see no hope of restoring peace and good order to this territory."

He requested that Sloat turn over to him the sloop of war *Cyane* in order to transport Frémont's California Battalion south of Los Angeles to head Castro off. After some grumbling and hand-wringing Sloat finally agreed. To Frémont's 250 men, Stockton added 80 of his marines, and he commissioned Frémont as a major and promoted Gillespie to captain. On July 25 the reinforced California Battalion embarked in the *Cyane* for San Diego, to Castro's rear. The plan was to then march quickly to Los Angeles to surprise him and cut him off. "This country has been trifled with long enough," Stockton declared.

As Frémont told it, "My men were all greatly pleased at the novelty of a voyage in a man-of-war, which they had anticipated would be very pleasant and there would be no prospect of storms."

However, no sooner had the *Cyane* cleared the bay and hauled southward than the wind began to blow and the ship began to roll and wallow in swells; after a few hours of this, Frémont said, "We were all very low in our minds. Carson was among those who were badly worsted by this enemy to landsmen, and many were the vows made that never again would they put trust in the fair-weather promises of the ocean."

Five hundred sea miles later, the bedraggled warriors at last staggered off *Cyane*'s long boats to lay foot on solid ground for the first time in three days and nights. Instead of the hostile reception they had anticipated, Frémont and his people were greeted as friends by the captain of the port, Santiago Argüello, and the suave, wealthy Don Juan Bandini, described as "the chief citizen of the place."

It was a good thing, too, since Frémont's party was entirely ignorant of the geography of the area or its resources. He was immediately in need of horses to mount his men and cattle to feed them but quickly discovered that the large ranches in this part of southern California were few and far between. Bandini and Argüello were "extremely valuable" in providing aid and information on these matters, but still it took Frémont a month to round up enough horses and provisions for his now 330-man army.

Conversations with Bandini and Argüello revealed that the "leaders"—meaning the wealthy—of San Diego were not pleased with the Mexican government, which had more or less abandoned them and had taken no steps whatever to exploit the value of the port in the bay or given any other economic help or encouragement. Thus these men welcomed the Americans and the notion of becoming part of the United States. Frémont convinced the two to use their influence with the rest of the population "to obtain quiet possession of the territory," and to convey Frémont's intentions of conciliation, which would "go far to allay the natural excitement created by our invasion."

In the meantime he familiarized himself with the country, reporting that while it was mostly arid, brush-covered waste, there was a surprising number of "little valleys converted by a single spring into crowded gardens, where pears, peaches, quinces, pomegranates, grapes, olives and other fruits grew luxuriantly together, the little stream acting upon them like a principle of life." The soil was so fertile in these oases, Frémont exulted, that "a single vine has been known to produce a barrel of wine, and the olive trees are burdened with the weight of the fruit." On the eighth of September they marched north, on Los Angeles.

The 140-mile expedition was a pleasant one, according to Frémont, with good weather, ample food obtained from the ranches, and frequent streams to water the stock. Juan Bandini had obtained information that General Castro was "encamped on the mesa near [Los Angeles] with a force of about five hundred men and ten pieces of artillery." Since Frémont had left behind the eighty marines Stockton had lent him, plus fifty of his own men, to garrison San Diego, he was feeling a little edgy that Castro might attack his reduced force. Not long after the expedition had gotten under way reconnaissance horsemen from Castro's cavalry began to shadow them. Frémont was relieved, therefore, when word came after several days' marching that Commodore Stockton had landed with 350 men and several pieces of artillery at San Pedro, about twenty-six miles from Frémont's present position.

As planned, these two forces united and on September 13, 1846, marched jointly on Los Angeles. Instead of the expected battle the American army waltzed into the city accompanied by a full brass band, "like a parade of home guards, rather than an enemy taking possession of a conquered town," as Frémont put it.

Castro, it seemed, had no stomach for a fight with the Americans and two days earlier had fled to Sonora in northern Mexico. In a letter to Mexican authorities he complained he had neither supplies for his men nor money to purchase them. For his part, Governor Pico "retired to one of his estates, lying about forty miles to the southward of Los Angeles." The American conquest was complete, and the U.S. flag now flew from San Diego to San Francisco and points in between.

Stockton issued a proclamation naming himself governor of California and commander in chief. Martial law was declared and all persons and their property were to be respected. Anyone not willing to obey or acquiesce to the new order would be expelled from the province, including military men, who were required to take an oath not to disturb the peace. Furthermore—and this would cause trouble later—there was a ten p.m. to dawn curfew. A few days later a second proclamation ordered public elections the following month for all *alcaldes* and municipal officers throughout the state. And a third named Captain Gillespie a military commandant for the territory, headquartered at Los Angeles, with broad discretionary powers under military rule.

Meantime, Stockton was growing anxious to get back into the war; in particular he wanted to sail south to blockade the Mexican coast and attack Acapulco. To that end he wrote Frémont saying he proposed to make him military governor of California in his absence, and that upon his return, "I will meet you in San Francisco and place you as Governor of California."

In order to convey the developments to Washington, Kit Carson was selected as courier and commissioned a second lieutenant in the army. Carson was to take the shortest route back east, traveling light and with fast horses about two and a half months' travel, which, Frémont pointedly reminds us, was also the most dicey as it "led through Mexican territory and through the dangerous Indians along the Spanish Trail."

Unknown to Stockton, Frémont, or any of the others was that this was the same route along which General Kearny was inching toward them with his Army of the West.

CHAPTER EIGHT

"The Dogs Bark, but the Caravan Moves On"*

Right around the time Commodore Sloat was hoisting Old Glory over San Francisco and Monterey, nineteen covered wagons of the Reed-Donner party creaked across a fair mountain meadow twinkling with wildflowers toward a stout bastion of civilization on the Oregon Trail known as Fort Bridger. Built three years earlier in 1843 by the celebrated mountain man Jim Bridger, the facility served as an Indian and trapper trading post and emigrant supply station on the Blacks Fork River in southern Wyoming. At 7,000 feet, and sandwiched between the Rocky and the Wasatch mountain ranges, the lovely little valley was like something from a storybook. Not many years back it had been a watery bog created by beaver dams, but the beavers were hunted out by the trappers, including Bridger, and the dams broken up, which opened the valley floor to rushing streams, cottonwoods, and high meadow grasses that had an almost Alpine aspect.

A week earlier there had been several hundred emigrants in the Donner train, captained originally by a forty-four-year-old "hellroaring orator" named William H. "Owl" Russell, a Kentucky lawyer, Black Hawk War veteran, and onetime secretary to Henry Clay. Russell would go on to become a major in Frémont's California Battalion, but there had been a parting of the ways, with the Donners and their crew peeling off southwest along a new, untested route, the so-called Hastings Cutoff. It turned out to be a fateful decision.

Most of their decisions had been fateful, though, since leaving Inde-

*Old Arab saying.

pendence, Missouri, seventy-six days and nearly a thousand miles ago; on the trail the blink of an eye could be the difference between life and death. The ominous warnings began in earnest when they reached Independence, according to Edwin Bryant, a forty-one-year-old transplanted Yankee who had given up his job as editor of the *Louisville Courier and Journal* to go west—where, it was said, a man had once immigrated long ago and lived to the ripe old age of two hundred years, so healthful was the golden California climate. But also, or so it was rumored—according to Bryant—a party of five thousand Mormons had recently marched across the prairies, "with ten brass field pieces, and that every man of the party was armed with a rifle, a bowie-knife, and a brace of large revolving pistols. It was declared that they were inveterately hostile to the emigrant parties and when the latter came up to the Mormons, they intended to attack and murder them, and appropriate their property."*

Another rumor was that "the Kansas Indians had collected in large numbers on the trail for the purpose of robbery and murder"; and finally "that a party of five Englishmen, supposed to be emissaries of their government, had started in advance of us, bound for Oregon, and that their object was to stir up the Indian tribes along the route, and incite them to deeds of hostility towards the emigrants; to rob, murder and annihilate them." And that was just the beginning, Bryant remembered. One day as a wagon train was leaving Independence, the headman of the local Masonic fraternity began an oration in which "he consigned us all to the grave, or to perpetual exile," while old Santa Fe traders warned that by the end of the long California trek everyone's hair "will have turned white as snow, and ten years will be taken from our lives."

Such frenzied tales, predictions, and rumors roiled in Independence, Missouri, in the spring of '46 as thousands of emigrants churned the mud of its streets on the cusp of the greatest mass migration the country had yet seen. The town was a bedlam of promiscuous commotion, with hundreds of prairie schooners clogging the roads and byways while teamsters and bullwackers polluted the air with a gale of

---

*This tale might have gotten its start when word spread around that the army was enlisting what would become the Mormon Battalion to go with Kearny's army and got confused and hyped from there.

horrible profanities. From stores and sidewalks traders sold, and emigrants bought, everything under the sun they had been told was needed for months on the lonesome trail: barrels of flour, molasses, crackers, salt pork, whiskey, and bacon; sacks of beans and rice, coffee, sugar, and cornmeal and bags of salt and spices. Gunpowder, priming caps, and lead for bullets were also high on the list; the men had brought their own weapons—tall "Kentucky long rifles" of high caliber, most of which were actually manufactured in Pennsylvania—and some few might have owned one of the new revolving pistols that Samuel Colt had started making in Connecticut a decade earlier. A yoke (of two) oxen went for $21.67, reported journalist Bryant.

The Reed-Donner party, including the wagons of James Reed and his family, had kicked off on May 12, in a torrential downpour, led by Owl Russell, crossing the Kansas River by ferry for $1 a wagon. It contained a melting pot of souls hoping for a better life—or at least a different life—on Pacific shores. Every manner of language was spoken by the emigrants—French, German, Italian, Spanish, and Scandinavian tongues in addition to English and its Irish and American versions. Among the travelers were two nephews of Daniel Boone, as well as former Missouri governor Lilburn Boggs, who had recovered from his assassination attempt by the Mormons and was taking his new wife, Panthea, on a hunt for greener pastures. The emigrant train's progress had been calculated at eighteen miles per day, what it would take to reach the Sierra Nevadas before the first snows of October closed off the passes for the winter. This was critical, for to be stuck on the eastern slopes, or high in the mountains themselves, was to invite death by starvation. Everyone, then, must pull together for this purpose and help his fellow travelers do the same, while the wagons creaked along, pulled by beasts of burden, flanked by outriders on horseback, guarded by an escort of dogs, and trailed by herds of cattle for meat and milk, which were trailed in turn by sullen packs of wolves, waiting for stragglers.

On June 14, 1846, about a month since the party had set out, Bryant experienced an epiphany. Late in the day, around sundown, as the wagon train headed toward its encampment, he was approached by several men from wagons up ahead who had been told that he was a doctor.

. . .

He wasn't, but he was well enough educated that he might pass for one in some instances. What constituted a doctor in those times was often presupposed by loose qualifications. But in this instance the medicine was well beyond Bryant's skill. Two days earlier, a boy of eight or nine had fallen off the tongue of a wagon and was run over by its wheels, shattering his leg. With misgivings, Bryant agreed to go with the men to see what he could do, not as a "doctor," he would remember, but as a "good Samaritan."

What he found was nearly beyond pity. The boy lay on a bench with his leg encased in a crude splint. It was a compound fracture, the jagged bone protruding through the skin. Gangrene had set in and the wound was swarming with maggots "from foot to knee, in a state of putrefaction." Doctor or no, Bryant told the distraught mother, it was too late for an amputation. The child was too weak to survive an operation, which he had neither the instruments nor the skill to perform.

But she was desperate and pleading and beseeched an old French-Canadian who offered up that he'd once been an assistant to a surgeon and seen such amputations performed. His tools, said Bryant, "were a butcher's knife, a carpenter's handsaw, and a shoemaker's awl to take up the arteries."

The operation was thus performed with no anesthetic, the leg removed above the knee, and the boy suffering through it "never offering a groan or complaint." But in watching his face, Bryant could tell the lad was fading, and just as the Frenchman finished, and drew the cord to tie the skin around the stump, he died. The grief of the mother and family was too much to bear, and Bryant ultimately left the scene only to run into acquaintances who invited him to, of all things, a wedding.

It was an unpretentious wedding by any standards, Bryant recalled, the bride being a Miss Lard, "a very pretty young lady," and the ceremonies performed in a bare tent with cheap candles and a cake "not frosted with sugar, nor illustrated with matrimonial devices." There was no music or dancing, either, and after being handed a slice of cake Bryant drifted off to the edges of the encampment, where in the dim twilight he "could see by the light of the torches and lanterns the funeral procession containing the corpse of the little boy whom I saw expire, to his last resting place in this desolate wilderness." As he stood ruminating on this "mournful scene," a man Bryant recognized passed by to announce that the wife of one of the settlers had "just been safely delivered of a son, and that there was in consequence of this event great rejoicing."

Here was Bryant's epiphany, as he suddenly reflected that within the space of two hours and the physical distance of two miles, he had in some fashion been a party to "a death, and a funeral; a wedding and a birth," and that tomorrow, "in this wilderness, the places where these events had taken place, would be deserted and unmarked except by the grave of the unfortunate boy. Such is the checkered map of human suffering and enjoyment."

On July 9, two months out from Independence, they got their first view of the Rocky Mountains, "which," said one of the crew, "seem almost to mingle their summits with the clouds." Another week and they found themselves at the crest of the South Pass, at an altitude of near 8,000 feet, where even in July the sunrise was cloaked in a veil of frost.

Descending the western slope of the Rockies, the cavalcade entered southern Wyoming, subsequently to become famous for its profusion of superb dinosaur fossils. Even in those days, more than a decade before Darwin published his thought-provoking treatise, it had become fashionable for erudite people to speculate on these absorbing relics. Thus Bryant told his diary, "Many ages ago, in the spot where we are encamped in a crater, there flowed a river of liquid fire [and] the thunders of its convulsions affrighted the huge monster animals which then existed."

Life on the trail was rarely easy, as we have seen from Kearny's march down the Santa Fe Trail. But the Oregon Trail, which was also the way to California, presented new challenges. First, it had been in general use for only a year or so, thus there remained many rough or steep sections of the track, while many river crossings had not been thoroughly worked out, often forcing travelers to improvise. Likewise, the trail led through arid deserts and steep mountains, which strained the stamina and resources of the emigrants. And of course there was the omnipresence of the Indians, whose raiding parties carried off stray or lagging cattle, causing the settlers to corral and guard their beasts at night, and who were often quick to prey on and kill or capture anyone who ventured too far from the train.

At one point in the passage a Pawnee chief pulled off a successful shakedown scheme by offering the company "protection." According to the account reconstructed by Eliza Donner, one of the five Donner girls, it worked this way. "Frequently [the Indians] walked or rode beside our wagons, asking for presents. Mrs. Kehi-go-wa-chuck-ee [the chief's wife] was made happy by the gift of a dozen strings of glass beads, and the chief also accepted a few trinkets and a contribution of tobacco, after which he made the company understand that for a consideration payable in cotton prints, tobacco, salt pork, and flour, he himself and his trusted braves would become escort to the train in order to protect its cattle from harm, and its wagons from the pilfering hands of his tribesmen. His offer was accepted," she added, "with the condition that he should not receive any of the promised goods until the last wagon was safe beyond his territory. This bargain was faithfully kept," Eliza said, "and when we parted from the Indians, they proceeded to immediate and hilarious enjoyment of the luxuries thus earned."

Numerous wagon trains that left from Independence that year soon invented a rude kind of post office in which informational notes from the leading trains were left for succeeding groups, written on the bleached skulls of dead buffalo or on trees that had been skinned of bark.

They covered the first three hundred miles in relative ease, but when they reached the Platte River in present-day Nebraska the terrain became a wilderness with just a two-rut track to hint that civilization had made any appreciable inroads, and hardly that. Yet the wagon train itself was like a miniature city on the move, encompassing the same joys, sorrows, antagonisms, and travails of everytown, U.S.A. A knife fight, for instance, between two men angry over who knew what was broken up before blood was drawn, but hostility remained. Axle trees cracked, iron tires around wheels slipped and had to be fixed by a blacksmith, teams of oxen entangled, wheels fell off. Days or even weeks were characterized by mud or dust or both. Tempers flared; Indians kept everyone on edge and men slept with their rifles and carried them during the day at the half-cock. A council was called and proposed to split up the Oregon-bound wagons from those headed to California. It was hoped this would relieve tensions. Bryant had started a journal in which he wrote, "The trip is sort of a magic mirror, and exposes every man's qualities of heart connected with it, vicious or amiable."

Before leaving Springfield, Jim Reed and the Donner brothers, George and Jake, had carefully read Lansford Hastings's *Emigrants' Guide to Oregon and California*. Now, out on the plains, a thousand miles from Independence, and another thousand from Sutter's Fort on the California side of the mountains, they took stock of the mileage and the distance and fretted over time. It was mid-July, they were behind schedule, and the shortened route that Hastings mentioned in his book began to look appealing.

When he'd written the book for emigrants a full year earlier, Hastings, an enterprising but not very honest Ohio lawyer, had set neither foot nor hoof along this alleged shortcut, the so-called Hastings Cutoff, but apparently had heard of it from mountain men. In fact, it was more or less the same path Frémont had taken when he'd sent Kit Carson ahead across the great desert near Salt Lake to report on Pilot Peak. But Frémont and his party were on horseback and with pack animals, unencumbered by large, heavy wagons pulled by teams of oxen, and, most important, Frémont and his people were seasoned explorers.

Jim Clyman was also a seasoned explorer, a mountain man of some renown, heading back east from California for the umpteenth time, guiding none other than Lansford Hastings, who now got to see first-hand the "cutoff" he'd touted in his book—the one that would "save 300 miles" but actually saved none. Clyman had spent nearly a quarter century in the mountains and had offered to raise a company in support of Frémont right before the Bear Flag rebellion, and coming back now to the States he found himself mistrustful of Hastings, whom he looked upon as a huckster. So when Hastings took his party up the trail from Fort Bridger to try to steer settlers to California instead of Oregon and by his much touted cutoff, Clyman went down the trail to try to steer them the other way. It was there, on June 27, some two hundred miles east of Fort Bridger, that he found himself before a roaring fire at a positive drunk-out near Fort Laramie, where the Owl Russell train, including of course the Donners and the Reeds, had for some cloudy reason decided to lighten their load by selling some of their whiskey to the Sioux and drinking the rest themselves.

Somehow the conversation got around to Hastings and his cutoff and Clyman, a man of few words, spoke to the subject, his voice rising against the inebriated whooping and yipping of the Sioux who were enjoying their own bonfire across the way. Clyman wasn't exactly sure what Hastings was up to, but it appeared he was determined to organize a large party of settlers that would give him hegemony when they reached California. That wasn't a word Clyman would have used, or even known, but he got the thought across. Hastings wanted to be some kind of empire builder, dreaming of the conquest of California, with himself as headman, like Sam Houston had been in Texas, and get rich off it—again, Clyman had his own way of saying it but the others got the drift.

Lansford Hastings, Clyman told them, had somehow decided that California was in play, that time was short, and he had a faster trail to get there, but don't believe him, Clyman said. De Voto has called the route Hastings was pitching "the ghastliest country in the United States," and Clyman felt duty bound to warn them. "Take the regular wagon track [via Fort Hall] and never leave it," he cautioned. "It is barely possible to get through [before the snows] and it may be impossible if you don't."

James Reed remained unconvinced, for he had read Hastings's book. Books spoke truth back then, and it is hard to change the mind of a man who has just read truth from a book. "There is a nigher route," Reed said to Clyman, "and there is no use to take so much of a roundabout course," referring to the Fort Hall trail.

Clyman tried to dissuade them—Reed and the Donners—but he might as well have talked to the fire. He had known Jim Reed and his stubbornness from the Black Hawk War when they'd served in the same infantry company.* "I told him about the great desert and the roughness of the Sierras, and that a straight route might turn out to be impracticable," Clyman said.

Professor De Voto extrapolates, probably correctly, that Clyman

---

*Also serving in this company was a lawyer from Springfield, Abraham Lincoln. "We didn't think much then about his ever being president of the United States," Clyman wrote in his memoirs.

continued in this way: "Told them about the glare of the salt plain under the sun and without water. Told them about the Diggers lurking outside the camps to kill the stock. Told about the chaos of the Wasatch canyons . . . which [he] and Hastings had just barely got through."

Clyman might have saved his breath. Among those who did not believe him was journalist Edwin Bryant, who that very day had decided to trade his wagons and oxen for a string of pack mules and get on toward California while the getting was good—meaning before the snow began to fall. Bryant and Owl Russell, who had turned the wagon train over to the former governor Lilburn Boggs, were going it with a half dozen others, with just their pack animals, hoping to make thirty or forty miles a day instead of the wagons' usual fifteen or twenty. They were riding ahead of the main train, but they were going to California come hell or high water. After listening to Clyman, Bryant lamented that many of the emigrants were ill-disposed to believe him. But Bryant said, "It was easy to perceive that [Clyman] had a motive for his conduct more powerful than his regard to truth." James Reed and the Donners agreed with Bryant. Clyman was a crank. The fire had died out, just the embers left. Even the Sioux had gone to sleep. Next morning they decided to make for the Hastings Cutoff.

There was one more chance.

Two weeks later, Bryant and his party on pack mules greeted a strange sight on the trail, a lone man riding a horse and leading a mule. He had come by himself all the way from Oregon—almost unheard-of—traveling by night and sleeping by day in brush and canebrakes to avoid Indians. His name was Wales B. Bonney and he carried an open letter from Lansford Hastings, who was at Fort Bridger with a large wagon train. "Come on quick!", the letter advised. It said there may be "trouble" with the Mexicans and it is best to arrive in a large group. It touted the Hastings Cutoff "that will save 350–400 miles," according to James Reed, later. The letter promised that Hastings would wait at Fort Bridger for the emigrant wagons and lead them through the wilderness Moses-like. But come on quick.

A week later Bryant and his party arrived at Fort Bridger, well ahead of the main wagon train. After talking with the fabled mountain man and his partner, a man named Louis Vásquez, Bryant decided to go the Hastings way. Bridger drew a glowing picture of the shortcut: plenty of grass for the stock to feed on and abundant water, except for one stretch of desert near the Great Salt Lake.

From what he'd learned, however, Bryant was apprehensive about the shortcut, especially for wagons and families. "We determined this morning to take the new route, with the South end of the Great Salt Lake." But he added, "I wrote several letters to my friends advising them *not* to take this route, but to keep to the old trail via Fort Hall. Our situation was different from theirs." And later in his journal he says, "We could afford to hazard experiments, and make explorations. They could not."

James Reed was one of the intended recipients, since Bryant knew he had contemplated using the Hastings Cutoff. Bryant gave the letters to Jim Bridger's partner, Vásquez, whom he supposed was an honorable man and who had promised to deliver them when the parties arrived at the fort. Vásquez put them in his pocket.

He knew, and Bridger knew, that the commerce of the fort depended in large part on the emigrant trains passing through. If the pilgrims began taking the Fort Hall route, Fort Bridger would wither and die. On July 26, the Reed-Donner company arrived at the fort to find that Hastings and the large train had gone already, anxious to beat the autumn snows in the Sierra passes. But, Reed wrote later, "Mr. Bridger informs me that the route we design to take [the cutoff] is a fine level road, with plenty of water and grass, with the exception before stated [the Great Salt Lake Desert]. It is estimated that 700 miles will take us to Capt. Sutter's fort, which we hope to make in seven weeks from today."

Edwin Bryant's warning, his letters to Reed and the others, stayed in Vásquez's pocket all the while the Reed-Donner train remained at Fort Bridger—a death warrant. It remains among the singular acts of treachery in U.S. history.

On July 31 the party shoved off into the unknown wilds in the customary haze of blue profanity from the teamsters. Seventy-four souls, their ages ranging from infants to sixty-two-year-old George Donner. It was the height of summer and the weather was fine but mornings were frosty at that altitude. Tamsen Donner, George's forty-three-year-old wife, didn't like it. She thought Hastings was a user and a fake and wanted to go with the others on the old tried trail. Taking off like this in the wilderness, alone, scared her.

In Santa Fe, after the American conquest, things had gone swimmingly for General Kearny, or so everyone believed. For many of the New Mexicans, Kearny was the knight in shining armor who had slain the dragon by sending fat old General Armijo and his clique tumbling down the Santa Fe Trail toward Chihuahua. In the days that followed, as promised, Kearny had sent out parties of U.S. soldiers to punish marauding Indians, something Armijo had singularly failed to do. On a promontory above the city Captain Emory and a Lieutenant J. F. Gilmer of the engineers had begun work on a fort with artillery positions that would command approaches to the entire town in case the Mexicans decided to send up an army to contest the conquest. This included nine pieces of artillery abandoned by Armijo when he fled the scene, one of them marked "Barcelona, 1778." When completed, it would be named Fort Marcy, in honor of the U.S. secretary of war.

Santa Fe took some getting used to for the Americans, who in general looked down on the Mexican way of life, and didn't think much of the Indians either. Emory, for example, informed his diary that "The fruits of this place, musk melon, apple, plum, are very indifferent, and would scarcely be eaten in the States." Visiting a pueblo inhabited by Indians of the same name, Emory observed, "The women of the village all dressed alike, and ranged in treble files; they looked fat and stupid."

He was more approving later, at a luncheon given by the padre of the pueblo, at which were served "grapes, melons and wine, with pure white napkins. We relished the wine, whatever its quality, [and] the sponge cake was irreproachable, and would have done honor to our best northern housekeepers." The women, too, at this *divertismo*, were a cut above the stupid fat ones Emory had encountered in the village. "The women seemed to me to drop their usual subdued look and timid wave of the eyelash for good hearty twinkles and signs of unaffected and cordial welcome. As neither party could speak the language of the other, this little exchange of artillery of the eyes was amusing enough," he wrote.

Captain Cooke, too, soon warmed to the women of Santa Fe, although he was likely alluding to what was routinely referred to as "the higher classes," as distinguished from the peons, who languished more or less like the untouchables of Calcutta.

After so many hard days on the trail, just-turned-nineteen-year-old Susan Magoffin was relieved to find herself "at home" in Santa Fe, in husband Samuel's Santa Fe house, a dirt-floored four-room adobe across from the cathedral. General Kearny was in and out on various business, as were a number of the younger officers, anxious to call on the pretty young newlywed bride, who appeared to remind them of their girlfriends or wives back home. Among these were Colonel Samuel C. Owens, battalion commander in Doniphan's regiment; Captains Abraham R. Johnston, Kearny's aide-de-camp; Henry S. Turner, Kearny's assistant adjutant; and Benjamin D. Moore; and Lieutenants Thomas C. Hammond, an aide to Kearny, and William H. Warner, assistant topographical engineer under Emory. With the exception of Moore, who was Hammond's brother-in-law, they were West Pointers all. Susan was delighted by the company and attention, except with the behavior of Lieutenant Hammond, who once became drunk and disorderly in her presence and had to be taken away. Little did she suspect at the time how few of those young officers would survive the expedition.

Two weeks after Kearny's army arrived in Santa Fe, the general gave a ball for the officers and "the citizens, generally [meaning the higher classes], at the government house; it was a political, or conciliatory affair, and we put the best face on it," Cooke said. "The women," he noted, "are comely—remarkable for [their] smallness of hands and feet; as usual in such states of society, they seem superior to the man; but," he added, gratuitously, "nowhere is chastity less valued, or expected."

The New Mexicans, Cooke said, quickly turned the ball into a fandango, their preferred type of party.

"There was an attempt at cotillions," continued the aristocratic Virginian, "but the natives are very Germans for waltzing; their favorite, called appropriately the *cuna* (cradle) is peculiar; it is a waltz, but the couple stand face to face; the gentleman encircles his partner's waist with both arms; the lady's similarly disposed, complete the cradle, which is not bottomless, for both parties lean well back as they swing around," said Captain Cooke.

Susan Magoffin remarked that the women "all danced and smoked cigarittos"; and the *cuna*, she said, "resembled the old Virginia negro shuffle." Private Isaac George of the Missouri Volunteers had this to say: "A kind of swinging, gallopade waltz was their favorite dance. If you were to read Lord Byron's graphic description of the Dutch waltz, and then use your imagination, a faint conception of the Mexican fandango may be formed. Such familiarity of position was repugnant to those accustomed to good society, but among the people of New Mexico nothing was considered a greater accomplishment than to pass gracefully through all the mazes of the waltz. The fandango had one republican feature in the fact that all classes rich or poor, met and intermingled on a common level."*

The next day was a Sunday, and Kearny had instructed his officers to attend church so as to dispel the persistent rumors (started by a few priests and associates of Armijo) that Catholicism would be abolished or subjugated under U.S. rule.

By most accounts the Americans were unimpressed by the sanctum and services, Captain Emory in particular: "The interior of the church was decorated with some fifty crosses, a great number of the most miserable paintings and wax figures, and looking glasses trimmed with pieces of tinsel." Captain Cooke concurred: "With the usual wax images, it is adorned with numerous paintings—one or two of some merit."†

As for the Mass itself, Emory was perplexed that "not a word was uttered from the pulpit from the priest, who kept his back to the congregation the whole time, repeating prayers and incantations [while] the band, the identical one used at the fandango, and strumming the same tunes, played without intermission."

Meanwhile, the air was still dark with rumors that Armijo had assembled a 6,000-man army to retake Santa Fe, but Kearny nevertheless was plotting his westward march, a thousand miles through broken,

---

*There appears to be some confusion on the part of the Americans about the Mexican class system, which was quite different from their own. When Cooke speaks of "the higher classes," he presumably means the Creole Mexicans, as distinguished from the mestizos and Indians. When Private George speaks of "all classes, rich or poor," he, too, excludes mestizos and Indians, whose ranking by the Mexicans was so low as to be almost nonexistent.

†As the scholar, author, Episcopal rector, and dedicated New Mexican Ross Calvin deliciously points out, most of these "miserable" pictures and icons have since been snapped up by savvy collectors and now hang in museums or on the walls of fashionable homes in Santa Fe and elsewhere as "notable specimens of primitive art."

uncharted, hostile territory, to reach southern California as quickly as possible. He had occupied Santa Fe for more than a month and it was time to move on; accordingly, he made a number of decisions that would have significant bearing on future events in the Mexican conflict.

First, Kearny determined that as a practical matter he could take only a limited number of troops across this vast and uncharted expanse of land, with no way of knowing how to provision them. As an old hand in western exploration, the general knew that the larger the party, the more difficult the supply problem, and in this case, after a short while on the trail during which they would use up what they could carry, they would have to live off the land.

Marching with the entire Army of the West was therefore out of the question; what was called for, Kearny decided, was a large battalion-sized "party of exploration," similar to Frémont's group, but with three hundred men instead of sixty. The three hundred were selected from Kearny's First Dragoons, the regulars. In addition he would take Captain Emory and his fourteen-man detachment of topographical engineers, as well as several prominent mountain men as scouts. The remainder of the First Dragoons would garrison Santa Fe against the possibility of any attempt at reconquest by the Mexicans.

Meantime, Colonel Doniphan's 1,000-man regiment of Missouri Volunteers would rejoin the Santa Fe Trail and march southward into Chihuahua, where they were to rendezvous with and reinforce Brigadier General John E. Wool, who was marching on Chihuahua from the east with a 3,400-man division to conquer and occupy this great northern state.

Wool's expedition was itself remarkable. The crusty sixty-two-year-old regular army officer, by authorization of the president, had personally recruited and organized ten regiments of volunteers from the Ohio Valley and, by dint of steamboats and boot leather, assembled them at San Antonio about the same time that Kearny was taking Santa Fe. From there, Wool began marching them due west, five hundred miles into Chihuahua.

The plan was thwarted, however, by a combination of terrain, political duplicity, egotism, misunderstanding, and backstabbing from Washington to Havana and from Veracruz to Monterrey, Mexico.

CHAPTER NINE

In Old Monterrey

In fact, General Wool never made it across the Sierras into Chihuahua; he was defeated by the mountains halfway there and recalled to join Zachary Taylor's depleted army, in consequence of actions devised by the Polk administration to win the war, which, by midsummer 1846, was rapidly sinking in public popularity. But this also left Colonel Doniphan and his Missourians, then entering Mexico's largest state alone, seriously in the lurch.

The Whigs, most of whom the previous spring had voted—however reluctantly—for Polk's declaration of war, were now repudiating their support and the Whig press was on the warpath, charging incompetence and bungling in the conduct of the war by the Polk administration, in spite of the fact that the Americans had not lost a battle. It had been anticipated, however, that the war would be short and limited; in particular that the U.S. Army's occupation of Mexico's northern provinces would quickly bring that dissolute nation to the bargaining table. In fact, it did no such thing. After the encouraging American victories at Palo Alto and Resaca de la Palma, General Taylor ran into a whipsaw at the city of Monterrey that delivered a jolt to the widespread impression that Mexican soldiers could not, or would not, fight.

On the Mexican side, the humiliations at Palo Alto and Resaca de la Palma were repaid by the court-martial and dismissal from the army of the popular general Mariano Arista, which prompted in turn the downfall of President Mariano Paredes. Both of these men were replaced with what for the Mexicans would prove to be unfortunate choices.

The Paredes affair involved possibly the greatest con ever perpetrated on a sitting U.S. president, certainly up until that time. Readers will recall Polk's meeting with the shadowy, slick-talking Alejandro Atocha, who had arrived at the White House on the evening of Friday the thirteenth of February, 1846, to inform a startled Polk that Atocha's friend Antonio López de Santa Anna, the recently deposed president of Mexico, had an exciting proposition to offer.

Atocha said that Santa Anna, who was living in exile in Havana, would entertain an offer of $30 million from the U.S. government in exchange for clear title to all of Texas and the New Mexico and California territories, if only the American navy would smuggle him back into his country to stage a coup and regain power. Polk had considered the offer seriously at the time, which was right before war had broken out, and even discussed it with his cabinet, but in the end he let the matter drop.*

When war finally came Polk had not forgotten the incident, and he dispatched the navy commander Alexander Slidell Mackenzie to Havana to parley with the irrepressible Mexican leader.† As we have seen, Polk's vision included the acquisition of California and New Mexico, by purchase if possible, by war if necessary, and he certainly preferred purchase over war. The meeting took place on July 6, 1846, about the same time John Frémont was raising the American flag over Sonoma and Kearny's army was eating dust down the Santa Fe Trail. The wily Mexican's views were all that Atocha had said and more; Santa Anna even suggested that the Americans should be more aggressive, so as to give Mexicans a face-saving excuse to trade their territory for money.‡

A month later, on August 8, Santa Anna, Atocha, and two other

---

*Polk does not tell us in his diary or elsewhere if alarms went off at the notion of Santa Anna ruling Mexico once more. After all, Santa Anna had been directly responsible for the massacre of hundreds of Texan prisoners at Goliad and the pitiless slaughter at the Alamo.

†Alexander Slidell Mackenzie was the Spanish-speaking brother of John Slidell, whom Polk had appointed U.S. minister to Mexico to try to smooth things over before hostilities broke out.

‡In fact, Santa Anna had frequently used the excuse of "imminent national danger"—including the invasion of Mexico by the French—to drum up support for his many returns to power. The deeper the Americans drove into Mexico, the easier it would be for Santa Anna to regain power.

conspirators became the only cargo sailing from Havana to Veracruz on the English merchant steamer *Arab*, deliberately "unmolested" by Commodore David E. Conner of the U.S. blockading squadron.

Citizens of Veracruz were startled to behold this controversial politician once again in their midst, even though he had been "met on the streets by a ragged honor guard" of shills prompted by bribes or other emoluments to support him. There was an anxious moment when somebody reminded the ex-*presidente* that he had been exiled under the penalty of death if he returned. But such was Santa Anna's magnetism that when he stomped one-legged over to the city hall and delivered himself of a powerful condemnation of the current state of affairs, the crowd forgot all about the firing squad and embraced his fulminations against the hated Gringo.

John S. D. Eisenhower, in his book *So Far from God: The U.S. War with Mexico, 1846–1848*,* sets the scene: "During the course of a week statues and portraits of him were brought out of hiding, [including his severed leg, which two years earlier had been disinterred from its resting place in an urn atop a stone column in Santa Paula and dragged through the streets by an angry crowd] and the name of Santa Anna appeared once more on numerous street signs. Mobs shouted pro–Santa Anna slogans, and a few threw rocks at the house of the former president Herrera."

Soon Santa Anna had regained control of the army, which would be followed closely by control of the country itself. And just as quickly he repudiated any notion that he might be willing to trade Mexican territory to the United States for cash or anything else. In fact, his intention from the outset had been only to drive the Yankee invader from Mexican soil and to reconquer Texas in the bargain—the ultimate double cross!

Following the battles of Palo Alto and Resaca de la Palma, Zachary Taylor took time to rest and reorganize an army that was quickly filling up

---

*Eisenhower wonderfully described Santa Anna as "a master of Mexican mob psychology," and his book is easily the most insightful about that conflict.

with volunteer regiments from the South and the Midwest, which were arriving on steamers out of New Orleans. By midsummer the American force consisted of some 3,200 regulars and 8,500 volunteers—an army of 12,000 spoiling for a fight. It was obvious to Taylor that the Mexicans had no intention of offering themselves up in battle again along the line of the Rio Grande, so he would have to take the battle to them—no easy matter in the harsh countryside of northern Mexico.

Most of the enemy army had now concentrated in or around Monterrey. That was about 250 miles west of Taylor's camp at Matamoros near the mouth of the Rio Grande, which the soldiers had derisively named "Baghdad." There in wretched, swampy living conditions the healthy along with the wounded and ill suffered and died with alarming regularity beneath the scorching sun, beset by flies, ants, mosquitoes, snakes, scorpions, tarantulas, and other subtropical unpleasantries.

Beginning in early June Taylor received separate instructions from Secretary of War William Marcy and General of the Army Winfield Scott (who were still not on speaking terms) suggesting an attack and occupation of Monterrey, capital of the state of Nuevo León.

Scott, in fact, suggested to Taylor that Monterrey would be an ideal jumping-off point for a campaign to capture Mexico City, a notion that Taylor found preposterous, given that the Mexican capital was a thousand miles to the south across immense mountains and wide deserts, let alone enemy opposition. Not wishing to offend his chief, Taylor merely responded that such an expedition would be "impracticable," but he agreed that Monterrey must be captured, as well as all the other northern capitals, which would put both an economic and a political squeeze on the Mexican government.

For a staging area halfway to Monterrey Taylor picked the empty riverbanks of Camargo, a hundred miles northwest of Matamoros by land, but some four hundred miles by riverboat, which was how Taylor planned to transport his men. There were on hand a few small steamers and these were pressed into service on the turbid swirling Rio Grande, which was fraught with quicksand, eddies, whirlpools, and dangerous shoals.

The camp at Camargo proved to be every bit as miserable and unsanitary as "Baghdad," and it was situated on reeking mudflats along the San Juan River where "the very name Camargo became synonymous with boredom, filth and tragic death. Diseases took a fearful toll and the dead march never ceased throughout the day."*

When Taylor arrived at Camargo he was horrified at the state of affairs, but since many of his troops and equipment had yet to arrive he was hamstrung. At last he could stand no more, and in late August the general issued orders for the army to march on Monterrey, about 120 miles to the southwest. It was before he was ready, but considering the alternative Taylor felt he had no choice.† From scouting parties the Americans learned that Monterrey had become a fortified bastion, occupied by the 10,000-man Mexican Army of the North now led by the ferocious Pedro de Ampudia, a forty-two-year-old Cuban-born sadist who two years earlier—and without so much as a court-martial trial—executed a rival general in one of Mexico's eternal civil wars, chopped off his head, and had it fried in boiling oil to preserve it for exhibition on a pike in the public square in the city of Villahermosa, Tabasco.

Ampudia had taken charge of the Mexican army after Arista's departure and right before Santa Anna assumed authority. Everyone knew that Monterrey was the key to the interior of Mexico and it had been recently fortified so as to become a formidable obstacle. The city was laid out rectangularly, in city blocks, and most of the houses and buildings were connected, flat-roofed, and built of stone, making each potentially a miniature stronghold. Guarding the Marin road, down which Taylor's army would have to march from the north, were two large forts, el Tenería (the Tannery, or slaughterhouse) and Fort Diablo (Devil's Fort). In front of the city, a gargantuan slab-sided edifice called the Citadel commanded all northern approaches. Walled in masonry thirty feet high with rectangular bastions and constructed on the foundations of an old cathedral, the Citadel's eight guns posed a fearful impediment for anyone trying to get at the city. Taylor's men called it the Black Fort.

---

*An estimated 1,500 American soldiers died at Camp Camargo—more than 10 percent of the army—and when these figures became known in the United States naturally it produced a reaction of anger, anxiety, and revulsion.

†Since his wagons had not come up, Taylor arranged to purchase one thousand mules from the nearest town and then hired one thousand Mexican mule drivers to pack and lead them.

As if that were not enough, on Independence and Federation hills, two elevations just to the west and behind Monterrey proper, were a pair of artillery strongpoints—one was called the Bishop's Palace and the other Fort Soldado—that further dominated the approaches to the city. Behind them, on the outskirts of town, the imposing Sierra Madres reared thousands of feet straight up out of the plain like a cresting basalt wave.

Taylor's army began marching from the dreadful Camargo encampment on September 4 and, after several stops to obtain shoes, blacksmith services, and provisions, the leading elements arrived before Monterrey on September 19, shadowed along the way by a squadron of Mexican lancers. The American army numbered fewer than seven thousand; Taylor had concluded that he could bring no more because of the difficulty of provisions and handling larger bodies of men. They brought with them eight days' worth of rations. The marching army was now composed of all 3,200 of Taylor's regulars and 3,000 volunteers—a total of 6,200 troops. Another 4,700 of the volunteers in his army had been left behind. By contrast, Ampudia had a full 10,000 men to defend Monterrey—7,000 regulars and 3,000 *rancheros,* or guerrillas.

Taylor's advance drew up on the plain of the Extremadura valley about three miles in front of Monterrey, with some of the men anxious to charge the city then and there, but Taylor held them back until the rest of the army was up. The Black Fort, a large Mexican flag flying from its ramparts, suddenly belched a cloud of dark smoke, which was followed immediately by a booming report that echoed down the valley, then by another, and another. The last shot caromed off the ground in front of Taylor and his staff and bounced over their heads. At this development they turned and retired out of range to a campground they called Walnut Springs, where Old Rough and Ready began sending out scouting parties to reconnoiter. Tomorrow would be a trying day. This was obviously quite different from what they had faced at Palo Alto and Resaca de la Palma—and more sinister too. By the end of the evening Taylor had his plan.

The key to Monterrey, Taylor concluded, was the Bishop's Palace and the other fortifications on Independence and Federation hills to the west and rear of the city. Once in American hands, they could be used to bombard Ampudia into submission. Accordingly, at two in the afternoon on September 20, a Sunday, General William Jenkins Worth led his division in a great hooking loop from Walnut Springs so as to come up on Federation Hill from the rear. In the lead was the Mounted Rifles regiment, volunteers from west Texas under command of Colonel John C. Hays. These would afterward become the fabled Texas Rangers.

It was a measure of Taylor's contempt for the Mexicans that he divided his army in the very face of battle, but his experience was that the Mexicans were far more inclined to defend than attack. In this he was correct; however, he had misjudged the extent to which the Mexicans were capable of defending.

Taylor's reconnoitering party had discovered a route that was defiladed behind some high ground from the fire of the Black Fort but soon the movement was reported to Ampudia, who rushed reinforcements to Independence Hill. By six p.m. General Worth halted the column for the night, and the men slept in the open, without shelter, fires, and not much food.* At daybreak they were again on the march. As the leading elements neared the Monterrey–Saltillo road, about two thousand Mexican cavalry attacked them. The Mounted Rifles dismounted and, with the help of two infantry companies and a pair of artillery batteries, decimated the Mexicans, who fled in a matter of minutes, leaving more than a hundred dead and wounded—along with scores of horses—on the killing field.†

Continuing their envelopment of the high ground, Worth's force by midafternoon had reached the steep base of 400-foot Federation Hill, the rearward of the two, and storming parties of some six hundred men began a grueling struggle through rough chaparral toward the crest. Fortunately, the steepness of the hill protected them from cannon fire since the artillery could not depress to that angle, as they staggered upward, stopping to fire volleys and shouting and yelling. An old military maxim holds that it is difficult to instill confidence in a beaten

---

*It is likely that Worth considered the distance (about ten miles) from Walnut Springs to the objective and timed his movement so an attack could be made early next morning, when the men would not be tired from the march and would have all day to fight for the hills.

†Once more proving what military commanders were just beginning to realize: cavalry was no longer a match for modern infantry trained to fire two or three shots a minute from their rifles, and especially not against fast-firing batteries of "flying artillery" employed by the U.S. Army.

army, let alone one that has been beaten twice, as Ampudia's men had been, and they proved it by fleeing "in terror" at the sight of the Americans charging wildly uphill. Atop the rise, Worth's soldiers used an abandoned Mexican piece to knock out a gun at el Soldado, and the day was theirs.

It was a brilliant, almost textbook victory, but during the same time that Worth was "covering himself with victory," Zachary Taylor was having a terrible day of it on the other side of town. Old Rough and Ready had kept command of the other part of the army, and to create a diversion to occupy Ampudia's attention while Worth turned his left flank Taylor had sent two divisions to attack or at least "demonstrate" against the Tannery and el Diablo strongpoints at the eastern fringes of Monterrey. This, Taylor properly concluded, ought to prevent Ampudia from rushing reinforcements from those positions to overcome Worth's men on the western hills.

Colonel John Garland had been instructed by Taylor to "keep well out of reach" of the enemy artillery. But, Taylor added, if he thought he could capture either or both of the strongpoints, "you'd better do it." Garland hadn't gotten far when the Black Fort opened up on his columns with a big 18-inch gun, but soon he was informed that a forward artillery position at the Tannery had been abandoned. What was he to do? He'd been ordered to keep out of range but also to take the strongpoints if possible. Here was a classic case of poor communication. Garland was a fifty-four-year-old veteran of the Seminole Wars, an earnest soldier who took orders seriously—and now this. It appeared that the Tannery could be captured, but not without putting his men in the range of enemy artillery fire. He did the soldierly thing and attacked the Tannery. But his line of assault was faulty.

Garland intended to get at the Tannery by going around it, to its rear. But that put his columns, 500-men strong, in a deadly double crossfire of artillery and rifles from the rooftops of the city itself, the Black Fort, the guns of the Tannery, and now the guns of el Diablo, which was behind the Tannery. It was sheer murder and confusion. Taylor arrived on the scene and threw reinforcements into the fray but by dusk he'd ordered a withdrawal.

Ironically one infantry company, commanded by Captain Electus Backus, tenaciously stayed the course and when the soldiers noticed a body of Mexicans fleeing the Tannery they rushed in and captured the fort, taking dozens of prisoners and five guns.* Still, the attack had been a trial for the army, which had sustained some four hundred casualties—nearly 10 percent of those committed to action. Among them were many of Taylor's best officers, and the carnage was deeply dispiriting for the men—heads torn off, limbs shredded, ghastly disfiguring wounds, and the unnerving cries for mercy and screams of pain. At day's end the general was forced to renew his respect for the Mexican army, which he had tended to trivialize after the two earlier encounters.

Next day Taylor's severely mauled wing of the army reorganized and regrouped, but Worth's division continued its attack with a dawn storming party on 800-foot Independence Hill. To their surprise, Worth's soldiers discovered that most of the defenders had retreated to the sanctity of the Bishop's Palace, which looked impregnable to infantry attack, and was. However, fifty of Worth's artillerymen using ropes and tackle blocks somehow grappled the disassembled parts of a twelve-pound gun up the hillside and began blasting the ramparts of the so-called palace several hundred yards distant on the eastern end of the hill. At the same time, U.S. artillery on Federation Hill also opened up on the stronghold, which compelled its defenders to flee with considerable loss of life. By late afternoon the American flag waved over the Bishop's Palace, and the morning of September 23 revealed that Ampudia had abandoned all of his outlying forts and strongpoints and was fortifying houses for a do-or-die defense in the main part of town.

Colonel Jefferson Davis's regiment of Mississippians was ordered into town to "carefully reconnoiter" beginning at the Tannery by using "the cover of walls and houses" (which was another way of saying, "Don't march down the middle of the street"). It was soon discovered that Monterrey city was a death trap to anyone showing himself in the open. Mexican riflemen manned the rooftops and windows of the adobe row houses. American artillerymen figured a way to blast them with cannons by loading a gun behind a wall or house, then running it out quickly and firing a round at a house down the street, then quickly

---

*As it turned out, the man who led the flight from the Tannery was its commander, who had also fled at the Battle of Resaca de la Palma.

hauling the gun back to cover by a rope from behind the wall. Davis's men quickly figured out that the best way to get at the Mexican defenders was to take a house and then, using pickaxes, crowbars, and mauls, batter their way through the next wall and toss in a lit artillery shell to clear out whatever Mexicans might be there, and then repeat the process from one house to the next. The U.S. troops penetrated block after block in this manner, breaking through scores of houses, until they were nearly to the town plaza, where most of the frightened women and children who had not evacuated had fled.

At some point in the midst of this frantic activity, Lieutenant Ulysses S. Grant made a name for himself with a notable act of bravery. Grant, who had been assigned as quartermaster for the Fourth Infantry, learned the leading parties were nearly out of ammo. One of the finest equestrians ever to graduate West Point, he jumped on his horse Indian-style with one leg slung over the saddle and the other under the horse's belly and, clinging sideways and protected from enemy fire, he clattered at a gallop down the deadly streets to order up the munitions.

From the eastern end of town, Worth's soldiers had begun similar block-clearing tactics and the two wings of the army were about to meet in the center plaza as the brutal street fighting continued all day and into the night. A gray misty morning found the streets littered with corpses, and the Americans poised to continue their grim excavations, when messengers arrived with orders to hold up the assault. Ampudia, it seemed, had decided to negotiate the surrender of Monterrey.

Trying desperately to save some sort of face, the Mexican commander agreed to hand over the city to the Americans, but he insisted that he and his army be permitted to leave with all their arms and government property. When Taylor refused and demanded unconditional surrender, Ampudia resorted to a trick. He had his negotiator falsely inform Taylor that authorities in Washington and Mexico City had formed a peace commission and that at that very moment peace between the counties was at hand. Taylor at first refused but Ampudia nursed this blatant lie throughout the day until Taylor, believing the Mexican officer would be good to his word, finally agreed that the Mexican army could march out of the city with just so many horses, so many artillery pieces, etc., not to be molested by U.S. forces for eight weeks. Thus, instead of a complete victory, Old Rough and Ready fell victim to a cheap con.

When news of these developments reached Washington, President Polk was furious. Grateful as he was for Taylor's victory and the capture of such an important Mexican capital, he condemned the armistice and release of Ampudia's army "which permitted them to retire from Monterrey . . . not as prisoners of war on parole, but at perfect liberty to reorganize and renew the war at their own time and place, and [giving] them eight weeks to effect this object." The president went on to inform his diary that Taylor had "committed a great error" and had "violated his express orders." As to Ampudia's claim of a peace commission, it was clear Taylor had allowed himself to be deceived, the president said. It was the opinion of Polk and his cabinet that after making Ampudia's army prisoners, Old Rough and Ready should have "pressed on into the country," and that if he had done so "it would probably have ended the war with Mexico."

Such was the judgment in the halls of the White House, but a ruder reality lay two thousand miles away where Taylor had lost a thousand men in the fighting, and before further offensive operations could be mounted the general felt the army badly needed rebuilding and resupply, which would take no fewer than six weeks. Polk and his cabinet sent orders for Taylor to call off the armistice, but by the time they arrived the truce period had run out anyway.

Meantime, much to Polk's annoyance and chagrin, the press and public were creating a great hero out of Zachary Taylor for the Monterrey victory. There was a presidential election coming up in 1848, and even though Polk had vowed to serve only one term, it did not sit well with his Democratic convictions that a Whig might take his place—most especially if he did so because of a war that Polk himself had promoted. To add insult to injury, General Taylor had somehow gotten wind of his newfound political status and began writing letters of inquiry to friends—and to acquaintances who were apparently not such close friends—who saw to it that the letters were published. Polk was infuriated. It was an unflattering measure of the president's personality that he became petty and vindictive in political matters but it was sometimes said that politics was Polk's "religion," and he was a stern master when it came to heresies.

During this time the president and cabinet had been contemplating the direction the war should take. Taylor, who was on the scene, had communicated his opinion that it would be a logistic impossibility for an American army to plunge south a thousand miles into enemy territory to take the Mexican capital, and that after conquering the northern provinces a strategy of "masterly inactivity"—one of Calhoun's expressions—would be the best and cheapest prospect to ultimately force Mexico to the bargaining table.

For Polk, such a policy had become increasingly unviable; the longer the war went on, the louder the Whigs squealed, and the press found fault, and the people grew restless and lost interest, especially if hardships were involved. It was a fairly axiomatic flaw of the political system that Tocqueville had pointed out a decade earlier in *Democracy in America*, his remarkable study of the new American institution. Unlike monarchies or dictatorships, the Frenchman wrote, democracy as a political system works well enough, "except in storms"—i.e., wars—where there is danger of the electorate losing its passion prematurely. It was a prescient observation that has generally borne itself out over time.

While Polk fretted over this prickly issue, he was paid a visit by his close colleague Senator Thomas Hart Benton, committed Democrat, father-in-law of John C. Frémont, often known by the military title Colonel.*

Benton was no more satisfied with the notion of "masterly inactivity" than Polk and used his considerable powers of persuasion to push for an amphibious landing at Veracruz on the Gulf Coast, which was more than two hundred miles from the Mexican capital. In fact, this option had been discussed at some length by the war planners but had not been exercised in order to see if the Mexicans might capitulate under the present strategy.

Benton insisted that it was both desirable and necessary in order to win the war quickly; otherwise, he warned, the conflict could go on interminably and sink the Democrats in the elections. Veracruz, however, was a risky, even dangerous, approach. It would demand an army

---

*Benton, a lawyer and planter, had held that rank in the Tennessee militia under Andrew Jackson during the War of 1812. He did not, however, see combat during Jackson's famous victory over the British army at the Battle of New Orleans. Instead, he had been detailed to duty as liaison between Jackson's forces and the military authorities in Washington.

of at least 12,000 men initially, which would mean another politically unpopular call for volunteers. It would require the quick capture of the port city, defended by its notorious fortress the Castle, and before the Mexicans could rush an army there to relieve it. It would then involve marching and supplying this large army to Mexico City through broken, often mountainous terrain that was ideal for defense. If the Mexicans somehow marshaled enough forces, the expedition could become a great calamity.

Who should command this force? asked Polk. Taylor's name came up and Polk dismissed him as "not a man of capacity enough." Benton agreed.* Winfield Scott's name arose and Benton nixed that by saying he had "no confidence in him," causing the president again to ask, "Who then?" At which point, in an act almost breathtaking in its megalomania, Old Bullion Benton drew up and suggested . . . *himself*!

There were a number of levels in this bizarre scenario, not the least of which was that Benton was a Democrat, while Generals Scott and Taylor were Whigs,† and in those times the man who commanded the victorious U.S. Army in a war was almost a shoe-in to become the next American president. This alone was enough to soothe whatever apprehensions Polk might have felt over Benton's startling presumption and total lack of qualifications. The way Benton explained it, Congress needed to create a new military rank of lieutenant general. This highest-ranked officer would be granted the authority to make peace with Mexico, he said, but not necessarily command combat troops in the field—in effect a kind of supernumerary man-on-the-scene who would let the generals do the fighting but step in whenever disputes needed settling or diplomatic decisions were called for. And also he would be dubbed commander in chief. It was a brilliant political ploy, if it worked.

But it did not work. Many in Congress saw straight through the thing and stalled, and after Polk and Benton hemmed and hawed for a few

---

*Everyone seemed to have political spies, and Polk certainly had his. "From all the information I have received," he told his diary, Taylor was "unfit" for the command, "had not mind enough," and "was a bitter political partisan and had no sympathies with the administration." As well, Polk insisted that Ṭaylor was controlled for political purposes by the Whigs, including the editor of the New Orleans *Picayune*.

†Taylor also seemed to have spies of his own and had spoken of "Polk, Marcy, and Co. as willing to discredit and ruin" him.

days it was decided to give command of the Veracruz expedition to Winfield Scott, a Whig—but not nearly so offensive as Zachary Taylor had become—and also an officer of proven field merit.

For months, Scott had made various overtures to get himself out of the doghouse with Polk and Marcy, but to no avail. He offered up a tactical sketch for a bombardment and amphibious landing at Veracruz, and on another occasion he suggested that he take command of newly recruited volunteers headed to Texas, but these ideas were coldly turned away by the secretary of war. But then, according to Scott, Polk summoned him to his office every day for nearly a week, tantalizing him with discussions of war plans but never hinting that he would be chosen to lead. When Polk at last called Scott in for the final meeting, he again toyed with him, cautioning him on the importance of victory in the Veracruz expedition—as if the commanding general of the army didn't understand this already—and ascertaining whether Scott had "the proper confidence in the administration." When Polk finally informed Scott that the command was his, "he was so much affected that he almost shed tears," the president told his diary, "and said he would show his gratitude by his conduct when he got to the field." The general departed, Polk wrote, "the most delighted man I have seen for a long time."

However, on the night of December 14, well after Scott had departed, Polk held a conference with several prominent members of Congress in which he pleaded with them to create a rank of lieutenant general for Senator Thomas Hart Benton, who would supersede Scott. Unfortunately for the president, the congressmen said it was "impossible," not only because Benton himself had made too many enemies but also because both Scott and Taylor had friends who would be against it, and the Calhoun faction would also be against it, in order to prevent Benton from becoming president. All this was still unbeknownst to Winfield Scott until he read it—or some version of it—in a newspaper as he boarded a steamer in New Orleans on his way to the war, after which, considering all the "gratitude" he had shown Polk, "his indignation was intense." In his memoirs Scott lamented, "a grosser abuse of human confidence is nowhere recorded."

In the coming days there was further acrimony between General Taylor and the administration, and Polk in particular, who seemed to have taken on a positive hatred of the man. "I am now satisfied he is a narrow-minded, bigoted partisan, without resources and wholly unqualified for the command he holds," Polk declared. Whether that had anything to do with it or not, Taylor was soon deprived of three-quarters of his army, including all of his regulars, who were to report to Matamoros for inclusion in Winfield Scott's Veracruz expedition. This of course left Taylor dangerously shorthanded, and so when General Wool's 3,400-man presence was made known Taylor ordered him to abandon the Chihuahua expedition and join him near Monterrey.

It was a good thing, too, because Santa Anna, who had by this time raised a 20,000-man army, had just intercepted a letter to General Taylor from General Scott revealing Taylor's glaring manpower weakness, and the Mexican commander now resolved to destroy him.

This in turn created a glaring weakness for Colonel Alexander Doniphan and his mounted regiment of one thousand Missourians who, unaware of all these developments, were at the moment struggling down the Santa Fe Trail to join up with General Wool so as to conquer Chihuahua.

Missouri senator Thomas Hart Benton, who had once nearly killed Andrew Jackson in a gunfight, was John C. Frémont's father-in-law, and an ardent expansionist. His friendship with President James K. Polk turned acrimonious after Frémont was court-martialed.

General Antonio López de Santa Anna, the perennial Mexican president, double-crossed President James K. Polk after Polk assisted him in his return from exile to Mexico.

On February 28, 1847, Colonel Alexander Doniphan and his 1,000-man regiment of Missouri Volunteers attacked and routed a 3,800-man Mexican army on the Sacramento River twenty-five miles north of Chihuahua City, capturing that enormous province for the American forces.

Bent's Fort was a bastion of civilization on the wild plains of the Southwest, along the Santa Fe Trail.

Brigham Young became the leader of the Mormons after the murder of founder Joseph Smith. Unlike Moses, who led his people out of the wilderness, Young led the Mormons *into* the wilderness of the Far West to escape the U.S. government.

Commodore John Drake Sloat was censured by the U.S. secretary of the navy for being a nervous Nellie during the Mexican conflict.

Left: "Old Rough and Ready" Zachary Taylor commanded the army in the north of Mexico and was afterward elected president of the United States.

Captain John C. Frémont was a topographical engineer with the U.S. Army whose writings about exploration in the Far West in the 1840s made him the most famous man in America. A run-in with his commanding officer nearly landed him in prison—or worse.

Sutter's Fort, built by a Swiss immigrant, was the center of civilization in California's Sacramento valley, and figured prominently in the Donner tragedy and, later, the Great Gold Rush.

James Reed was one of the leaders of the doomed Donner party, from which he luckily became an outcast after killing a fellow traveler.

Winfield Scott, hero of the War of 1812, was commander of the U.S. Army, but nearly lost his reputation over a "hasty plate of soup."

No American embraced the concept of manifest destiny more than President James K. Polk, who made a list of four things he wished to accomplish during his presidency, then retired after his first term. When he left office, America was a nation "from sea to shining sea."

Left: Brash and arrogant, Robert F. Stockton was commodore of the U.S. Pacific Fleet during the American conquest of California. Right: David Wilmot, an obscure congressman from Pennsylvania, set off a firestorm when he proposed an amendment that would have outlawed slavery in any territory acquired during the Mexican War.

The first battles of the Mexican War at Resaca de la Palma and Palo Alto were mere tune-ups to the big battles later on.

BATTLE OF RESACA DE LA PALMA,
MAY 9TH 1846.

BATTLE OF PALO ALTO,
MAY 8TH 1846.

Polk's contrarian secretary of state, James Buchanan, was often at odds with the president in matters of foreign policy. As a diplomat, he frequently balked at what he believed was rashness on Polk's part.

A fanciful drawing of Monterrey right before the battle. Seen in the foreground is the Bishop's Palace. It was during this battle that General Taylor learned the Mexican army was no pushover.

Kit Carson, a legendary mountain man and scout for Frémont's expeditions, rose to become a general in the U.S. Army.

Polk and his cabinet during the Mexican War. This is the first photograph of a president and his cabinet. Seated (from left): Attorney General John Y. Mason, Secretary of War William L. Marcy, Polk, and Treasury Secretary Robert J. Walker. Standing: Postmaster General Cave Johnson and the dapper Secretary of the Navy George Bancroft.

An "Adonis who made women swoon" was how they described Colonel Alexander Doniphan, who commanded the First Missouri Mounted Volunteers during the war with Mexico, in what came to be known as Doniphan's Expedition.

Opposite: There was tough hand-to-hand combat in the streets of Monterrey, where both Jefferson Davis and Ulysses S. Grant distinguished themselves in battle.

San Francisco, 1846

Sketch of the Old Spanish Palace in Santa Fe, where Governor Manuel Armijo lived and held court until the arrival of General Kearny

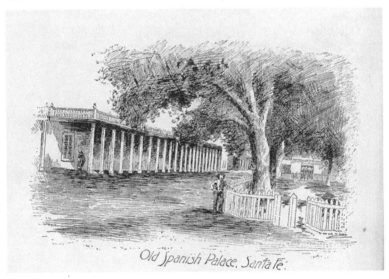

Sketch of a typical Santa Fe–territory ranch of the 1840s,
built to ward off depredations by Indians

Kearny's march: Frederic Remington's drawing
of U.S. troops going to Mexico

Top: Klamath Indians attacked Frémont's expedition as they attempted to survey Klamath Lake in Oregon Territory. Unbeknownst to Frémont, President Polk had wrested control of the territory away from the British.

Above: Kit Carson and others in Frémont's party were startled and alarmed high in the Sierra Mountains when an old Digger Indian woman suddenly appeared in the light of their campfire.

Lieutenant Edward F. Beale of the U.S. Navy led a relief expedition to Kearny's embattled party near San Diego, then walked barefoot for more than thirty miles across a rocky, cactus-strewn desert to find aid at the U.S. garrison.

There were tense moments in Monterey Bay in 1847 when a powerful British battleship (left) appeared. But the two American frigates need not have worried. The English ship rounded up and anchored, peaceful as a yacht.

Jessie Benton Frémont, the fervent booster and defender of her husband, John C. Frémont, the fabled "Pathfinder"

Eighteen-year-old Susan Shelby Magoffin was a recent bride, and newly pregnant, when she embarked with her husband down the Santa Fe Trail in 1846. She kept a fine diary of her trip.

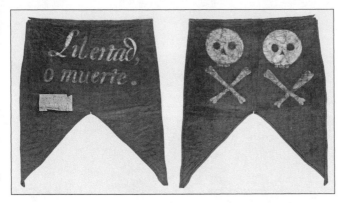

The infamous black flag of "no quarter," captured from the Mexicans following their defeat by Doniphan's First Missouri Mounted Volunteers at the Battle of Sacramento, February 28, 1847.

Stephen Watts Kearny, ca. 1820s

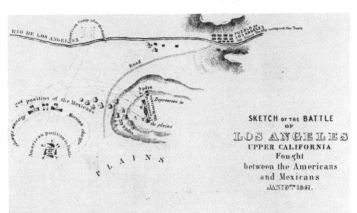

Lieutenant Emory's plan of the Battle of Los Angeles

SKETCH of the BATTLE
OF
LOS ANGELES
UPPER CALIFORNIA
Fought
between the Americans
and Mexicans
JAN. 9TH 1847.

Civil War photograph of William Emory, Kearny's chief of topography on the march, who kept a detailed notebook later published as *Lieutenant Emory Reports.*

Trapped by snow in the High Sierras, the miserable Donner party began eating their dead, and were rumored to have eaten their living as well. Half a dozen parties of relief were only partly successful in bringing them out.

End of the Santa Fe Trail after months—and a thousand miles—of hard traveling

Cuban-born General Pedro de Ampudia, who once chopped off a rival's head and fried it in oil for exhibition in a town square. He was a tough customer, but was defeated by Zachary Taylor at the Battle of Monterrey.

Phillip St. George Cooke, who was tapped to command the Mormon Battalion on its fantastic march to California, 1846–1847

Lieutenant Emory's plan of the Battle of San Gabriel

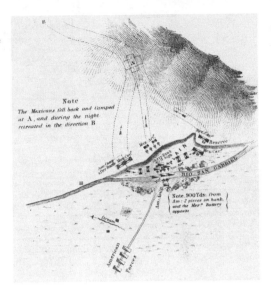

Entrepreneur Lansford W. Hastings led the Donner party to its doom by touting the "Hastings Cutoff" route across the Sierra mountains. Hastings had never traveled the route when he claimed, in a widely distributed pamphlet, that it would cut three hundred miles off the trip to California.

General John E. Wool and staff in Mexico, 1846; this is thought to be the first photograph of the U.S. military in action. General Wool raised a division in the Midwest and marched them nine hundred miles to join General Taylor at the Battle of Saltillo.

General Stephen Watts Kearny as he would have appeared in 1846 at the time of his march

General Manuel Armijo, the corrupt governor of Santa Fe, who was described by an English traveler as "a mountain of fat"

The "camp of death" for a group of the wretched Donner party, seeking to descend from their winter trap in the Sierra mountains

CHAPTER TEN

Dancing on Air

After five weeks in Santa Fe, General Kearny felt comfortable enough to resume his march to California, even though rumors persisted that Armijo had raised a large army of reconquest. Fort Marcy was complete, its artillery fan bristling above the city, fully armed against invaders. Kearny's Code had been laid down and, apparently, was being followed. The former Mexican citizens appeared pacified. Accordingly, at two p.m. on September 5, 1846, Kearny marched out of Santa Fe, south following the Rio Grande for a hundred miles, before dropping down to the west along the Gila and into the unknown.

Riding with him were three hundred handpicked cavalrymen of the First U.S. Dragoons Regiment, a small detachment of field artillery, half a dozen mountain men as scouts, and Captain Emory's party of topographical engineers, consisting of fourteen people, including two "servants"* for Emory and his assistant Lieutenant Warner.

Following closely behind Kearny, but by a different route, would be the five hundred men of the Mormon Battalion, which was to be commanded by Captain Philip St. George Cooke after the death of Colonel James Allen. The battalion was expected in Santa Fe any day.

Left behind was Colonel Doniphan's thousand-man mounted regiment of Missouri Volunteers, who were waiting to be relieved by a newly raised Second Regiment of Mounted Missouri Volunteer Cavalry, which was also expected any day, coming down the Santa Fe Trail.

---

*Military officers in those times were permitted to bring a servant along with them. Since Emory was from a slaveholding family in Maryland, it is highly probable that his servant was a bondsman. Likewise with Lieutenant Warner.

Colonel Sterling Price, a thirty-seven-year-old St. Louis lawyer, congressman, and friend of the president, who had resigned his seat in Congress to fight in the war, commanded it. Once Price's regiment arrived, Doniphan could begin his march down the Rio Grande into Chihuahua, where ostensibly he would join up with General Wool and conquer the province.

Meantime, Kearny had left Colonel Doniphan in overall charge of all the military forces at Santa Fe and appointed Charles Bent, of Bent's Fort renown, as governor of the New Mexico Territory, which would be administered from the pueblo town of Taos, where Bent had a home.

When Kearny's little army reached the rude pueblo of Albuquerque, four days and seventy-five miles from Santa Fe, they crossed to the western side of the shallow Rio Grande and camped "on a sandy plain, destitute of woods, and with little grass." More than one diarist remarked on the "myriads of sand crane, geese, and brant." The weather had turned mild, a sort of Indian summer, when it could be quite cold at that altitude (7,000 feet) at that time of year. They used the occasion to trade their tired, thin mules to the townspeople for better stock. Emory reported, "The more liberal were our offers for the animals, the more exorbitant were the demands of the Mexicans."

When it was ascertained that General Armijo's wife had fled to the city, Kearny directed Captain Emory "to call and see Madam Armijo, and ask her for the map of New Mexico, belonging to her husband, which she had in her possession."*

Emory said, "I found her ladyship sitting on an ottoman, smoking, after the fashion of her country-women. She said she had searched for the map without success; if not in Santa Fe, her husband must have taken it with him to Chihuahua."

With that, Kearny's caravan moved on, soon arriving in Indian territory, a sobering experience. While the citizens of Santa Fe had appeared pacified with their abrupt change of government, the Indians had used the occasion to run amok. Not only were different tribes

*In Santa Fe it had been learned that a map of sorts had been constructed of at least the central part of New Mexico. At that point, anything would have helped. When officers would ask villagers about trails, terrain, and directions they simply shrugged their shoulders. Few, if any, had ever been far outside their own village.

attacking Mexicans, they also began fighting with one another. The warlike Navajos in particular launched a fresh rampage of thieving, murder, and kidnapping throughout the province, presumably on the notion that the Mexicans would be unsettled by Kearny's arrival and thus more vulnerable to raids. On October 2, for example, a large band had fallen upon a Mexican village near the town of Socorro, "killing seven or eight men, taking as many women and children, and driving off 10,000 head of sheep, cattle and mules," according to a report by General Kearny, who arrived at the scene shortly after the crime. Two U.S soldiers detailed to track stolen livestock were eventually found shot through with nearly a dozen arrows, their skulls crushed by large rocks and their bodies otherwise mutilated.

Nevertheless, Captain Emory was in an exploratory mood and rode away from the line of march out of topographical curiosity, reporting, among other things, of finding a strange, empty land filled with "*Obione canescens*" (ragweed).

"I saw here the hiding places of the Navajoes," he wrote, "who, when few in numbers, wait for the night to descend upon the valley and carry off the fruit, sheep, women, and children of the Mexicans. When in numbers they come in daytime and levy their dues."

Kearny was outraged by the barbarous turn of affairs. He was certainly no stranger to Indian violence, having seen a life's worth on the plains, yet for the most part it had been Indian against Indian. Now it was Indian against "civilization," so to speak, which to Kearny's and practically every other white American's mind meant that civilization must eradicate savagery.

Eradication for Kearny, however, did not equate with extermination, as it did with some frontier whites. Instead, Kearny issued invitations for the chiefs of the various tribes to come to Santa Fe for a council of peace between them and the Mexican (now American) citizens of the territory. Many of the chiefs came, including some Apaches, but not the Navajos, who remained defiant and aloof.

The latest outrage prompted Kearny to consider a major change in plans. He sent instructions to Colonel Doniphan that before he left for Chihuahua he was to organize a punitive expedition against the Navajos, "who had continued killing the people and committing depredations on their property," the purpose of which was to reclaim all possible stolen livestock and kidnapped persons.* Furthermore, Doniphan was ordered "to require of [the Navajos] such security for their future good conduct as he may think ample and sufficient by taking hostages or otherwise." It was a tall order, since never in living memory had these Indians been tamed, but Doniphan took it in stride.

Trouble with the Indians, mainly Navajos, had been brewing for years, ever since the Mexicans ejected the Spanish, who at least had made efforts to protect the province. Accordingly, the fertile areas of New Mexico were slowly being depopulated by Indian raids, which everyone agreed had greatly increased in brutality under Armijo's rule. According to Captain Cooke, the sheep population had decreased by about 80 percent—amounting to hundreds of thousands—due to theft and raids, and "the people are almost confined to the villages." Worse, it was said—and by more than one person—that Armijo was using the Indians as "a check to any resistance [by citizens] on his arbitrary oppression," and it was a fact that Armijo had forbidden the citizens from making war on the Navajos without special permission.

Accordingly, Colonel Doniphan sent out several mounted columns to fan out and chastise the recalcitrants within a 200-mile arc west of Santa Fe, then converge in six weeks at a place called Ojo del Oso, or Bear Springs, with as many hostage chiefs as possible, for the purpose of making a peace treaty. Most of the Indian bands lived in the remotest part of the province, barely accessible through steep mountain passes that became treacherous as the weather turned. Here is one striking account, by the regiment's self-styled historian Private John Hughes, of a party of Doniphan's men attempting in early November to reach Bear Springs, which was said to lie in a mysterious secret valley, across mountains 6,000 to 7,000 feet high.

"They encamped on a rivulet whose waters came leaping down in foaming cascades from the mountain and disappeared into the sands of the valley. Having no tents the soldiers quartered on the naked earth in the open air, but so much snow fell that night that at dawn it was not possible to distinguish where they lay until they broke the snow which

*The Navajos were the most numerous tribe around Santa Fe, numbering an estimated 12,000.

covered them, and came out as though they were rising from their own graves. In less that 12 hours the snow had fallen 13 inches deep in the valleys and 36 inches in the mountains.

"On the 17th they marched more northwesterly over the Sierra Madre. When they came to ascend the steep spurs and bench lands which led up to the mountains a horrid, dreary prospect opened up above them. The men and their commanders were almost up to their waists toiling in the snow, breaking a way for the horses and mules to ascend. The lowest point in the main mountain rose to a sublime height, and to the right still towering far above this projected stupendous, colossal columns of ragged granite and iron-colored basalt."

After an all day and night struggle the soldiers reached the other side, and it was only then, when they saw that the stream flowed west, toward the Pacific, that they realized they had just crossed the western Continental Divide. They continued on across "gently rolling hills, then rocky bluffs, then bench lands, then crags and bleak knobs, and then barren, naked giant masses of gray granite and dark basalt and a heavy forest of pines and cedars, always verdant, spreading over the low lands. In many cases these colossal granite peaks shoot almost perpendicularly out of the plain more than 6,000 feet high." In two days at last they came to an enchanted-looking glade. "Here the Navajos pasture their immense droves of horses and mules and keep their numerous flocks of sheep and goats." This was Bear Springs.

Along the way, Doniphan's men had encountered various tribes of Indians without serious incident, except that a number of soldiers died of typhoid fever, cholera, or exposure. In much of the territory there was no wood for coffins, so the corpses would be buried wrapped in blankets and the grave "covered in broad stones to prevent the wolves from disturbing the dead."

One hundred miles north of Taos, one of Doniphan's columns encountered a village of "Yutas [Utahs], a fierce and numerous tribe of Indians, with the view to conciliate them and dispose them to a friendly intercourse with the Americans." Sixty of their chiefs were taken to Santa Fe by the soldiers, where a treaty of peace was signed. Others came across a tribe of six thousand Zunis, as well as seven villages of Moquis, each with the same results. They crossed vast deserts and steep mountains and lands that looked like they belonged on the moon. They discovered a petrified forest and ancient ruins from who knew what or when, which remained vibrantly deserted in the rarefied desert air, and they chanced on flora and fauna unknown to Western civilization.*

At Bear Springs Doniphan held a powwow with a dozen Navajo chiefs, the object being to make an official, permanent peace between themselves, the Mexicans, and the Americans. One hundred and eight U.S. soldiers and five hundred Navajo warriors were present. The negotiations went on all day, and into the evening, with each chief having his say. After a time it became apparent that the Navajos had no ax to grind with the Americans and were willing to make peace, but they detested the Mexicans. One chief named Sarcilla Largo, who seemed to speak for the others, summed up the situation in logic that was hard to defeat.

"We have been at war with the Mexicans for years," he explained. "We have plundered their villages and killed many of their people and made many prisoners. You [Americans] have lately commenced war against the same people, and now you turn upon us for attempting to do what you have done yourselves. This is our war," he said. "We have more right to complain of you for interfering in our war than you have to quarrel with us for continuing a war we had begun long before you got here."

A lesser man might have been nonplussed by this straightforward argument, but not Doniphan. In his firm, lawyerly manner he explained to Largo and the other chiefs that the Americans' war with the Mexicans in this territory had ended; that the Mexicans had surrendered and were now American citizens; and that everyone in the territory, including Navajos, would be accorded equal protection under the laws of the United States. He went on to say that New Mexico was now part of the United States and that stealing from or killing the Mexicans was the same as stealing from or killing Americans. Furthermore, Doniphan said, the Americans would now open a trade with the Indians in New Mexico and everyone would prosper.

Largo digested all this, then made his pronouncement. "Then let there be peace between us," he said and promised to stop the wars

---

*Catalogued later on the march to California by Captain Emory.

against the Mexicans and everyone else. Shortly afterward, a formal document of peace was drawn up, containing five articles, including promise of free travel, exchange of prisoners, return of stolen property, and an agreement for "mutual trade." Doniphan signed it as did two of his battalion commanders and the Navajo chiefs, each of whom made his *X* mark at the bottom. Following this ceremony, Doniphan began distributing gifts that he had brought from Santa Fe, "explicitly stating they were made, not by way of purchasing the [Indians'] friendship, but as a testimony of personal good will." To his surprise, the chiefs in turn presented Colonel Doniphan with several fine Navajo blankets, then among the most prized textile fabrics in the world, and with that the Treaty of Bear Springs became history, and the Indian troubles in New Mexico were at an end, or so it was hoped.

Around the same time that General Kearny ordered Doniphan on his Indian-pacifying mission, on October 7, 1846, the 300-wagon trading caravan, which included Susan Magoffin's party, rumbled out of Santa Fe toward Chihuahua in hopes of selling its wares before war came to that province. But three weeks down the trail the train's new wagon master, Susan's husband, Samuel Magoffin, was instructed by the army to wait for Colonel Doniphan's regiment to escort it into Mexico. The train's former wagon master, Samuel's brother James Magoffin, had gone ahead down to Mexico on another secret mission.

In the meantime rumors flew like trail dust in the wind: General Wool has taken Chihuahua. General Wool has not taken Chihuahua. Paredes is still president of Mexico. Santa Anna is president of Mexico. Frémont and Commodore Stockton have taken California. Armijo has organized an army of three thousand men and "the Chihuahuans will rise en masse and murder us all."

Susan was actually glad to be back on the trail. "I am most tired of Santa Fe, and do not regret leaving," she told her diary. But now, as they were stuck waiting for the army, a pathetic episode presented itself one morning when a Mexican boy of nine or ten began asking if someone would *buy* him. Three years earlier, it seems, Apaches had murdered the boy's father and kidnapped the boy. His mother had died earlier, so he was orphaned. "After three years of hard servitude among the Apaches," Susan said, "the little fellow ran off, and found his way to the house of an old Mexican, who resides here on the bank of the river in a lone hut, the picture of misery." But the boy soon discovered that life under the old Mexican was as bad if not worse than under the Indians, and he was looking for somebody to pay $7 (about $200 in today's money) that he owed to the old man and he would become their servant. The Magoffins were so touched that they paid the money and gained a serving boy.

Then a chilling rumor came flying up out of Mexico that Samuel's brother James—who had arranged for the capture of Santa Fe—was in jail in Chihuahua, on trial for his life, charged with being a spy. The rumor turned out to be true.

After pulling off the stunning coup of persuading Armijo to abandon his province to the Americans, James Magoffin had ridden along with Kearny and his dragoons on the first leg of his march to California. When they reached the village of Socorro near where the latest Navajo atrocities had occurred, Kearny's army met up with, of all people, Kit Carson and a party of Indians and mountain men headed east with urgent dispatches from California. These contained the staggering news that Americans had conquered the province and that Old Glory was flying from every important California port and town.

Kearny's reaction to Carson's report is not recorded, but it is safe to guess that his feelings were mixed. He had been handed a golden opportunity to conquer one of the great prizes on the North American continent, only to discover that others had beat him to it. If Kearny was disappointed he did not show it, but some of the younger officers openly lamented that they would no longer be permitted to fight Mexicans. Since Kearny had no clear idea how to get to California, and Carson had just come from there, he told the recently commissioned U.S. Army officer to hand over his dispatches to one of Kearny's officers and join the general's staff as chief scout.

It was a severe blow to Carson, who had a home, wife, and child in Taos, only a few days away, whom he had not seen in more than a year. He had been looking forward to a well-deserved homecoming, as well as traveling to Washington and meeting the president and other dignitaries. Carson, whose sole military training had come from watching Frémont, protested that he had given his promise to deliver the dispatches personally and could not relinquish them to anyone else.

This was not the kind of response that commanding generals wish to hear from second lieutenants and, despite Carson's indelible reputation, Kearny abruptly ordered him to turn over the dispatches to his own chief scout, who would carry them to the nation's capital. There was apparently a moment—probably more than a moment—in which Kit Carson considered slipping away and meeting his wife. But this he did not do, prompting Captain Johnston, Kearny's aide-de-camp, to declare, "It requires a brave man to give up his private feelings thus for the public good; but Carson is one such! Honor him for it!"

In the face of Carson's momentous news, Kearny made a fateful decision. After consulting with Carson on the nature of the route to the Pacific, the deserts, the barrens, the mountains, and so forth, he concluded that the more men he took, the more perilous the trip would become owing to the scarcity of food, water, and fodder. So he ordered two hundred of his dragoons to return to Santa Fe, while he would carry on the journey with the remaining hundred men. With California conquered, it seemed a logical judgment, so long as California stayed conquered. As we shall see, this was not a given certainty by any stretch of the imagination.

In the meantime, suave James Magoffin, who had been traveling with Kearny, made his departure to the south with a party of four men. His purpose, according to letters and other documents, was to perform the same charismatic sleight of hand in Chihuahua that he had in Santa Fe and persuade the governor to hand over control to General Wool with nary a shot fired.

Thus charged, Magoffin wended his way down the Rio Grande to El Paso del Norte (Juárez), and then another 250 miles south to Chihuahua City, where he expected to be feted by the governor with dinner and cordial conversation. This time, however, his wit, charm, and repartee failed him utterly. Soon as Magoffin set foot in town he was arrested for espionage, a crime that in Mexico, as elsewhere, is a capital offense. And it seemed they had him dead to rights.

The evidence was a letter signed by General Kearny that detailed Magoffin's surreptitious role in the surrender of Santa Fe. Authorities in

Chihuahua were in no laughing mood about the loss of the New Mexico province and had in fact court-martialed Armijo for dereliction and cowardice when he'd skulked into town after the American conquest. The fact that Armijo was acquitted in no way assuaged the Mexican authorities—they had been snookered.

Kearny's letter had been captured from the personal effects of a friend of the Magoffin brothers, a Dr. Henry Connelly, longtime resident of Chihuahua, to whom Samuel Magoffin had entrusted it for delivery to James in Juárez. Unfortunately, Connelly had arrived before Magoffin and was arrested, and his possessions were searched.

The letter was sufficiently damning that James Magoffin was condemned to the firing squad. Nearly at the stage of saying his final prayers fate intervened in the most unlikely form of Governor-General Armijo himself, who, recently cleared of similar charges, interceded on behalf of Magoffin and managed to arrange a temporary stay of execution. Still, Magoffin was not yet off the hook and remained in the Chihuahua calaboose, awaiting developments.

Captain Philip St. George Cooke, as we have seen, was a capable, earnest army officer, somewhat patrician, somewhat conventional, who kept a daily journal that he liked to sprinkle with Dickensian allusions. So far during Kearny's march he had performed admirably in command of his troop in the First Dragoons and in his role as military escort for James Magoffin in the Santa Fe subterfuge. But beneath his masterful West Point bearing and confident mien Cooke was roiled and discontented.

Like many company-grade officers at the onset of war, Cooke's blood was up, as the expression went, to get into the thick of battle. And that was precisely where he and his dragoons had been headed—down the Mississippi on a steamboat to the seat of war in Matamoros under Zachary Taylor—until, as Cooke put it, Kearny had "demanded" two additional troops of cavalry for his Army of the West, of which Cooke's was one. This left him "inexpressibly disappointed," since the sole object of Kearny's column at that point had been New Mexico, which Captain Cooke considered a backwater to the real fighting war.

Soon new orders arrived extending the mission all the way to California, which might present a more proper martial challenge for a West Point–trained officer. Traveling down the Santa Fe Trail, Cooke mused in his diary about what might lie in store for a mounted troop crossing unknown mountains and deserts and, once in California, to engage in battle with the vaunted Mexican lancers, some of the finest light cavalry in the world.

So it was all the more a surprise—or shock—to Cooke when, into the camp along the Rio Grande from which Kearny had sent orders for Doniphan to march against the Indians, there arrived a dispatch from Colonel Sterling Price, commanding the Second U.S. Missouri Volunteers, who had just entered Santa Fe. Among other things he reported the good news that the Mormon Battalion was marching behind and would be in Santa Fe directly. The bad news was about the death of Lieutenant Colonel James Allen, which left the battalion without a proper commander. It did not take long for Kearny to locate his favorite special detail man, Captain Cooke, and bestow upon him the title of lieutenant colonel and command of a battalion of five hundred Mormons.

It was a terrible time in the short history of the "Saints," as Mormons sometimes described themselves, whose existence dated back to 1830 when a man named Joseph Smith put on sale a 500-page religious tract called the Book of Mormon. Its revelations were so original that even Mormons still refer to themselves as "a peculiar people," a characteristic that at the time did not endear them to their fellow citizens. Mormons, Smith had informed his followers, were the true descendants of a lost tribe of Israel, alone chosen by God to inherit the earth. This news Smith had divined from a book of golden plates that he told people he had found in 1823, when he was eighteen years old, in a box buried on a hill near Manchester, New York.

The plates were engraved in an ancient hieroglyphic that Smith said was of Egyptian origin, and that after he had translated them into English, with the aid of magic eyeglasses given to him by an angel named Moroni, he returned them to the angel and proceeded to incorporate the Church of Jesus Christ of Latter-Day Saints, with himself as chief prophet and revelator. According to the golden plates, the Mormons had arrived in America fourteen hundred centuries earlier and formed a

Hebrew tribe in Central America, but in time the group separated into two factions, Nephites, who were fair-skinned, intelligent, and industrious, and Lamanites, who were so lazy, mean, and warlike that God had cursed them with dark skins.

In time, the two clans went to war and the Lamanites got the better of the fight. The Nephites were wiped out, the last one remaining alive being Mormon, who set down the history of the tribe on the golden plates and for safekeeping gave them to his son, Moroni, who was turned into an angel. For their part, the Lamanites devolved into the ancestors of American Indians, who over time lost any memory of whatever remained of their heritage and culture.

In themselves, these beliefs did not generate friction between the Mormons and other citizens, but when the sect began to attract a large following the clannishness and smugness of its members began to grate. The golden plates had also revealed that any church other than the Latter-Day Saints was the "church of the devil," and that everyone but Mormons was an "apostate," attitudes that did not go down well with many of the Saints' fellow Americans. Mormons were forbidden to drink alcohol, gamble, or smoke tobacco,* which was for the good, and they were hard workers, but they sometimes aggravated their neighbors by what were then called "sharp business practices" (i.e., dishonesty) and a feeling of distrust ensued toward the Mormons. A further grievance was that the Mormons voted en bloc, for whichever candidate gave them the most money. Moreover, they attracted among their number a significant smattering of shady characters who became involved in such activities as counterfeiting, fraudulent land deals, and the like.

Joseph Smith began to receive converts soon as his Book of Mormon was published, but once the citizens in his neck of the woods got a gander at its contents their open hostility was enough to convince him that the flock better be moved as quickly as possible. The group of about fifty settled for a while in a town near Cleveland, Ohio, but soon enough it was on the road again. Seeking someplace isolated and remote from the scorn and fury of people that Smith had termed "Gentiles,"† he led his band west toward the frontier, then located on the Missouri River,

---

*They were, however, allowed to chew, and their temples at the time were supplied with spittoons at the ends of pews.

†Anyone not aspiring to the Mormon faith was a "Gentile," Jews included.

beside the Kansas border. Along the way Smith was inundated with more revelations, including one disclosing that the Garden of Eden was not located on the Tigris and Euphrates rivers as once supposed but in northwest Kansas.

By the time Smith got his people settled in Jackson County near present-day Kansas City, there were more than a thousand. Eight years later, they numbered 10,000 and some had come from as far as Europe and Scandinavia, having seen the light from the Book of Mormon. But as in the Mormons' previous relocation, the local citizens did not welcome this great flood of Israelites with open arms—most especially since, in addition to reasons previously enumerated, Missouri was a slave state and the Mormons were abolitionists. Also, since they were evangelicals, the Mormons at first went around trying to convert their Gentile neighbors, but this was not well received either and before long the Missourians began to beat, tar and feather, stone, shoot, and otherwise molest the Mormons.

By 1836 things had gotten so bad that the Missouri legislature decided to relocate the Mormons north, to remote Caldwell County, and within two years most had moved there, but it didn't help. Wherever they went, riots and violence broke out. Thus far Smith had forbidden retaliation, but finally he had enough and whipped his Mormons into a carnival of boiling vengeance, which in turn prompted Missouri governor Lilburn Boggs to order state militia general Alexander Doniphan to either "exterminate" the Mormons or "drive them from the state."

By then local militias had slaughtered seventeen Mormons, including three children, in a single massacre, incarcerated Joseph Smith and nine of his associates for treason, convicted them by court-martial the same day, and ordered their execution by firing squad next morning.

General Doniphan, however, was a fair man, and also a lawyer, and he wasn't about to shoot down men like dogs after a drumhead court, no matter what he thought personally about Mormons. So he not only refused to obey the execution order, he informed the head of the court that "if you execute these men, I will hold you responsible before an earthly tribunal, so help me God!"

There the matter rested until Smith and his comrades managed to escape and flee eastward into Illinois, where the remainder of his miserable and now destitute followers had settled on an isolated peninsula on the Mississippi River that they named Nauvoo, or "Place of Peace." In the coming decade, through dint of hard work, industriousness, and communal living, they built a substantial city of architecturally pleasing brick and stone buildings and neat and often elegant homes, in which they hoped at last to settle in for the long haul.

It was not to be. The same antagonisms that had bedeviled the Saints in Missouri bedeviled them in paradise Nauvoo. By then Smith's congregation had swelled to 15,000, making Nauvoo second only to Chicago in Illinois population, which so encouraged Smith that in 1844 he declared himself a candidate for the U.S. presidency. He lost, to James K. Polk, but the Mormons had clearly established themselves not only locally but nationally as a force to be reckoned with.

Then somebody sneaked up to a side window of the home of Missouri governor Boggs, who had sicced the state militia on the Mormons back in 1838, and shot him multiple times. Fortunately for the governor, even with two balls entering his skull, another in his neck, and yet another in his throat, which he swallowed, he didn't die, despite the obituaries that appeared in local papers. Unfortunately for Joseph Smith and the Mormons, the would-be assassin was traced back to Nauvoo and that got people's dander up all over again.

The straw that finally broke the back, however, was when it was revealed that Smith had been acquiring multiple wives—or "celestial marriages," as he called them—from the beginning, and that between 1842 and 1844 alone he married forty women and sired innumerable children. There was an immediate uproar, both within the Mormon community and without. Moreover, Smith had been encouraging selected elders of the church to do the same.

One of the Mormon newspapers published an angry denunciation of Smith "and his abominations and whoredoms." It was its last publication. An organized mob of the Mormon leader's followers—the Nauvoo Legion—broke into the newspaper office, smashed the press and type to smithereens, then burned the building and ran the offending editor out of town.

All this riled the Gentiles into an outrage beyond reconciliation. Locals tended to be Methodists, Baptists, or Presbyterians, and the revelation that Mormons kept multiple wives in addition to everything else was a clear call for action.

Warrants for the arrest of Joseph Smith and eleven other elders were again issued on June 24, 1844, on charges of, among other things, treason. Following a clumsy escape attempt, Smith turned himself in to a local sheriff after the governor of Illinois warned that, if he fled the state, militias probably could not be restrained from exterminating the entire body of 15,000 Saints. Three days later a vigilante party of 125 militiamen, politicians, clerics, and law enforcement officers broke into the jail and murdered Smith and his brother Hyrum, which presented the congregation with a crisis. The chief prophet and leader of the church of Mormon was dead at the age of thirty-eight, and practically the entire rest of the state was up in arms and talking genocide. What to do? Where to go? It was then that elder Brigham Young, the new leader, got the idea of moving west—so far west they would be forever out of the reach of the detested Gentiles.

When Young took the reins of the beleaguered sect as chief prophet he reversed a page from Moses and vowed to lead his people *into* the wilderness. A forty-three-year-old New Englander, Young was short, fat, and practical, and it was his conclusion that nowhere within the United States would Mormons be safe and left to their own devices and, worse, there was no appeal to government or law enforcement for help—state, federal, or local. No better example could be held up than the recent acquittal of all nine defendants in the murder of Joseph Smith, including several Illinois military officers, a newspaper editor, and a state senator. Afterward a predictable bloodbath was drawn between still irate citizens and the Mormons of Nauvoo. Dozens of Mormon homes were burned down and their occupants bushwhacked by vigilantes. For their part, a number of Saints went on killing sprees in which their Gentile victims were mutilated with knives, and a blood oath of vengeance was permanently incorporated into the Latter Day Saints' church litany.

By early 1846 the situation was completely out of hand. Hundreds of homes had been torched and dozens of citizens were dead, Mormon and Gentile alike. At last the governor called out the militia, never a good sign, and Brigham Young finally threw in the towel. He sent a letter telling the governor that the Saints were abandoning Nauvoo en masse for more collegial climes and would be gone by the following spring. Like many Americans, Young had read Frémont's earlier published exploits and was enticed by the notion of forming a private, secure Mormon nation somewhere beyond the western slopes of the Rocky Mountains. In other words, he desired a place so far away and outlandish that nobody would bother to come there.

But even this did not satisfy the authorities, who issued a warrant for Young's arrest on charges that, as headman of Nauvoo, he was harboring counterfeiters within the city, which happened to be true. This prompted the onset of the greatest concerted mass migration in the nation's history, as six thousand disgruntled Mormons and their various wives and children began crossing the frozen Mississippi, trudging westward across Iowa to the land of the Potawatomi and Omaha Indians. When they reached the banks of the Missouri River, most chose to encamp for the winter because they were too worn out and broke to continue.

This they called Winter Quarters, which remains famous in Mormon history for the hardships people endured. They were "surrounded by the Lamanites on all sides," declared a Mormon wife named Perrigrine Sessions, but "over one hundred miles from the cursed Gentiles." The Lamanites were Omaha Indians, "an unmilitary but thievish race who constantly stole the cattle of their Nephite brethren." Many Saints were able to construct rude log huts but some lived in tents, caves, and dugouts through the terrible Nebraska winter, and hundreds perished from illness and the elements. It was there that the U.S. government found them on July 1, 1846, in the person of Captain James Allen, First U.S. Dragoons, who was under orders to recruit a battalion of five hundred men for a march to California with the Army of the West.

At first the Mormons were highly suspicious of such an idea, since during their entire existence the government had provided them virtually no protection from the violence of their neighbors. But Brigham Young and other elders gradually persuaded men to volunteer, explaining that their pay and clothing allowances would provide dearly needed cash for food and supplies needed to cross the Rockies. In fact, their combined pay and allowances totaled more than $70,000—some $2 million today—a sizable grubstake. Furthermore, following a quaint custom of the times, each of the five rifle companies was authorized to bring along four women as laundresses, who would receive rations and allowances same as in the regular army. In all, when the 543-man Mormon Battalion marched out of Winter Quarters toward Fort Leavenworth, it included thirty-three women and fifty-one children.

After drawing weapons and equipment at Leavenworth, and receiving minimal instruction in military courtesy, marksmanship, and close order drill, the Mormon entourage departed on the Santa Fe Trail. Their commander, Captain Allen, now an acting lieutenant colonel, had become ill and remained at the fort. In less than a week he was dead. Lieutenant A. J. (Andrew Jackson) Smith assumed command. They were about six weeks behind Kearny and the weather had turned dry nearly to the point of drought. On the twenty-eighth of August, 1846, Jane Bosco, one of the laundresses, died of illness. Two days later her husband, John, one of the soldiers, was laid in a grave next to hers. Others would follow. On October 9, 1846, the Mormon Battalion arrived in Santa Fe, where it was met by its new commander, formerly a captain but now Lieutenant Colonel Philip St. George Cooke, who had been out rounding up mules. He was not pleased with what he saw.

The battalion contained "too many families," he said. "Some [soldiers] were too old, some feeble, some too young. It was embarrassed by many women; it was undisciplined; it was much worn by traveling on foot; their clothing was very scant; their mules were broken down."* In other words, Cooke summed up, "Everything conspired to discourage the extraordinary undertaking of marching this battalion eleven hundred miles through unknown wilderness, without road or trail and with a wagon train."

That was about the size of it, but orders were orders, and Cooke understood that General Kearny was not a man who scrupled at excuses. Cooke and his fellow West Pointers A. J. Smith, a lieutenant once again, and Lieutenant George Stoneman picked through the rabble and weeded out eighty-six men as unfit, plus all of the children and nearly all of the women, and sent them under the care of two officers to stay in a town called Pueblo near Bent's Fort.†

---

*The Mormons' clothing was poor because they hadn't purchased any. Instead they sent all the money received for their military clothing allowance back to Winter Quarters for the purchase of emigrant supplies.

†Five wives of Mormon officers were allowed to accompany their husbands, but they had to provide their own mules.

In less than a week they were off. From the army's quartermaster Cooke had procured mules and packsaddles and rations for sixty days, after which they would be on their own. He also acquired road building equipment, since in addition to simply getting the battalion to California Kearny had also charged Cooke with the stupendous task of building the rudiments of a wagon road along the way, a daunting challenge to say the least. Cooke was *"determined,"* he said, "to take through my wagons," but, he continued, "The experiment is not a fair one, as the mules are nearly broken down at the outset."*

Cooke was fortunate, however, in having for a guide one of the more experienced mountain men of the era, forty-one-year-old Jean Baptiste Charbonneau. He came by his reputation honestly, being the half-breed son of the legendary Indian woman Sacagawea, whose exploits with the Lewis and Clark expedition of 1804–6 had already thrilled a generation of schoolchildren. Charbonneau, whose father, Toussaint Charbonneau, was that expedition's interpreter, had been born during the early days of the journey and rode as a papoose on his mother's back during the great exploring trek to the Pacific. Having explored with Frémont and trapped with the crème of the mountain men at Bent's Fort, Charbonneau was said to be "the best man on foot on the Plains or in the Rocky Mountains."

On October 3, 1846, when Colonel Sterling Price and the Second Regiment of Mounted Missouri Volunteers arrived in Santa Fe, it freed Doniphan to begin his march against the Indian uprising. Price's orders were straightforward and unromantic: stand guard over the city. This pacific duty did not last long, however, and when the uproar came it was from an unlikely source.

The Pueblo Indians were known among western Indians as "civilized" tribes who had given up warring against white men, adopted the Catholic faith, and lived in adobe apartment houses, growing grains and vegetables and raising livestock. In fact, when Doniphan drew up the Treaty of Bear Springs with the Navajos, Article 2 specifically

---

*Cooke had managed to purchase twenty "good" mules in Albuquerque, but almost immediately Kearny requisitioned them to take Frémont's dispatches on to Washington.

stated, "The people of New Mexico and the Pueblo Tribe of Indians are included in the term 'American People'"—as opposed to the Navajos and other "wild" Indians who were considered savages without standing.

So it was with the greatest surprise that Colonel Price and the authorities in Santa Fe learned that Pueblos had risen up in Taos and brutally murdered Governor Charles Bent and many of his staff in an insurrection designed to expel or exterminate the Americans in New Mexico.

Word had come down to U.S. authorities just before Christmas that an uprising was possibly afoot in Santa Fe, but quick reaction by the military averted actual revolt. A former officer under Armijo arrested on an informant's tip was found to have a list of hundreds of disbanded Mexican soldiers.* After questioning, a number of others were also arrested and it was revealed that an insurrection was planned for the day after Christmas, which was to commence with the midnight ringing of the church bells. The conspirators decreed that every American in the territory would be murdered. Meetings had been held in the wee hours by various cells. Colonel Price and Governor Bent were to be assassinated first. It was rumored that Catholic priests, who feared an influx of Protestant americanos, were deeply involved. The two ringleaders were identified: the wealthy Tomás Ortiz and Don Diego Archuleta—Armijo's former military commander who had wanted to resist Kearny's advance but relented after listening to Magoffin. Both of these men escaped into the mountains, Ortiz said to be disguised in a woman's dress.

Bent, a Taos resident who knew the natives well and felt trusted by them, had been forewarned about the possibility of revolt. Weeks earlier he had written in a letter to Price that the U.S. soldiers needed to be restrained in their actions and attitudes toward the citizenry, especially after they had been drinking. The Missouri Volunteers, mainly, had adopted an attitude of disdain and superiority toward the Mexicans, which, on top of Armijo's disgraceful surrender, reignited a smol-

---

*The tipster was forty-six-year-old Mme. Gertrudis "La Tules" Barceló, an infamous card sharp and gambling hall operator in Santa Fe, known for her prominent wig and false teeth, who had heard it from her mulatto servant, who was married to someone involved in the conspiracy.

dering humiliation and frustration that burst into anger and a desire for revenge.

After the plot was uncovered, Santa Fe was basically locked down and martial law declared. The plaza bristled with artillery aimed in all directions and manned night and day. Guards were posted and suspicious persons questioned. More conspirators were arrested. It was in this atmosphere that Governor Bent after Christmas decided to travel to Taos, where his wife and family were living, along with Kit Carson's beautiful new wife, Josefa, who was Bent's sister-in-law. He was warned that it was dangerous, because there were signs that the conspiracy was still alive. But Bent felt he knew his people and that, after twenty years among them, he would be respected and trusted. On January 14 he set out for Taos, eighty miles north.

As he entered the town Bent was accosted by a throng of Pueblo Indians who asserted that two of their tribe had been wrongfully arrested for stealing and demanded that Bent release them. He replied that he held no authority to release prisoners and that they would receive fair justice at the bar, which seemed to placate the mob and it dispersed. After an amicable evening with his wife and family and several houseguests, Bent was awakened at the crack of dawn by someone warning that the Indian mob along with some Mexicans had reassembled, drunk and bloodthirsty, and was headed his way. Bent met them at the door and asked their purpose. The answer was direct and not good.

"We want your head, gringo, we do not want for any of you gringos to govern us, as we have come to kill you."*

"What wrong have I done you?" Bent responded. I have always helped you. I cured you when you were sick and never charged you."

"Yes," cried an Indian, "and now you must die so that no American is going to govern us!" With that, a shower of arrows enveloped Bent at his door, which he managed to slam shut and bolt. His family, now thoroughly alarmed but still dressed in nightclothes, was horrified to see three arrows sticking out of the governor's face and blood streaming everywhere.

---

*The colloquy here is from Eisenhower's book, quoting from an unpublished manuscript of Teresina Bent Scheurich, Charles Bent's daughter, who was a witness to the event.

The mob began breaking the thin mica windows of the Bents' adobe home while rocks and more arrows flew inside and cries of "kill the Americans" rose to a pitch along with war whoops and curses in both the Spanish and Pueblo tongues. The family could hear people clattering on the roof, trying to smash through. In desperation, someone suggested they endeavor to break through the wall the adobe shared with the house next door, and the women frantically set at this task using fire pokers and iron kitchen tools. Bent, meantime, was shouting out a broken window, trying to reason with the mob, but they only laughed and cursed at him. Gunfire coming through either a window or the door hit Bent in the face and stomach, while the women hysterically beat and clawed at the soft adobe bricks.

Soon they had cracked a hole large enough for a human body and after the children had gone through Bent's wife, Ignacia, was adamant that the governor should go next. But the arrows still sticking out of his head would not fit through the narrow opening and Bent was obliged to withdraw and pull them out from beneath his skin before reentering the hole "holding his hand on top of his bleeding head." Just then some Indians burst into the house and confronted Ignacia with a gun. Her servant, an orphaned Navajo woman, jumped in between her mistress and the gunman and was shot.

The shooter then struck Ignacia with the gun butt and was about to finish her off when one of his companions discovered the hole broken into the wall and crawled through. Other Indians had already broken into the next-door house and were wandering its rooms. By then Bent was enfeebled from his wounds and lying down, his head cradled by Mrs. Thomas Boggs, one of his houseguests. With his stunned and horrified family watching, a Pueblo named Tomás Romero burst in and seized Bent by his suspenders and jerked him up, only to smash him to the floor, pounce on him, and scalp him alive. Other Indians riddled Bent's body with arrows and still others finally put him out of his misery in a hail of gunfire.

The assailants stripped Bent of all his clothes and began to mutilate him with knives. Some reports said he was decapitated. A plank was brought out and Bent's bloody scalp was stretched upon it, nailed with brass tacks. This was then proudly paraded through Taos by the drunken mob, as the early rays of sunlight dappled the adobe-lined streets. Before leaving, the Indians took all the belongings of the Bents and the next-door house, including all the food. The Bent family and their guests were then warned not to leave their house, and the townspeople were warned not to give them food or any other kind of assistance. The mob then fell on the Taos sheriff, Stephen Lee, and murdered him on his rooftop as he sought to escape. They seized the United States attorney, J. W. Leal, stripped him naked, and paraded him through the town, singing, as they stuck him with lances and arrows before scalping him alive. "Praying them to kill him, he instead received arrows that drove delicately into his eyes, mouth and nose. He was thrown broken and alive to freeze in a ditch for several hours. At last the rebels in their terrible sense of virtue returned from other work and killed him with a few final arrows. His body was then given to hogs who feasted upon it."

Taos prefect Cornelio Vigil was chopped into pieces. Two boys, Pablo Jaramillo, a nephew of Bent's, and his friend Narciso Beaubien, who had just returned from boarding school in Missouri, had hidden under some straw in a stable when they were discovered. They were tortured, scalped alive, and killed. The mob then began to loot the town, cleaning out Bent's store and Kit Carson's home. Hundreds of others descended on a liquor distillery just north of Taos and murdered its American owner, Simeon Turley, and seven of nine mountain men who had been staying there on a toot. But not without a fight. The trappers held out all day, completely surrounded and picked off one by one, until the last two managed to get away that night. Likewise, another bloodthirsty horde fell upon an American pack train and massacred eight American men. Next day the mob, Mexican and Indian alike, now more than a thousand strong and drunker than ever thanks to the proceeds of the Turley distillery, marched on Santa Fe, gaining strength at every town and village and swearing to liberate the territory from American rule.

Next morning, word of the calamity and the impending rebel attack reached Santa Fe through Governor Bent's personal slave, a black man named Dick Green, who had somehow escaped the Taos massacre. Donaciano Vigil, brother of the slain Taos prefect, was appointed acting governor by Colonel Price, and he and Price laid plans to strike the rebellion a mighty blow. Because of the lack of animal fodder at Santa

Fe, it had been necessary for Price to scatter his troops as far as Albuquerque and the Pecos River. Now he began desperately calling them in. A furious Ceran St. Vrain, partner in the Bent's Fort enterprise, organized a grim and grizzled company that included the trappers, mountain men, merchants, friendly Mexicans, and Dick Green, keen to avenge the murder of his master. Numbering sixty-five men, and mounted, they took the company name Avengers. For many of them, in addition to Green, it was personal, and their eyes must have glinted like the steel in their knives.

It took Price three days to organize his response force, which at that time consisted of 353 men, all dismounted except for St. Vrain's company, as well as four small but effective mountain howitzers and a six-pounder gun. On January 23 he marched out of Santa Fe and early next day encountered fifteen hundred Mexicans and Indians, led by a Hispanic named Pablo Montoya who called himself "general," waiting behind entrenchments at a village called Santa Cruz de la Cañada. With fire and maneuver, and furious infantry assaults with house-to-house fighting, Price soon scattered these people, killing thirty-six and driving the rest back toward Taos, at a cost to himself of two killed and eight wounded. Fortuitously, the U.S. Dragoons that Kearny had sent back from the California expedition arrived on the scene, led by Captain J. H. K. Burgwin. Price now commanded a not insignificant force of 480 men, some of them mounted regulars.

His task was immensely complicated by heavy winter snows, which clogged the high mountain passes and fell in clumps from green mountain pines. The Americans invariably met resistance by the rebels, who then fought a rearguard guerrilla-style action. At Embudo Pass in freezing cold Price drove the rebels again, slaying twenty and capturing sixty wounded and pressed them on again toward Taos, where he arrived February 2 to find the enemy, numbering in the thousands, drawn up at the Pueblo to make a final stand.

The thousand-year-old Taos Pueblo, about two miles north of the city in the shadows of the snowcapped Sangre de Cristo Mountains, consisted of two massive facing adobe pyramids, seven stories in height, with a creek running between them. It was a formidable defensive position, with walls up to three feet thick and reached only by ladders, which could be drawn up. The Pueblo itself was enclosed by an adobe wall, forming a square, with a sturdy adobe mission, San Geronimo, along the north section of wall. The rebels had concentrated in the courtyard and in the mission church.

With his light mountain artillery, Price began to batter at the stout outer wall of this imposing citadel, but without much effect, and at sundown, to the jeers of the Pueblo's defenders, he retired across the windy plain to Taos to rest and regroup. He was confident at this point that the rebels had no other place to go.

Next morning, Price ordered St. Vrain's Avengers—as he had in the previous two engagements—to circle around behind the rebels so as to swoop down on any fugitives. Captain Burgwin's dragoons were posted to the west of the mission, just out of gunshot range. The artillery was positioned both east and west, in order to obtain a crossfire that converged on the church where a majority of the rebels congregated, apparently intending to make a last stand. At nine a.m. on February 4 the guns began to fire.

For the next two hours the artillery bombardment increased in intensity. At eleven o'clock Price ordered a cease-fire to assess the damage. When the smoke cleared he was disgusted to find that the mission appeared practically undamaged. Its thick adobe walls had simply absorbed the cannonballs without crumbling. Meantime, the rebels had punched out loopholes in the mission walls to shoot from and were also sniping from the roof. Having run out of options, Price ordered a plain old infantry charge. From the west Captain Burgwin's two hundred dragoons dismounted and formed in ranks. Along the north wall a similar formation dressed ranks. At the signal, nearly four hundred U.S. soldiers moved out in perfect marching formation, "flags waving, drums and fife marking the tempo, with officers leading the way, drawn swords gesturing overhead."

As they came within rifle range the American companies broke into a run until they were flat against the huge earthen walls of the church, which they immediately began attacking with pickaxes and crowbars. Others found ladders and managed to climb atop the church and light it afire. In the meanwhile, Captain Burgwin—who as described by a mountain man who knew him was "as brave a soldier as was ever seen on the frontier"—took a party round to the huge wooden entrance door, only to find it securely bolted. As the men undertook to break through,

Burgwin was shot dead by a gunman in the adjoining pueblo, but this so enraged his soldiers that they managed to hack a hole in the wall, through which they pushed artillery shells with the fuses lit. Lieutenant Alexander Dyer, Price's artillery officer, moved the six-pound gun to within fifty yards of the church and fired a dozen rounds, which blew a gaping hole in the building.

By midafternoon the roof of the mission was engulfed in flame, and amid all the roaring and banging and racketing Lieutenant Dyer wheeled his six-pounder to within ten yards of the ragged breach in the church wall and began blasting away with grapeshot. This produced a fearful slaughter inside the church, and the air was punctuated by the shrieks and howls of men being torn apart by the shot.

Dyer ceased firing and American soldiers stormed inside the mission through the gaping fissure to behold an appalling sight. The floor, walls, and bench pews were drenched in blood and pieces of flesh and the air was thick with gunpowder and hung heavy with the stench of gore. The nave and apse were strewn with scores of the dead and dying and those few still able to resist were quickly dispatched.

Nevertheless, in the face of the point-blank cannon fire, several hundred had managed to escape into the Pueblo apartments. Fifty-four of the insurgents ran through the back door toward the foothills of the mountains; unluckily for them, St. Vrain's Avengers had stationed themselves in a large semicircle around that part of the Pueblo, in contemplation of just that eventuality. Hidden in brush or behind rocks with their weapons at the ready the Avengers made short work of these fugitives, mostly without quarter, slaughtering fifty-one out of the fifty-four in what amounted to a kind of impromptu turkey shoot. Those who weren't gunned down outright were fallen upon with knives and hatchets.

By sundown the roof of the church had caved in and the blackened beams hung down crazily as clouds sailed overhead against the bright azure sky. An American flag was planted at the entrance to the church, which had become a smoldering ruin. While bodies were still being cleared, the U.S. troops bedded down for the night in and around the church, expecting the fight to continue the next day.

But upon arising Price noted a number of white flags flying from the rebel pueblos, and soon he was beseeched by elders of the tribe, accompanied by women and children, pleading for peace. This Price granted, "thinking that the severe loss they had sustained would prove a salutary lesson," but only on the condition that they give up the instigators of the rebellion. This stipulation was agreed to and seventeen of the leading rebels were put on trial for murder and treason.

The battle at the Taos Pueblo had cost Sterling Price twenty killed and twenty-nine wounded, including several outstanding officers. It cost the rebels 150 killed and nearly that number wounded. Price left a powerful force to ensure the peace in Taos and returned to Santa Fe with the main part of the army. The revolt had turned into one of the bloodiest episodes of the Mexican-American War, and afterward there was speculation that the clergy had played a large hand in its instigation. Priests held huge sway among the Pueblos, nearly all of whom were illiterate and susceptible to influence. In particular a long accusatory finger has been pointed at Padre Antonio José Martínez of Taos by no less than Kit Carson, who remained convinced that the powerful priest was involved in the uprising and in Bent's murder. The evidence is slim, but it was well known that Martínez disliked Bent and opposed his requests for land grants from the Mexican government. It has been suggested that the animus began when Bent refused to convert to Catholicism when he married Ignacia.

Others saw deeper involvements. The religious makeup of New Mexico nurtured many strange and almost inscrutable tentacles of Catholicism, including a branch or sect called Penitentes, a cult of self-flagellates that Padre Martínez oversaw. Then there were the so-called Marrano Jews of New Mexico, who seemed strangely evocative of the accursed Lamanites, who, according to the golden tablets of Mormon founder Joseph Smith, had lost all memory of their culture. Like all good Mexicans, the Marranos (or Crypto-Jews) were, by law, practicing Catholics, but still they atavistically washed their hands on Fridays and lit Hebrew candelabras without ever knowing why. It was said that they were descendants of *converso* Jews from Spain, who had converted to Catholicism but then, beginning in the fifteenth century, nevertheless became targets for the Spanish Inquisition. To avoid torture or burning at the stake, so the story went, these people joined up with the early conquistadors for expeditions to the new world and somehow managed to escape to the more remote parts of Mexico.

In any case the Church in New Mexico was deeply suspicious of Americans and America, with its secular policies and heavy concentration of Protestants. With good reason the priests feared a loss of power and influence and, like powerful and influential men everywhere, they came to hate what they feared.

The trials of the rebel conspirators took place in the spring of 1847. By modern judicial standards it could easily be deemed a kangaroo court, but in those times justice often worked with what it had, which, in the case of New Mexico, wasn't much. Among the judges, for instance, were Charles Beaubien, father of the slain and scalped boy Narciso, and Joab Houghten, a close friend of the deceased governor. The foreman of the jury was none other than Charles Bent's brother, George, and the jury was composed of a number of Bent friends as well as the famed trapper and mountain man Lucien Maxwell, who was married to Narciso Beaubien's sister. The court interpreter was Ceran St. Vrain. The verdicts seemed foregone.

The two principal conspirators were Tomás Romero, the Pueblo who led the Taos mob and harangued Governor Bent on his doorstep, then scalped him alive, and Pablo Montoya, the Mexican who served as so-called general of the rebel band. However, on the day before trial an impatient dragoon named Fitzgerald murdered Romero in his cell, leaving Montoya to face the music alone. After a fair trial he was sentenced to death by hanging. Court was in session fifteen days, during which another fifteen rebels received the death sentence. The executions were carried out starting April 9 when six of the condemned, "miserable in dress, miserable in features, miserable in feelings," were trundled to the town plaza in the back of a donkey wagon. Seventeen-year-old Lewis H. Garrard, who left his St. Louis home a few months earlier for a little western adventure, had joined up with St. Vrain's Avengers and, along with a battalion of Price's soldiers, had the duty of escorting the prisoners to the gallows, which was nothing more than a long, bare tree limb in the plaza square.

The sheriff had borrowed the lassos of Garrard and some others to do the hanging and greased the nooses with Mexican soft soap to make the knot slip quickly. The method of hanging in Taos did not involve a proper gallows in which the condemned fell through a trap that instantly broke his neck. Instead it consisted of a prolonged, twisting strangulation when the donkey cart was moved out from beneath him.

Such was the fate of this first crew of six. About nine in the morning they were given a chance to say their last piece; then each turned to the others to bid *adiós* before the sheriff started the mules and, one by one, they were dancing on air in the bright New Mexico morning. There they twisted for a long while; as Garrard tells it, "The bodies swayed back and forth, and, coming in contact with each other, convulsive shudders shook their frames, the muscles contracting, would relax, and again contract, and the bodies writhed most horribly. While thus swinging," he continued, "the hands of two came together, which they held with a firm grasp till the muscles loosened in death."

This was the gruesome reality of life and death along the frontier, where the lofty thoughts of civilized men dwelled on putting down native rebellions and pacifying the Indians. And the Treaty of Bear Springs? It was broken almost immediately by the Navajos, who redoubled their outrages against the Mexican farmers and stockmen as soon as Kearny's and Doniphan's soldiers were safely out of sight.

CHAPTER ELEVEN

Doniphan's Expedition

Alexander Doniphan was the kind of man writers of Westerns dream about. President-elect Abraham Lincoln summed it up niftily some twenty years after Doniphan's legendary exploits in the Mexican-American War when he met the distinguished Missouri lawyer in February 1861. Doniphan was part of the so-called Peace Commission composed of prominent men from twenty-one states that went to Washington in an eleventh-hour effort to head off civil war and, at least, managed an audience with Lincoln.

"And this is Colonel Doniphan," Lincoln intoned, "who made the wild march against the Navajos and Mexicans. You are the only man I ever met who in appearance came up to my expectations."

It was true enough. At six feet four Doniphan was a giant of a man, especially for his day and time, dashing and ruggedly handsome with piercing hazel eyes, a nose straight as an ax handle, and thick auburn hair that he often wore collar length. It was said, without verification, that women swooned when he entered a room. Celebrated for his eloquence and quick legal mind, the thirty-eight-year-old Whig was also renowned for his sense of fairness. It was he, after all, who as state militia commander had broken up the Mormon kangaroo court-martial and saved Joseph Smith and the other Saints from the firing squad during the 1838 dustup in Missouri, then wound up representing the Mormon Church in its efforts to save its property.

Most of the thousand-odd men Doniphan commanded were Missouri farm boys who had enlisted to see the world, or at least some part of it, before they got married or died, and to fight the Mexicans, just for the hell of it. Doniphan, though educated, was still one of them and joked and talked their turkey, settled disputes, and called them "boys." He took into consideration that they were undisciplined compared with regular army troops and, when not under Kearny's direct orders, often asked their opinions of military matters large and small. They loved him for it.

It was 236 hard miles due south from Santa Fe to El Paso del Norte, the foremost city in northern Chihuahua. During the first part of the march the First Missouri Volunteers, presently 856-strong, would have to contend with Indians, rough terrain, freezing cold, and the overwhelming Mexican army that was eternally rumored to be coming up to meet them. But at least they would have water, as they followed the Rio Grande south out of the mountains and onto the plains.

The second half of the trip, however, they would leave the river as it turned east and contend with the dreaded and aptly named Jornada del Muerto, "Dead Man's Journey," across a barren arid desert of ninety-three excruciating miles. Along the way they would encounter petrified forests and steaming earth, ferocious wolves and the inevitable Indians and rattlesnakes.

The expedition got on the march December 4 from Santa Fe, but a large part of the First Missouri Volunteers was already well down the trail owing to the Indian treaty expeditions. Also strung out along the trail were Magoffin and the other traders and their three hundred wagons, waiting for an army escort in case of trouble. Doniphan had planned to travel light and quick to join General Wool, without his artillery, but persistent rumors suggested that Wool was not in Chihuahua at all. What this portended, Doniphan did not know for sure and could not divine.

The traders, many of whom had made the trip numerous times and were well acquainted with the Mexicans, almost unanimously said Doniphan would be "crazy" to order his small force into Chihuahua unless Wool's army was already there. But Alexander William Doniphan was not a man to welsh on an order. Kearny had told him to go into Mexico and, after carefully weighing the risk, he intended to do it—first ordering a mounted company to ride hastily ahead and scout things out.

He also sent a "fast post" (messenger) to try to find Wool and bring back news of his location and intentions, but meantime he took the precaution of ordering his ten-gun artillery battalion and 125 artillerymen to join him on the march. It consisted of two five-gun batteries commanded by two West Pointers, Captain Richard H. Weightman and Major Meriwether Lewis Clark, Kearny's brother-in-law. At Santa Fe there was a brief delay caused by Colonel Sterling Price, who was busy putting down the Taos rebellion and did not wish to part with the guns, but after a bit of a wrangle both Weightman and Clark started their caissons down the Santa Fe Trail.

Moreover, Doniphan first wisely decided to send out one company of cavalry, under Captain William Gilpin, then another under Captain John Reid, as forward reconnaissance. Aside from the cold, and the rough nature of the ground, and horse-thieving Indians at night, the march wasn't so bad because it was almost all downhill as they descended the mountains. The singular feature noticed by all the men was the abandoned and forlorn nature of the countryside.

A few brave New Mexican souls clung on in the 150 or so miles of fertile valley along the river that led into Chihuahua, but because of the Indian terror most inhabitants had long since fled to the relative safety of Santa Fe, Albuquerque, or some other large town. Ranchos that had once boasted orchards, fields, and vineyards now everywhere lay fallow, their haciendas' roofs caved in and vines overtaking their windows. Flocks and herds were nowhere to be seen. Once thriving copper, silver, iron, and coal mines were deserted, as were furnaces, smelters, and smithys. Everything seemed in decay. Even the population, such as remained, "are in a state of decline and degeneracy." One diarist compared it with the northern frontiers of ancient Rome, "as the Goths, Vandals, or Huns overran her territory," adding "only that the Indians are far more savage." Such was the level of protection that the government in Mexico City had provided its citizens.

As the traders' caravan and First Missouri Mounted Volunteers traversed this remote and unhappy valley southward out of the mountains an improbable character came trotting up on horseback from the opposite direction. He was Lieutenant George Frederick Augustus Ruxton, twenty-five, late of Her Majesty's Eighty-ninth Foot, decorated hero of the Carlist Wars in Spain, African explorer, and member of the Royal Geographical Society. Six months earlier, the ever-inquisitive Ruxton had steamed out of Southampton on a Royal Mail packet bound for Veracruz, where he embarked on a single-handed overland journey of observation in northern Mexico and the American West. After an informative tour of Mexican cities and countryside, Ruxton ventured north into Chihuahua, with his horses, mules, a Hawkin rifle, and a dog as his favorite companions, crossing the dreaded Jornada and eluding rampaging Apaches. At one point he had encountered the party of Governor-General Armijo, fleeing Santa Fe with his wagon train full of loot. The general, whom Ruxton described as "a mountain of fat," suddenly "rolled out of his American Dearborn" and "inquired as to what they were saying in Mexico respecting its [New Mexico] capture by the Americans without any resistance." Unfazed, Ruxton replied, "There was but one opinion expressed—that General Armijo and the New Mexicans are a pack of arrant cowards; to which the former governor answered, 'Adios! They don't know that I had but 75 men to fight 3,000. What could I do?'"

After parting company with General Armijo, Ruxton continued up the Rio Grande, encountering from time to time the bodies of dead Mexicans massacred by Apache and Comanche, their corpses being picked over by flocks of repulsive *zopilotes,* or Mexican turkey vultures. Presently he came upon a laager, or encampment, of the First Missouri, which, to Ruxton's Sandhurst-educated sensibilities, left much to be desired.

"From appearances, no one would have imagined this to be a military encampment," he wrote later in a journal of his travels. "The tents were in a line, but there all uniformity ceased. The camp was strewn with the bones and offal of the cattle slaughtered for its supply, and not the slightest attention was made to keeping it clear from accumulations of filth. The men, unwashed and unshaven, were ragged and dirty, without uniforms, and dress as, and how, they pleased. They wandered about listless or were sitting in groups playing cards, and swearing and cursing, even at the officers, if they interfered to stop it (as I witnessed)."

These were serious enough charges, but Lieutenant Ruxton was just getting warmed up.

"The greatest irregularities constantly took place. Although [they were] in enemy country, sentries, or a guard, were voted unnecessary;

and one fine day, during the time I was here, three Navajos ran off with a flock of eight hundred sheep belonging to the camp, killing two volunteers in charge of them. The most total want of discipline was apparent in everything." Sandhurst it was not.

Now Ruxton got on his soapbox, as if he had drawn a crowd in Piccadilly Circus. "The American can never be made a soldier," he exclaimed. "His constitution will not bear the restraint of discipline, neither will his very mistaken notions about liberty allow him to subject himself to its necessary control."

Ruxton observed (correctly) that America had ample natural resources and easy opportunity for all; he concluded (incorrectly) that military service in the United States was "unpopular, and only resorted to by men who are too indolent to work, or whose bad characters prevent them seeking other employment."

"Of drill and maneuver," Ruxton lamented, "the volunteers have little or no idea. 'Every man on his own hook,' is their system." But, he finally conceded, "These very men, however, were as full of fight as game cocks."

What, if anything, the maligned Missourians would have made of Ruxton's evaluation of them is not known, but after wining and dining him for several days they sent him on his way north toward Santa Fe, in the company of a military engineering detachment.

The Jornada del Muerto, which the main body of Volunteers entered on December 18, was pretty much as advertised, which is to say that it was an ordeal. "The Jornada being an elevated plain," wrote Private Jacob Robinson, "the climate is extremely cold, and many of us suffered very much on our march through, being obliged to travel by night as well as by day."

"Good as the road was," remarked Lieutenant George Gibson, some of my oxen gave out, and were abandoned. We marched until about nine o'clock at night, when we camped on the open prairie." And Lieutenant John T. Hughes told his diary, "In passing this dreadful desert, there was neither water to drink nor wood for fire. Hence it was not possible to prepare anything to eat." At night, the wolves were so bold they would creep right up to the campfires, and men shooting them set off many false alarms of enemy attack.

The First Missouri departed the Jornada several days later at a place they came to call the Dead Men's Camp, after two Mexican spies who were slain there by an American sentry. There, beside clear streams, they "feasted and reposed" and recruited their animals for a few days before moving off toward El Paso del Norte, fifty miles south, present-day site of Juárez, Mexico. On Christmas Eve, after a march of fifteen miles, they picked up the Rio Grande again and soon word came back from the forward reconnaissance that a considerable Mexican force was being assembled at El Paso, under a general with the familiar and imposing name of Ponce de León. There would be no bloodless conquest, then, as at Santa Fe, but the Volunteers "were in fine spirits" and "their blood was up."

On Christmas Day, "a brilliant sun, rising above the Organ Mountains to the eastward, burst forth upon the world in all his effulgence." So said Private Hughes. In celebration, "the men had turned frolicksome," and some fired off their weapons, while others "sang the cheering songs of Yankee Doodle, and Hail Columbia." The weather had turned pleasant, and they took up the march in the wide fertile valley of the Rio Grande, not expecting to meet the enemy until they entered the Great Pass itself, between the mountains that led into El Paso del Norte. The mood of the men matched the weather as they ambled along in route step, reins slack, casually laughing and boisterous, more like adventurers than man killers. In the distance were low-lying hills; thick, dried, brownish chaparral covered them like the fur of some bush-dwelling animal.

After eighteen miles they camped alongside an arm of the river called the Brazito. They were nine miles northwest of El Paso and Doniphan gave them the rest of the day off for Christmas. It was early yet, and many of the men were sent out to graze horses or gather water or wood for their supper fires. To the east and slightly south of them was a series of sandy hills beyond which rose the Organ Mountains; to their rear was the river. At this point the column was spread out for several miles along the Camino Real.

A detachment of cavalry scouts had brought in a handsome white stallion captured from a Mexican reconnaissance detail. Several officers, including Doniphan, were gambling for it in a game of three-card loo when an odd cloud of dust appeared on the southern horizon in the direction of El Paso. At first they thought it was prairie dust blown up by the wind, but it soon dissolved into a chilling tableau that must have shivered Doniphan to the bone. As the dust settled, it revealed the dressed infantry lines of a Mexican army, more than thirteen hundred strong, drawn up about half a mile away, accompanied by flags and banners and resplendent in their uniforms, as opposed to the ragged and bedraggled First Missouri, which looked like a rabble.

There was Mexican cavalry, too. As Private Hughes recalled it: "They exhibited a most gallant and imposing appearance, for the dragoons were dressed in a uniform of blue pantaloons, green coats trimmed with scarlet, and tall caps plated in front with brass, on the tops of which fantastically waved a plume of horse hair or buffalo's tail. Their bright lances and swords glittered in the sheen of the sun. Thus marshaled, they paused for a moment."

If this disagreeable development had nonplussed Doniphan he didn't show it. "Boys," the colonel said, throwing down his cards and jumping to his feet, "I held an invincible hand, but damned if I don't have to play it out in steel now!" He buckled on his saber and began giving orders. Buglers blew the call to arms, but the men were scattered hither and yon, up and down the column and on all sides of the road. Some dropped their wood or water buckets or rushed their horses to the remuda, but others took their time, assuming it was just another of the false alarms that had been caused in recent nights by sentries shooting at threatening wolves.

If the Mexican commander had immediately marched on Doniphan he likely would have prevailed in victory for, as it was, only about 500 of 850 First Missourians were able to scramble into a line of battle. Worse, Doniphan was naked of artillery, since the regiment's guns from Santa Fe had not yet caught up.

Instead, the Mexican general sent out a rider, dressed in all his martial finery, "who approached on a furious steed, bearing a black flag" tied to his lance, which, when he was sixty yards from the American line, "he waved gracefully in salutation."* The flag, a pennant actually, was inscribed on one side with the slogan "Libertad o Muerte" (Liberty or Death) and on the other was a pair of skulls and crossbones.

---

*In international military parlance, a black flag is a signal that no prisoners will be taken or that no quarter will be given in battle.

Doniphan, who did not speak Spanish, sent out his interpreter, Thomas Caldwell, and his adjutant, James DeCourcy, to see what the man wanted. Turned out he wanted Colonel Doniphan to come with him into the Mexican lines and see General Ponce de León.

"If your general wants to see him, come and take him!" Caldwell told the Mexican, "unwittingly using the phrase of the Spartans at Thermopylae," according to a lieutenant who witnessed the exchange.

This seemed to enrage the Mexican, who exclaimed, "Then we shall break your ranks and take him!" "*Carajo!* [A curse on you!] Prepare for a charge! We give no quarter, and we ask none!" he cried as he dashed back to his lines waving the black flag of death.

The episode was a welcome delay: as Caldwell translated the conversation to Doniphan, more and more American troops fell into line and prepared to receive the charge as infantry, in what would soon become the Battle of the Brazito. Several dozen slaves also joined the battle line, including one who belonged to Doniphan. There were two ranks in line, actually, and as they watched the Mexican army wheel right to fall full force on the American left flank they loaded and cocked their weapons. Then Doniphan gave them a curious order, nowhere to be found in the military handbooks.* "Prepare to squat!" he shouted, and the men, unsure of the meaning, thus prepared themselves, as the order was repeated by captains, lieutenants, and sergeants all down the line.

Forward marched the Mexican army as if on dress parade, with a band playing in the background. A brass six-pounder howitzer in the center of their formation began belching rounds that passed over the Americans. The Mexican dragoons, in their shakos and fine green-and-red-trimmed jackets, swooped down upon the American left but the Volunteers fired off a tremendous volley that knocked the head of the column to eternity. The rest wheeled and began to flee, pursued by a detachment of twenty First Missouri horsemen that Captain Reid had hastily assembled, which "hewed them to pieces with their sabers."

On the American right more Mexican columns came on but were slowed by a patch of thick chaparral that they undertook to pick their way through. Whenever they formed and raised their rifles to the ready,

*Doniphan, having no formal martial training himself, had borrowed some military handbooks from Kearny covering such subjects as drill, tactics, and strategy.

the order "prepare to squat—*squat*!" was given by U.S. commanders and the rounds sailed overhead. The Mexicans, believing that the
squatting Americans had actually fallen from their volleys, advanced
thusly through the chaparral, stopping five times to fire more volleys
and shouting "Bueno! Bueno!" until they came to within sixty yards of
the First Missouri line, whose first rank suddenly rose up and blasted
them in the face with a deadly sheet of fire, hitting dozens. The next
U.S. rank quickly rose and fired, a rabble of Missouri coon hunters and
squirrel barkers,* facing down the haute-coutured ranks of Mexican
regulars and volunteers who outnumbered them three to one, until they,
too, began to drop their weapons and flee back toward the pass. The
enemy center also caved in, and an American party took their howitzer
and turned it on them as they fled.

Then the whole American line quickly formed and, cheering,
advanced onto the rise where the Mexican army had first appeared and
took and held this ground for symbolic sake. Meantime, Captain Reid
and his cavalry returned to report that he had chased the Mexicans into
the mountains, along roads "marked by streams of blood" from carrying off their wounded, adding that a band of Apaches who had been
watching the proceedings from afar had begun to swoop down upon the
Mexican stragglers.

The whole Battle of the Brazito had taken no more than thirty minutes. Doniphan's people counted forty-one dead Mexicans and enemy
documents later acknowledged that another 150 had been wounded.
Seven of the First Missouri had flesh wounds. At last, after all the
marching down the trail and waiting at Santa Fe and the Camino Real,
they'd been bloodied and had acquitted themselves well. It was a crush-
ing victory for the Americans.

Before dark they had collected a great amount of booty that the
Mexican army had left in its flight—in addition to small arms and
ammunition, blankets, horses, tack, and other military accoutrements,
there were kegs of wine and cigars and stores of bread and beans.
Doniphan and his fellow officers returned to their game of three-card

---

*Squirrel barking was a hunter's technique from colonial days, when backwoodsmen
discovered that the .50-caliber ball from their rifles would blow a squirrel to smithereens. So they learned to aim instead for the branch right below where the squirrel was
perched, and the concussion and splinters from the bark would kill the animal.

loo, only to discover that the fabulous white stallion had run off in the confusion of battle. As night fell the men gathered around their fires beside the river and celebrated Christmas with dinner amid the chaparral and dead Mexicans. Private Robinson set the scene in his diary. "We ate their bread, drank their wine, and went to bed as comfortable as if no Mexicans were near."

Next morning the First Missouri took to the trail once more, half expecting a fight when they reached the pass. Instead, they were greeted by a man bearing bread, wine, and a white flag. He was the *alcalde* of El Paso del Norte, who begged Doniphan not to destroy his city. It was an easy request to grant, as it was not the practice of Americans to destroy cities, and as the regiment entered El Paso, "the people came from their houses giving us apples, pears, grapes, &c," said Jacob Robinson. "We encamped in an old corn field amid plenty of burrs and sand. These Mexicans are a singular people; but yesterday, up in arms against us—today, every man said *omega* [*amigo*], or friend."

Doniphan had the Stars and Stripes hoisted over the town's official building and settled his regiment in to await the arrival of his artillery. The slaves who had fought in the battle came to Doniphan with a request that they be allowed to form a company of their own in case of future fighting. The request was granted and as captain they elected the personal servant of one of the lieutenants.

An important addition to the expedition was the arrival outside of El Paso of a fifty-four-year-old Scots-Irishman named James Kirker, described as "an unprincipled opportunist of legendary proportions." For decades Kirker had lived on the frontier as a trapper and trader, known for shady political dealings and shiftable allegiances. In recent years he had been employed by the authorities in Chihuahua as an Apache hunter "at the rate of $40 per scalp, and half price for squaws and children," and it was generally acknowledged that "he had succeeded in ridding at least the more populous areas of the state of Apache annoyance."

Kirker now offered his services to Doniphan as guide, if the Americans intended to march on Chihuahua City, the state capital, as he had intimate knowledge of the terrain and Mexican military capability.

Kirker explained his duplicity by saying that the governor of Chihuahua had not paid him for a number of Indian scalps he had turned in.
Doniphan agreed to take him on—somewhat reluctantly, for Kirker's
reputation had preceded him—but told his lead company commander
to shoot the Irishman dead at the first sign of treachery.

Doniphan kept the First Missouri in El Paso for six weeks, the
length of time that it took for Major Clark to struggle his artillery out of
the mountains and rejoin the regiment. During their stay the men had
thoroughly enjoyed themselves, so much so that Doniphan had been
obliged to outlaw gambling and drinking in the public streets. Three of
the soldiers even took the time to marry Mexican señoritas, but another
was convicted of "ravishing a woman."

On the eighth of February 1847, to use the descriptive words of Lieutenant Hughes, "The whole army, the merchant, baggage, commissary,
hospital, sutler, and ammunition trains, and all the stragglers, ama-
teurs, and gentlemen of leisure, under flying colors, presenting the most
martial aspect, set out with buoyant hopes for the city of Chihuahua."

When final confirmation came that General Wool was not, and
would not be, anywhere near Chihuahua, it was a bold decision for
Doniphan to abandon his lines of communication and press forward,
even if, with the reinforcements, his command now numbered twelve
hundred. Scouts belonging to the Scots-Irishman Kirker reliably
informed Doniphan that an army of about 3,500 Mexicans—regulars
and militia, artillery and cavalry—had gathered in Chihuahua, rallied
by Governor-General Angel Trias, who had informed them by proclamation that, among other unpleasant things, the American soldiers
intended to "abolish the church, molest the women, and brand the
men's faces with the mark of Cain."

But Doniphan had his orders, and Kearny had said for him to go
to Chihuahua City and meet up with Wool. Chihuahua City was 250
miles south, with two other *jornadas* to cross, the first sixty miles long,
but much harder than the earlier one, and with many canyons, drifts,
and hills where they might be subject to surprise attack. Doniphan
therefore employed several mounted companies as cavalry to screen,
reconnoiter, and report on enemy activity.

They were taking all the traders with them, the Magoffins included,
in 325 wagons. To provide additional firepower, 150 of the traders were

organized into a battalion of two civilian infantry companies, plus the company of slaves. These men elected as their leader Doniphan's old friend Major Samuel C. Owens. They were well supplied: while in El Paso the regiment had liberated some 20,000 pounds of gunpowder, lead and cartridges, cannon cartridge, grape and canister shot, four pieces of artillery, and various small arms—plus abundant stores of food, all properly bought and paid for in chits payable on the U.S. Quartermaster.

Thus combobulated, they entered the first *jornada* and right away ran into trouble. The sand was so thin and powdery that the mules sank up to their knees and the wagon wheels to their hubs, so the men had to roll the wagons by hand. The pace was excruciating; over days they dumped out 8,000 pounds of flour and barrels of salt but the animals were still breaking down or dying from exertion and thirst and the going was so slow that consideration was given to abandoning the mission. Then, providentially . . . Well, let us turn once more to the lavender-tinged pen of now Captain Hughes: "But the God who made the fountain leap from the rock to quench the thirst of the Israelitish army in the desert now sent a cloud, which hung upon the summits of the mountains to the right, and such a copious shower of rain descended that the torrents came rushing and foaming down from the rocks, and spread out upon the plains in such quantities that both the men and the animals were filled. Therefore they stayed all night at this place where the godsend had blessed them, and being much refreshed, next morning passed out of the desert."

On the eighteenth the regiment entered a country of such strange rock formations that the men speculated it must have been formed by the Great Flood of the Bible. It featured an exotic spot called Ojo Caliente, with a large natural basin where the troopers, including Colonel Doniphan, and later the women of the traders' wagons, could at last wash away the dust and grime of the prairies and desert. The pool of the gushing natural spring was about 75 by 120 feet and a little above waist deep, with "crystal clear" water and a sparkling sandy bottom, and to top it off the water was geothermally heated "to about blood temperature," which made for a perfect bath.

It was just as well because next day they entered the second desert *jornada*, forty-five miles long, ringed in by snowcapped mountains and "containing neither wood, water, or grass." As they pushed on, Doniphan's reconnaissance, including Kirker's men, reported large bodies of Mexican soldiers concentrating to meet them.

On February 25 they left the desert and entered a grassy plain featuring a large lake beside which they camped and were watering their stock when suddenly they were assailed by a shocking and dangerous prairie fire, "which came bursting and sweeping terribly over the summits of the mountains, and, descending into the valley, united with a fire on the margin of the lake." Flames roared twenty feet high, boomed like cannon shot through the tall, dried grass, and "threatened to devour the whole [wagon] train." In the panic to get away, teamsters lashed the mules and oxen and mounted troopers dashed ahead while infantry ran afoot, but the fire was gaining as a powerful wind blew the conflagration in the same direction the army was traveling.

"The column of flame, displaying a front of many miles, steadily advanced, raging and sweeping like a wave, more terrible than an army with banners," said the Bible-loving Captain Hughes.* "The ammunition wagons narrowly escaped. The artillery was run into the lake."

Doniphan and his entourage attempted to build a firebreak by riding into the lake and then trampling down the grass with their dripping horses, "but the flames passed over and heedlessly swept along." Captain Reid, meantime, had his mounted troopers gallop two miles ahead, dismount, and chop down the grass with their sabers, creating a break thirty feet wide. Then they set fire to the grass on the windward side, which burned until it met the advancing wall of fire and, with one great, last explosive burst, exhausted itself for lack of fuel.

So passed this horrifying tick of fate; at least they would not have come all this way to be roasted alive by a phenomenon. The quick-thinking action of Reid's saved the train and the army, and in their profound relief the people parked their wagons on the scorched and smoldering ground to pass a dreamlike night, shaking their heads in awe and wonder as other, larger fires raged, flared, and boomed up and down the valley and mountainsides all around them.

*Song of Solomon, 6:10: "Who is she that looketh forth as the morning, fair as the moon, bright as the sun, and terrible as an army with banners?"

. . .

The day after the prairie fire, Doniphan's cavalry reconnaissance reported a 4,000- to 5,000-man Mexican army drawn up for battle in a narrow pass at the Sacramento River, about twenty miles north of Chihuahua City. The American horsemen had scaled a tall butte a mile or so away and scanned the enemy position with telescopes. The position looked to be dangerous, if not impregnable; the encounter would become known as the Battle of the Sacramento.

The Mexicans had constructed heavy fortifications of earth and logs, complete with redoubts and redans, to protect their infantry, and their artillery was composed of sixteen pieces, ranging from small culverins, or wall cannons, to large nine-pounders. About 1,200 Mexican cavalry were in and about the encampment, including several hundred lancers. The enemy commander, Major General José A. Heredia, had selected this spot to throw back the U.S. invasion because it was the strongest possible position on the El Paso–Chihuahua road and a perfect trap for the arrogant Americanos. The only problem was that to spring it would require the American commander to come down the Chihuahua road.

Because the regiment was in broken country it made the wagon train vulnerable to surprise attack, and Doniphan had devised a defensive scheme that was more or less an updated version of Macbeth's Birnam Wood come to Dunsinane. The train, including the army's wagons, now included nearly four hundred prairie schooners. Doniphan arranged these in four columns of one hundred wagons each. He set his artillery marching between the two outer columns and the infantry between the inside ones, protected from, if not impervious to, long-range shot—the whole affair was almost Roman in character. The mounted troopers rode at the head and rear, so that the cavalcade now slouched down El Camino Real like a great creaking tortoise which, if attacked, could immediately draw itself in and lash out with blazing cannons and rifles while the cavalry rode round to flank the enemy. It was reported that during its march on the morning of February 28 an eagle overtook the column, "sometimes soaring aloft and sometimes swooping down amongst the fluttering banners, followed all day and seemed to herald the news of victory. The men regarded the omen as good."

Just as he was supposed to veer into General Heredia's trap, Doniphan swung his entire force off to the right, tortoise train and all, west of the Chihuahua road and into a dry gulch, then up onto the mesa, arriving at an angle completely contrary to what the Mexicans had anticipated.

This required the Mexican commander to shift positions, forcing many of the units to come from behind their fortifications, which unsettled the soldiers. Leave it again to Hughes to set the scene: "Nothing could exceed in point of solemnity and grandeur the rumbling of the artillery, the firm moving of the caravan, the dashing to and fro of horsemen, and the waving of banners and gay fluttering guidons, as both armies advanced to the attack on the rocky plain."

About noon the Americans reappeared from behind a *cerro* in full view of the Mexican army, including a gallery of an estimated thousand spectators, "women, citizens, and rancheros—perched on the summits of the adjacent hills, watching the events of the day." The opening gambit was a full-scale cavalry attack by General Pedro García Conde's 1,200 horsemen, certainly an intimidating stratagem. But when they closed within a thousand yards, the artillery batteries of Major Meriwether Clark and Captain Weightman lashed out with such scathing fire that it destroyed the head of the column and the rest fled, leaving heaps of dead horses and the bodies of soldiers on the field.

Next the Mexican guns opened up, beginning an artillery duel that was unquestionably won by the Americans. Even though they were badly outweighed in artillery, the batteries of Clark and Weightman managed to fire a relentlessly accurate combined twenty-four rounds per minute, which, according to an astonished Doniphan, actually "drowned out the sound of the Mexican guns." Many of the First Missouri's horses and mules were killed, and one man had both legs broken by a cannonball, but it was nothing compared to the carnage in the Mexican ranks where more than a hundred were killed and wounded.*

*As the Mexican guns began to fire the Americans noticed a curious phenomenon. Owing most probably to a combination of poor Mexican gunpowder and the rarefied mountain atmosphere, the enemy cannonballs left a blue streak behind them, often allowing Doniphan's men to dodge the danger. It struck the men as being so remarkable that afterward they began using the phrase "blue streak" to describe anything that had great speed or intensity, thus introducing a new expression into the common lexicon.

General García Conde at last pulled his army back behind its fortifications, whereupon Doniphan immediately ordered an attack by his entire force led by, of all things, the artillery, which was run out to the front escorted by cavalry. This textbook no-no worked like a charm, as the American guns began reducing one Mexican battery after the other into silence.

In the meantime, a force of some three hundred lancers suddenly appeared in the rear of the American columns, among the traders' wagons.* They were gallantly beaten back, however, by the merchants' battalion and company of slaves, which then marched to the front to join in the attack on the main enemy position.

This took place directly when Doniphan gave the order and about eight hundred of the Volunteers began an uphill march to close with the enemy. Normally, the force that commands the heights has a distinct advantage, but not in this case because the steepness of the ground prevented the Mexicans from depressing their remaining artillery pieces low enough to sweep the field. At one point a trooper who had been detailed to hold horses out of the range of fire threw down the reins of his seven mounts and grabbed his sword and rifle, exclaiming, "Hell, I didn't come here to hold horses—I can do that at home!" before rushing off to join the battle.

When the First Missouri was within a quarter mile of the Mexican positions Doniphan ordered a cavalry charge by three companies of horsemen on a key enemy bastion, intended to break the enemy lines. About halfway there, however, the horsemen ran into such a heavy crossfire that the regimental adjutant ordered a halt. But the ubiquitous Captain Reid, "either not hearing, or disregarding the order, leading the way, waving his sword and rising in his stirrups," roared, "Will my men follow me?" and with that the entire company charged up the hill at the gallop and took the battery and silenced the guns.

They were too weak to hold the position, though, and a strong Mexican counterattack drove them off with several casualties, including Doniphan's friend Major Owens, who was killed instantly along with his horse. Reid's horse was shot from under him but he remounted and

*These were said by some to be criminals released from Chihuahua jails in exchange for service to their country.

was about to escape when a deadly volley of American rifle fire coupled with grapeshot and canister from the U.S. artillery cleared the enemy redoubt and this time it was taken for good.

Now the American troopers began pouring over the enemy entrenchments and a great slaughter commenced with bayonets, gun butts, knives, rocks, fists, gouging fingers, and strangling hands. General Heredia pitchforked more soldiers into the fray but it was useless; the Mexican army was beaten and no amount of encouragement or threat could rally them. Soon a general retreat turned into a rout in which the Americans "beat the Mexicans from their strong places and chased them like bloodhounds," until nightfall put an end to it.

When the butcher's bill was tallied, 303 Mexicans lay slain on the field of battle and at least that many had been wounded, of which about a third later died. Fifty prisoners had been taken, including a brigadier general. The Americans suffered two killed and seven wounded, of whom three later died. It was one of the most lopsided victories in U.S. military history.

Large numbers of weapons and ammunition were confiscated, including all of the enemy artillery, wagons, stores, livestock, $6,000 in gold, and seven fine carriages, as well as General Heredia's own fancy writing desk and engraved stationery.* Also captured were a number of Mexican flags and regimental colors, including the infamous double-crossboned black flag of the previous battle.† That night, as after the Battle of the Brazito, the Americans camped on the bloody field and "feasted sumptuously on the enemy's wines and poundcakes." Next day, to the tunes of "Hail, Columbia" and "Yankee Doodle" played by the regimental band, they marched into the capital city and accepted its surrender, ran up Old Glory, and fired a twenty-eight-gun salute to the United States.

Doniphan's expedition was one of the most singular feats of the Mexican-American War; with an army of barely a thousand he had captured the vast state of Chihuahua. More important, his entrance into that part of Mexico had tied up five thousand enemy troops at the Battle

---

*It was said that the soldiers later delighted in using the general's personal stationery to write their letters home.

† This "Take No Prisoners" black flag hangs now in St. Louis in the museum of the Missouri Historical Society.

of the Sacramento, including regulars and artillery, which, had they not been required to remain and defend against Doniphan, would have been available to turn the tide at the crucial Battle of Buena Vista, on February 23, 1847, five days previous, against Santa Anna himself, which had been a near run thing for General Zachary Taylor.

CHAPTER TWELVE

The Fight of Their Lives

While Doniphan's force was savoring its victory, Kearny's greatly reduced Army of the West was six hundred miles away, straining toward California in cold and high winds through a landscape of desiccated New Mexican barrens and tablelands so desolate they were forsaken even by the Navajos and Apaches. There was no road or trail, only the broken earth and compass and sextant. Thick mesquite and fremontia* made it doubly difficult for the wagons. The compass route led through gullies, ravines, buttes, and sharp escarpments, and Kit Carson informed Kearny that, if they continued with the wagons, at this rate it would take at least four months to reach California. After another frustrating day of it, Kearny ordered a halt and sent an express rider back to Santa Fe with orders to bring up mules and a couple of hundred packsaddles. The wagons were unloaded and sent back. The party waited. At night the thermometer dropped into the mid-twenties; in daytime it would rise to eighty degrees.

A week later they found themselves in high country, a long pack train snaking single file through the hills. Presently they came into a region of supposedly rich gold and copper mines that had been abandoned years earlier after Apaches descended on the place and killed the Mexican workers. They rode through the ghost town—twenty or thirty adobe houses and a dozen mine shafts were all that remained. Captain Emory, whose engineering detachment was mapping the expe-

---

*A low, feathery shrub also known as flannel bush, named for John C. Frémont. It is ubiquitous throughout the Southwest.

dition, named an exceptionally high and striking escarpment Moore's Bluff, after his good friend in the First Dragoons, Captain Ben Moore, a recent widower with two young children. It was one of the perks of being a topographical engineer in uncharted territory—you got to name things. It did not mean superiors wouldn't overrule you later, but at least for the moment you could officially name mountains, rivers, and anything else on your map as you wished.

On October 20 they reached the Gila River, which bent off south-westward toward California. That morning they were met in camp by a band of Apaches who claimed they came to trade. According to Emory, "They swore eternal friendship to the whites, and everlasting hatred to the Mexicans." The head chief was Red Sleeve, who addressed Kearny with some version of this speech: You have taken New Mexico, go on then and take Chihuahua, Durango, Sonora. We will help you. You fight for land, we fight for Montezuma, and plunder. The Mexicans are rascals and we hate them, and we will kill them all.

Emory noted that the Apaches were "elegantly dressed, with beauti-ful helmets with black plumes, which, with the short skirt, waist belt, bare lags and buskins, gave them the look of pictures of antique Gre-cian warriors." But, he added, "These men have no fixed homes. They hover around the beautiful hills that overlook the Del Norte, and woe to the luckless company that ventures out unguarded." Kit Carson took one look and whispered, "I would not trust a one of them."

Some miles behind, and on a parallel course farther south, struggled Colonel Cooke and his Mormon Battalion, charged not only with bring-ing the wagons along but with building a road all the way to California.

On November 15, "It blew a gale, with snow, sleet, rain and sun-shine alternately," Cooke wrote in his journal. "The despairing wan-derer whose life depends on finding water, always turns with hope to a mountain, to a tree, or to broken ground."

Their guide Charbonneau, Cooke said, "has come in. His mule gave out, he says, and he stopped for it to rest and feed for half an hour; when going to re-saddle it, it kicked at him and ran off, he followed a number of miles and finally shot it; partly I suppose from anger and, partly, as he says, to get his saddle back, and pistols, which he brought into camp."

Cooke and his Mormons pressed on into the Mexican state of Sonora, far to the west, traveling past buttes and mesas from the tops of which ominous smoke signals rose to mark their passage. As on the Santa Fe Trail, the men soon were bewitched by mirages. "A distant mountain range became the shore of a luminous lake," Cooke said, "in which nearer mountains or hills showed as a vast city—castles, churches, spires! Even masts and sails of shipping could be seen by some."

At spots they had to lower the wagons down from precipices by blocks and tackle and ropes around rocks and other levers. On one of these occasions, Cooke reported, "I discovered Charboneaux near the summit, in pursuit of bears. I saw three of them up among the rocks. Soon he fired and in ten seconds again, then there was confused action one bear falling down, the other rushing about with loud fierce cries, amid which the hunter's too, could be distinguished; the mountain fairly echoed. I much feared he was lost, but soon, in his red shirt, he appeared on a rock; he had cried out, in Spanish, for more balls [lead shot]. The bear was rolled down and butchered before the wagons passed."

Suddenly bad things began to happen to them. On December 1 a Private Allen disappeared, and that night, "thick ice formed in the tents." Next day they entered an enormous valley, ringed by mountains, and covered with mesquite, the site of a hundred-year-old plantation ("Nothing but the old adobe walls standing," said Private Henry Bigler), now abandoned due to Apache depredations and said to have once contained 80,000 cattle.

The descendants of those cattle still wandered the valley, eating and propagating, with few natural enemies other than the Indians, who would kill one when they felt like it. "The ox, in a perfectly wild state, abounds here," Cooke reported. "As we descended an immense red bull rushed by in front, at great speed; it was more novel and exciting than the sight of buffaloes."

It was apparently not a moment too soon, either, because by then the provisions they had brought with them had almost given out, including the cattle and sheep that had been driven behind the march. According to Private Bigler, "It had become a common thing to eat head, heels, hide, and tripe. Even the very wool was pulled off from sheep skins that had been used under the pack saddles, and the thin hide roasted and eaten. Poor give-out beef cattle that could not be driven another inch were killed, dressed and eaten to save men from starvation." Bigler informed his diary that a Corporal Green from B Company had "lost his reason."

As the battalion crossed the valley a band of Apaches appeared. "They are poor, dirty, Indians," Cooke remarked, "[but] they wear fine moccasins, with tops or leggings attached. Their tongue," he continued uncharitably, "is by far the most brutal grunt that I have ever heard; their lips scarcely move, and the words come out a stuttering, jerking, gutteral [sic]."

Cooke had hoped to employ some of the Indians as guides, but they did not come in as promised next day: however, the missing Private Allen did, and with a harrowing story to tell. It seems hunger had driven him to go off hunting. Almost immediately Allen—the only enlisted member of the battalion who was not a Mormon—lost his way. Next he came across the road the battalion had made but, as Cooke put it, "his great misfortunes seem to have turned on his taking for granted we could not have come that way." Allen then encountered Indians who robbed him of his gun and clothes. Thus, five days and sixty miles later, according to Bigler, "he overtook us at this encampment naked, and almost starved to death." To survive, noted Colonel Cooke, "having no knife, he had eaten of a dead horse, in the fashion of a wolf."

The battalion's ill luck continued when, several days later, while crossing a prairie "through a northwester that cut us to the bone," they were attacked by, of all things, a herd of wild cattle. In battalion lore it became known as the "Great Bullfight."

In midafternoon of December 11 the column was moving through a sea of tall grass when, without warning or provocation, dozens of wild bulls came charging out of the west, much as the herd of buffalo had attacked the First Missouri Volunteers along the Santa Fe Trail.

Wrote Colonel Cooke, "One ran on a man, caught him on the thigh, and threw him clear over his body, lengthwise; then it charged on a team, ran its head under the first mule, and tore the entrails out of the one beyond. I had to direct the men to load their weapons to defend themselves."

A bull ran down a sergeant who narrowly escaped serious injury as he was struck between the animal's horns. Another charged a horse tied behind a wagon, but the horse broke free and the bull hit the wagon head-on, knocking it out of the road. One bull killed two mules, then charged on a "Private Amos D. Cox of Company D, [who] was thrown several feet in the air, the bull passing on, taking no further notice of him," according to Bigler, who noted that "Cox was severely wounded in the thigh." Many of the bulls seemed to go for the wagons and the mule teams. "I saw a bull make a charge," said Bigler, "and it appeared to me he threw the near mule slick and clean over his off mate."

By now the men were shooting at the bulls, with mixed results. Lieutenant Stoneman, Cooke recorded, "was accidentally wounded in the thumb." Another bull, "after receiving two balls through its heart, and two through its lungs, ran on a man. I have seen the heart," Cooke said, after the animal was finally killed.

To escape being gored, a soldier "fell flat to the earth [and] the bull ran lengthwise over him, hooking down at the same time and caught the soldier's cap on his horn, and carried it off, I suppose in triumph," said Bigler. Colonel Cooke wrote, "I was very near Corporal [Lafayette] Frost when an immense charcoal-black bull came charging at us, a hundred yards. Frost aimed his musket, a flintlock, very deliberately, and only fired when the beast was within six paces; it fell headlong, almost at our feet." According to Bigler, who saw the incident, "The Colonel turned round and swore that man was a soldier!"

After the dust had settled it was found ten bulls had been killed— tough meat but more than enough for several days on the march. After the bulls had been butchered, the wounded tended to, and the battalion settled down beside its campfires to assess the incident, Colonel Cooke, who was himself an accomplished topographer and in fact was making his own map of the journey, recollected that they had just crossed "a pretty stream." He drew it in on his map as "Bull Run."*

Two days later, well into Sonora, the scouts encountered a shack at a well in the desert, about twenty miles from the line of march, where some Mexicans and Apaches were operating a still to make mescal. The Mexicans informed them that about two hundred Mexican soldiers were garrisoned at a fort called Tucson, about sixty miles to the northwest. To

---

*De Voto says these originally Spanish cattle belonged to the stock "that gave rise to the famous longhorns of Texas, which were to be the basis of the Cattle Kingdom that reigned before oil."

avoid capture (or death) the scouts lied about who they were and what they were doing, and one returned to tell Cooke while the other went on to Tucson to see if the Mexicans had been telling the truth.

Cooke immediately ordered the march turned toward Tucson, about four days distant. On the way, the men began to encounter an "extraordinary" flora that none had seen before. It was "a straight column thirty feet high, near two feet in diameter, fluted very similar to a Corinthian column, only the capitol wanting," Cooke marveled. "Some throw out one or more branches, gracefully curved and then vertical, like the branches of a candelabrum."*

That night a Mexican sergeant arrived with a request from the commandant at Tucson that Cooke avoid the fort and the town by marching either north or south of it. Cooke told the sergeant to go back and tell the people they wanted to buy flour. Then about sixteen miles from Tucson two officers from the garrison came to try to arrange an armistice before any fighting got started. Cooke told them they could surrender a few arms as a symbolic gesture and he would leave them be. Next morning the battalion was met by "a fine looking [Mexican] cavalryman, well armed," who carried a message refusing Cooke's offer.

Cooke therefore brought the battalion to arms and began marching on the garrison when a few miles out he encountered two peons who informed him that Tucson had been evacuated by the Mexican forces, which had carried off two brass cannons along with their stores and ammunition. That was okay by Cooke; his orders were to go to California, not get into a scrape with Mexicans in the desert. Besides, he had a wagon road to build.

Kearny's army had reached the Gila, which snakes westward from New Mexico across Arizona to a confluence with the Colorado at the California border. They were 342 miles out of Santa Fe, and Kearny's march continued with the men's faces now turned due west toward the setting sun. Captain Henry Turner, Kearny's aide, thought the Gila was "a

*He was of course describing the famous saguaro cactus (*Carnegiea gigantea*) native to Arizona and the Sonoran Desert, which can grow to fifty feet tall and live up to 150 years. They are today prized as lawn or garden specimens in the Southwest, and wild ones are protected from destruction or molestation by stringent state laws.

beautiful mountain stream—perfectly clear water, and about 30 steps across, timbered in cottonwood principally, it abounds in fish."

But soon the ground became difficult as they wound their way "over the most broken, stony, and precipitous road I have ever traveled over, making it most dangerous for our mules," Turner complained. But when they camped that night the men were relieved to find abundant game and fish in the river bottom—partridge, turkey, deer, bear, and beaver. "The United States will place a high value on this country," Turner wrote, "affording a highway from the United States via New Mexico to California."

Almost everyone commented on the fresh air, how deep and clean it was, rarefied at the dry altitude. According to Turner, "There never was a purer atmosphere than I am breathing at this moment."

To avoid an impassable canyon that the Gila flowed through, they entered sixty miles of mountain-studded semi-desert in what is now southern Arizona. Freezing at night and hot by day, it sustained various small nomadic Indian tribes, which the Army of the West encountered from time to time. On one occasion they met up with an offshoot band of Apaches who called themselves the Pinaleños, which translates as "those who live in the pine forests." Captain Turner, a harsh man, thought them "a worthless, squalid-looking set, their physical appearance greatly inferior to that of any Indians I have ever seen." Among them was a middle-aged woman saddled on a fine gray horse and "wearing a gauzy white dress trimmed with the richest and most costly Brussels lace," according to Captain Emory, "pillaged no doubt from some fandango-going belle of Sonora."

Anxious to trade with the soldiers, the woman dashed about on her horse until her dress slipped off her shoulders and, seeing the soldiers laugh and shout, she then carefully removed the whole thing, tucked it between herself and her saddle, and sat on it. And, said Emory, "In this state of nudity she rode through camp, from fire to fire, until at last she attained a soldier's red flannel shirt, the object of her ambition, and made her adieu in that new costume."

They also came across a sad, complicated situation. "A boy of about 12 years of age," Emory said, "of uncommon beauty, was among our visitors."

The boy, obvious to everyone of Spanish origin, had been kidnapped by the Apaches at a very young age. Now he seemed to be the darling of the tribe—"an idol with the Apaches," as Emory put it in his diary. "We tried to purchase him," Emory continued, but "he said it was *long, long,* since he was captured, and he had no desire to leave his master who, he was certain, would not sell him for any money. All attempts were vain, and the lad seemed satisfied both at the offer to purchase, and the refusal to sell. Here," Emory concludes, as if to block the incident from his mind, "we found the mountains chiefly of red ferruginous sandstone, altered by heat."   .

As they took up the Gila again, for his part Captain Turner ruminated on the bleak fate of the Indians after coming across fresh tracks of cattle and mules, "supposedly stolen by the Indians from the settlements of Sonora.

"Should this country ever be in the possession of the U.S. there will be much difficulty keeping these Indians in order," he predicted, "their only subsistence is stolen cattle, etc. from Sonora, and if they are cut off from this resource I cannot perceive how they are to live—the U.S. may buy them up with annuities, and cause them to be subsisted, and in this way purchase permanent peace with them—they live in such rough country their hiding places are in such fastnesses that a war with them would be almost as endless as was the Florida war with the Seminoles."

It was here, in the floodplain of the Gila, that the men began to see signs of an ancient and lost civilization; shards of pottery, some of it exquisitely fired, littered the ground "for hours in every direction." Then, on the morning of November 10, ahead and slightly southward, loomed the remains of a huge primordial structure, which Indians later told them was the ruins of the House of Montezuma, the sacred Aztec ancestor of all the peoples of the region.

Several of Kearny's more curious officers visited the place. The structure, about sixty feet square, had long ago been burnt out and consisted of four buildings three or four stories high, one of which was still standing, built of a kind of lime, pebble, and clay tabby with smooth plastered walls four feet thick. Neither the joists nor any other part had been made with modern tools. Nearby were two large man-made circular mounds about a hundred yards around. One seemed to contain a well in the center and the other a pyramid. On the second story of the main house Captain Emory noticed a line of hieroglyphics, which some of the men thought might be a curse.* In any case, Emory said, "It was, no doubt, built by the same race that had once so thickly peopled this territory, and left behind the ruins."

That evening they stopped to make camp, 640 miles from Santa Fe, according to the primitive but effective little odometer that Captain Emory had affixed to a wheel of one of the two mountain howitzers attached to the army. It was only by the greatest strains and exertions that the 225-pound howitzers had kept up over so many miles of rough ground, and most of their carriage parts had been repaired or replaced more times than anyone cared to remember. The guns were usually still struggling along behind hours after everyone else had made camp, "under the charge of Lieutenant Davidson," Emory recorded, "whose post has been no sinecure."

Not long after they got their campfires going, a large body of Indians appeared from the west. To everyone's surprise and delight, these were not the suspicious and untrustworthy Apaches but men from a tribe of Pima Indians, bringing armloads of corn, beans, honey, and watermelons to trade. Kit Carson, scouting ahead, had found their village earlier, and when he tried to buy some fresh bread the chief informed him that "Bread is to eat, not to sell—take what you want." Several thousand Pima lived in this part of Arizona and impressed Captain Johnston as "more industrious than I have ever found Indians—they have all the necessities of life, produced by their own industry— they raise cattle and horses, corn, wheat, beans, melons quite enough for their own consumption," and also for trade. Turner found himself surprised by the sophistication of the irrigation system constructed by the Pima. Moreover, he said, they also "raise cotton and manufacture a very substantial blanket of that material."† Unlike Navajos and Apaches, the Pima lived in houses, "resembling what is termed a root house in our country," said Turner, and the people "generally

*The symbols remain undeciphered.

†This may be a forerunner of the luxurious Pima extra long staple cotton that produces a cloth of silky softness.

have kind, amiable expressions" on their faces. Their only known enemies were the Apaches, but the Pima were a tough and substantial
tribe, whom Apaches mostly left alone.* "Theft seemed to be unknown
among them," Captain Emory observed.

Their chief was a tall, spare sixty-year-old named Antonio Llunas
who, according to the normally critical Turner, "exhibit[ed] more of
human kindness in his face, air, and manner, than I have ever seen in
any other individual." Through his interpreter Chief Llunas told Kearny
how in the past he had tasted the whiskey of Sonora and of New Mexico, and he wondered "if he could have a sample of that of the United
States." The liquor was produced and, according to Captain Emory,
"the effect was electric; brightened his eye and loosened his tongue."

Emory asked about the origin of Casa Montezuma and the chief
waxed eloquent on the subject. As Emory noted, "The Indians do not
know the name Aztec. Montezuma is the outward point in their chronol-
ogy; and he is supposed to have lived and reigned for all time preced-
ing his disappearance." The great Montezuma, Emory went on, was
as familiar to every Indian of the Southwest as Jesus Christ or George
Washington was to United States citizens. "In the person of Montezuma," he said, "they unite both qualities of divinity and patriot."

Whiskey glass in hand, Chief Llunas divulged, through the interpreter, the tradition of the ruins attributed to Montezuma, "that in
bygone days a woman of surpassing beauty lived in a green spot in the
mountains. All the men paid her tributes in devotion, gifts, food &c.
but she did not return their love or favor. Then came a drought which
threatened the world with famine, and in their distress the people
applied to her. She gave freely of her food and the supply was endless,
and her goodness abounded.

"One day she was lying asleep with her body exposed and a drop
of rain landed on her stomach, which produced conception. A son was
the issue, who was the founder of a new race that built this house," said
Chief Llunas.

Emory, who had copied down the hieroglyphics from the wall of

---

*In fact, when Kearny's army arrived the Pima had on display eleven fresh Apache
scalps and thirteen Apache prisoners, whom they intended to sell to the Mexicans as
payback for some recent Apache outrage.

Casa Montezuma, showed them to the chief and asked if he knew what it meant. He did not, he said, and the men continued to insist that it was a curse.

Next morning, Emory and the chief's interpreter were out riding, away from the column, when Emory "asked if he believed the fable he had relayed to me last night."

" 'No,' said he. 'But most of the Pimas do. We know, in truth, nothing of our origins. It is all enveloped in mystery.' "

Kearny wrote out an official letter to the chief, stating that "he was a good man, and directing all United States troops that might pass his way to respect his excellency, his people, and their property." They also left behind several broken-down mules for the Pima to bring back to serviceable use for Colonel Cooke's Mormon Battalion, which was expected to pass by presently.

Now the army was about to enter the Tesotal, a forty-mile *jornada* without water or grass. But first they encountered the nation of the Maricopa Indians, a tribe very similar to the Pima but with a different language, and its men had distinct aquiline noses. Like the Pima, they were a friendly people. To prepare for the *jornada* many of the soldiers tried to acquire gourds from the Indians to fill with water, and soon a brisk trade began and the value of gourds steadily began to rise. "One large gourd cost me four strings of glass beads, which was thought to be a high price," Emory grumbled.

They started across the desert at moonrise, three a.m., and as the sun came up so did mirages, the first this party had seen since the Santa Fe Trail. The most interesting was a mirage of the U.S. Capitol, "with dome, wings, and portico, all complete," which presented itself in the far distance "for about twenty minutes," Emory said, adding that he went hungry, "having given my breakfast, consisting of two biscuits, to my even more hungry mule." By that evening they had crossed over the *jornada* and encamped at a spot with both water and forage for the animals, but they had been warned by the Indians that for the next three hundred miles, to where the Gila joined the Colorado, there would be no more grass. Six or eight mules had died during the *jornada*, "and those that survive give little promise of future service," Emory warned.

Kearny ordered that from here on half the command would dismount and walk and use the mules for packing purposes.

The expedition now entered a landscape as foreign as another planet. Huge dark mesas, hundreds of feet high, trailed off in rows like a fleet of dreadnoughts, and the surface changed every so often from sand or dust so fine "it felt as though we were marching through a bed of flour, or ground-up plaster of Paris," to ground "strewed as far as the eye could reach, with black, shining, well-rounded pebbles."

November was ending, and day after day they plunged ahead, consuming the irreplaceable foodstuffs they had brought along, as well as any mule or horse that happened to die from hunger or exertion. Captain Turner lamented to his diary that "our animals are now in a half-starved condition, skin and bone. I really do not perceive how they will get to California." The weather was mostly pleasant during the day, with noon temperatures in the mid-seventies, but at night in this desert it dropped into the twenties or below. At one point Kit Carson killed a mountain sheep near a protuberance that Captain Emory named Goat's Spur. On the afternoon of November 22, General Kearny's horse gave out, "and he was obliged to mount his mule."

Not long afterward, the forward elements of the march made a chilling discovery that "left every man straightened in his saddle." About ten miles from the junction of the Gila and the Colorado they came across a freshly abandoned camp that appeared to have been occupied just that morning by at least a thousand men. Everyone concluded that "It was General Castro and his troops, who must have succeeded in recruiting an army in Sonora, and was now on his return to California." Since there were only 110 dragoons, Kearny decided it would be foolhardy to try to fend off an attack by that many soldiers, so their only recourse was to go on the attack themselves and hope surprise would even the odds a little. As it was getting dark, Kearny put the dragoons into camp in a little depression in the ground where he hoped they would not be discovered. About nine p.m. Lieutenant John Davidson finally caught up with the party and brought his howitzers in. He reported seeing campfires about five miles north on the other side of the Gila. Kearny dispatched Captain Emory and his topographical party, as well as fifteen dragoons, to discreetly find out exactly what in hell they were up against.

Emory and his men "thrashed around" in the dark and the mesquite for a while, finally nearing the enemy camp, where he sent a man up a tall tree who came down to report seeing not so many campfires but hearing the neighing of many, many horses. Pursuing this interesting development, Emory and his squadron eased up to one of the campfires in the dark and, to their relief and delight, discovered that it was not General Castro's army at all but a party of Mexican wranglers with some five hundred California horses on their way to Sonora to mount an army that General Castro was supposed to be recruiting there.

Emory and his men seized what appeared to be the four head horse herders and brought them before General Kearny. "But as usual," Johnston reported, "they lied so much we could get very little out of them."*

One of the drovers claimed there had been a revolt in California and that the Americans no longer controlled the country. He even gave details, including a rumor that the Americans had been expelled from Los Angeles and were congregated at San Diego with three warships and a force of soldiers and sailors who were being challenged by a rebel Californio army. All of this was of course disturbing news and, if true, quite the opposite of the situation Kit Carson had described when he left. Kearny let the quartet return to their camp and next morning sent details to requisition new mounts from the Mexican herd. Nobody knew quite what to make of the revelations of the previous night, but it was obvious that from now on the army should be on its guard.

Meantime, Captain Emory and his people were sent out to reconnoiter. Reaching the junction of the Gila and the Colorado, Emory found the remains of an old Spanish church, "whose mission was eventually sacked by the Indians and the inhabitants all driven off or murdered," but he nevertheless concluded that, being at the confluence of two such important rivers, the site would "probably be the seat of a city of wealth and importance.†

Emory discovered various tribes of Indians in the neighborhood, whose names per Emory are worth repeating: the Coyotaros, or wolf eaters; Cochinears, or dirty fellows; Tontears, or fools; and the Garrote-

---

*One of these men was later identified as José María Leguna, a colonel in the Mexican army.

†It is today the site of Yuma, Arizona.

ros, or club Indians. "These last cultivate melons, beans and maize," the captain noted.

On his way back to the main party Emory made a valuable discovery. He came across a Mexican, mounted of a fine horse, who was carrying extra water and other items indicative of a long journey south through the Sonora desert. He also seemed nervous, so Emory invited him to return to the dragoons' camp, "much against his taste." There he was searched and determined to be an enemy courier, and in his satchel was a treasure trove of military intelligence in the form of letters the man was carrying to Sonora, including one to General Castro himself.

From these letters it became apparent that indeed there had been a counterrevolution in California since Kit Carson had departed there, and that the Americans were no longer in firm control of the province. The letters, Emory said, "all spoke exultingly of having thrown off 'the detestable' Anglo-Yankee yoke, and congratulated themselves that the tri-color once more floated in California." The letters were at least several weeks old and some much older than that, but to Kearny it was plain that a situation awaited him. Also it could have been overtaken by subsequent events. He made no mention in his official reports then, or afterward, of having regrets for sending back two hundred of his dragoon regulars soon after he met Carson. But on balance, with all the trouble he was having feeding and watering his present force, perhaps the question was moot.

The story of the revolt was too true. Like the New Mexicans in Santa Fe and Taos, the Californios soon rebelled against American rule. In fact, they never considered themselves conquered in the first place, only that events had quickly subsumed them in the form of U.S. warships and upstart American settlers who had taken them by surprise.

After the easy fall of Los Angeles, Commodore Stockton had named Frémont military governor and installed Lieutenant Gillespie as *alcalde* of Los Angeles, with a force of forty-eight men to keep order. Stockton decreed that California was now part of the United States, published a set of laws, established a newspaper and a school. Then he went off to Monterey. Frémont, with thirty-five of his mountain men, rode north to the Sacramento River valley. It looked like laurels were in store for everyone; California was certainly a jewel to be prized in America's crown.

Meantime, however, Gillespie mucked things up. In addition to Stockton's laws he imposed a number of various unwelcome rules, curfews, and behavior-governing regulations that caused any goodwill between the freewheeling native Californians and the Americans to evaporate. Not only were the Mexicans unaccustomed to following strict rules, they quickly came to resent the superior attitude of their conquerors, who behaved as precisely that—just as the Missourians had in Santa Fe—and not as benevolent friends come to free them from the bonds of an oppressive government. From the outset, the Los Angelenos were the least pacified of any of the Californios, and two highly respected Mexicans, José María Flores, a captain in the regular Mexican army, and General Andrés Pico, brother of the former governor, began raising troops in the countryside. Gillespie was about to find out that you cannot hold a large section of populated country with harsh rules and forty-eight men.

On September 30, a mere six weeks after the relatively bloodless American conquest of California, Gillespie found himself besieged in Los Angeles by Flores and a force of three hundred angry Californios. Seeing no other choice, he negotiated for himself a rather generous surrender, which allowed him and his forty-eight men to march out of the city to San Pedro, where they were picked up by an American ship and taken north to Monterey. It was a humiliating comedown for the Americans, and Flores capitalized on it by moving swiftly to reestablish Mexican rule in San Diego and Santa Barbara.

Stockton was infuriated when word of the revolt reached Monterey. It spoiled his plan to sail his fleet south to begin capturing Mexico's Pacific ports, then march overland and link up to shake hands with the American commander in chief who would by then have conquered Mexico City. Stockton immediately sent a midshipman, Edward Beale, with a fleet of longboats to fetch Frémont out of the valley "with all the men, rifles and saddles" you can carry. The idea was to ship Frémont's men south from Monterey. Frémont began preparations to move his California Battalion, now some 450-strong, when another messenger arrived informing him that the Californios had stripped the entire area around Los Angeles clean of horses and mules, which would make it impossible to mount the battalion once it arrived. Frémont then made the decision to bring his force to Los Angeles overland, already mounted, a distance of some 350 miles, a two-week march.

Meantime, Stockton had assembled a naval battalion of nearly four hundred sailors and marines that he placed under the command of fifty-five-year-old Captain William Mervine, of the frigate *Savannah*. Mervine landed at San Pedro and marched his force afoot toward Los Angeles. They were met by a body of Flores's Californios, "who almost playfully frustrated the Americans from the outset."

The Californios had brought with them a small piece of artillery from the garrison at Los Angeles. With this they fired on the Americans advancing across the open plain, wounding a few of them. But just as Mervine's force stopped to return fire with their muskets the Californios—displaying their famously adroit horsemanship—would lasso the muzzle of the cannon and quickly drag it out of small-arms range, then set it up again to repeat the procedure.

After losing four men killed and ten wounded this way Mervine gave up, realizing there was no way he could overcome this infuriating tactic. He withdrew his men to the ship to await Stockton. Upon his arrival, the commodore decided to make his base in San Diego, instead of San Pedro, where he could sweep the flat terrain with his naval guns and possibly find livestock to mount his men from farther south.

Flushed with victory, Flores returned to Los Angeles to be elected provisional governor and commanding general by the Californio legislature. From there he sent a hundred men under Castro, who had at last returned, north of San Luis Obispo, and another hundred under Andrés Pico south to San Diego to keep Stockton in check. He himself remained in Los Angeles to await developments.

It was about this time that General Kearny and his tattered, worn-down, half-starved dragoons appeared on the scene.

After weathering yet one more *jornada*, this by far the worst of all, they staggered out of the desert to the civilization of Agua Caliente, an immense cattle and sheep ranch owned by an American named Warner, where, observed Captain Johnston, "the labor is performed by Indians, who are stimulated to work by $3 a month and repeated floggings." The desert had been an appalling strain on man and beast, a hundred miles of fetid waterholes and footsore marching across a landscape strewn with the bones of livestock and the occasional human skull or bone. Near the end the dragoons themselves ran out of food and had begun to eat their own starving horses.

At Agua Caliente, near present-day Palm Springs and about a hundred miles from Los Angeles, they learned the latest news about military conditions in California, not the least of which was that they themselves had arrived within the enemy's rear lines, for the Californios were busily recruiting food, livestock, and other stores from all the ranches in the area.

Kearny instantly realized they would need reinforcements for the remaining sixty miles to San Diego. Word came that an Englishman named Stokes, who lived on a nearby ranch, was headed to San Diego next morning. Kearny sent a dispatch rider to him, and three hours later a strange and striking apparition appeared in the dragoons' camp. "His dress was a black velvet English hunting coat, a pair of black velvet trousers, cut off at the knee and open on the outside to the hips, beneath which were drawers of spotless white; his leggings were of black buckskin, and heels armed with spurs six inches long. Above the whole bloomed the broad merry face of Mr. Stokes, the Englishman." So noted Captain Emory. Stokes confirmed that the Americans held San Diego and not much else and agreed to take a letter to Stockton when he left for the town—about forty-five miles distant—next day.

"The morning was murky and we did not start till 9'o'clock, about which time it commenced to rain heavily, and the rain lasted all day," Emory began his diary for December 4. They were now in "a region of rains" and the vegetation had changed. Late next day on the march they met a detachment from San Diego in response to the letter Kearny had sent and the Englishman Stokes, true to his word, had faithfully delivered to Stockton. The force consisted of Captain Gillespie; Beale, now a lieutenant; a midshipman Duncan; and thirty-five members of the California Battalion who had been chased out of Los Angeles and found their way to San Diego with Gillespie. They had brought with them a small artillery piece that came to be known as the "Sutter

Gun," a four-pounder with a forty-inch-long barrel and three-inch bore. It was wheeled but also had handles and could be carried by two men.*

The rumor was, Gillespie said, that a party of Californio cavalry were encamped nine miles away. They pressed on, night fell, then fog rolled in; they were looking for grass for the animals. It began to rain again.

At last after nine o'clock they halted in a narrow canyon and a reconnaissance squad was sent out to scout the Californios, but it was discovered and "the enemy placed on the qui vive." Captain Johnston wrote in his diary, "We heard a party of Californians of 80 men camped a distance, but the informant varied from 16 to 30 miles, rendering it too uncertain to make a dash on them in the dark, stormy night."

About two a.m. the call to horse was sounded, and after a hasty breakfast they assembled, marching orders were given, packs stowed, and an attack formation got under way. Captain Gillespie remembered, "The weather had cleared, the moon shone bright as day, almost, but the wind coming from the snow-covered mountains made it so cold we could scarcely hold our bridal reins."

It was Kearny's intention to attack these horsemen, they hoped by surprise, and drive them back to Mexico. Soon they reached the upper edge of a large valley and caught sight of the enemy campfires, "which shone brightly," about a mile away. "The general and his party were in advance," Emory recorded, "preceded only by the advance guard of twelve men under Captain Johnston. He ordered a trot, then a charge, and we soon found ourselves in hand-to-hand conflict with a largely superior force."

That was to say the least. Lieutenant Hammond, who had led the reconnaissance, told Kearny upon his return that the Californios had discovered his party, but the general was determined to attack regard-

---

*The gun was cast in St. Petersburg, Russia, in 1804, just in time to help repel Napoleon's siege. It was then taken across Siberia and shipped to a Russian outpost in Alaska, and from there by sea to a Russian fort near Sonoma. In 1841 Captain John Sutter bought the property, and with it the cannon, which he put on a boat up the Sacramento to his own fort. In 1845 Sutter helped the Mexicans put down a rebellion, during which he carried the gun to Los Angeles and, for reasons unexplained, left it there in someone's garden, "overgrown with roses and covered with dust thrown up by horses in the street." When Captain Gillespie got the call from Stockton to meet General Kearny in the desert, he sent a couple of his men for the gun, almost as an afterthought. No one then knew how useful it would become.

less. Worse, Hammond had been unable to determine the size of the Mexican force before being exposed, so Kearny could not be sure of what he was up against. But both Captain Gillespie and Kit Carson had predicted that, based on their experience, the Mexicans would run at the first sign of an organized attack by a well-mounted, well-armed force of U.S. cavalry.

But Kearny's men were anything but well mounted or well armed. Only a few of the dragoons had horses; the majority were riding bony and emaciated mules, jaded from more than a thousand miles on the trail from Santa Fe, including the last *jornada*. Indeed, one of Kearny's reasons for attacking was to get trained horses from the Mexicans to remount his dragoons. Furthermore, "their Hall breech-loader carbines had become useless because of the rains of the previous night," which had wet their paper cartridges.

It was under these obvious handicaps that Kearny set his force in motion before sunup toward the Indian village in the valley of San Pasqual, thirty-eight miles northeast of San Diego. Encamped in the village were 160 Californios, mostly cowboys, under the able command of General Andrés Pico. These men were gloriously uniformed, as most Mexican mounted militia were, and armed, principally, with lances, a holdover from European armies but deadly effective on the battlefield in close quarters. Before the age of firearms, lancers were the elite and most feared of an army's troops. The lance itself was made of stout wood, about nine feet long, with an eight-inch razor-sharp blade embedded in its business end. The California cowboys used them to kill bulls and were highly skilled in their employment.

Kearny's total command numbered 160 men, equal to Pico's but, as we shall see, fatally disordered in battle. The thirty-six-year-old Pico, like his older brother, was a mixed breed of Indian and African, with a little Spanish and Italian thrown in, and he had an irascible temper. The discovery of U.S. forces operating this far out in these hills was both perplexing and disturbing, because all intelligence so far had been that the Americans were bottled up in San Diego under cover of their naval ships. There had been rumors among the Indians that a column of American cavalry was approaching from the east, but it was almost unthinkable that an army had come all the way from the east, considering the many *jornadas*, starvation stretches, hostile Indians, and other obstacles. Still, Pico could not discount the possibility. He roused his men before sunrise and had them saddle up. Scouts were sent out to the east, who soon reported an approaching force of mounted men.

Pico deftly placed a fourth of his horsemen in line astride the cart road leading into San Pasqual, then positioned another fourth in a hidden ravine to the left of the road and another in a ravine to the right. The rest he left in reserve as he awaited developments, which were not long in coming.

Just as the first gray streaks of dawn began to lighten the landscape, Captain Johnston suddenly shouted the charge, and twelve Americans—including Kit Carson—lunged forward at a gallop through a light fog. What apparently prompted Johnston to abandon the trot and go hell-for-leather was the sight of several of Pico's forward mounted scouts, or pickets, in the roadway ahead. Of course the pickets dashed off ahead of the dragoons, but it was a full mile of flat-out running before Johnston's men came into contact with Pico's force, and when they did it was less a clash than a head-on collision. Johnston didn't live to see it. A number of Pico's horsemen carried firearms and some lucky shot toppled Captain Johnston with a bullet right between the eyes. Thus began the Battle of San Pasqual.

The mile-long dash had exhausted and lathered the horses and when the killing clash of man-to-man combat began they were not up to strength. The order to charge had also caught Kearny and his men off guard, but they spurred on at the gallop, too. The order of battle was as follows:

Advance Guard, led by Captain Johnston, mounted on horses.
General Kearny and his party: Captains Turner, Emory, and John
    S. Griffin, the surgeon. Scout Antoine Robideaux and Navy
    Lieutenant Edward Beale—all mounted on horses.
Main Attack Force: Captain Benjamin Moore and his brother-in-
    law Lieutenant Thomas C. Hammond, with about a hundred
    First Dragoons—mounted on mules.
Rear Guard: Captain Archibald Gillespie and George Gibson
    leading about thirty of the California Battalion volunteers—
    mounted on fresh horses and towing the little Sutter Gun.

Artillery: Lieutenant John Davidson and his two mule-drawn
six-pounder howitzers with six to eight men to man them.*

About thirty men, led by Major Thomas Swords, the quartermaster, stayed behind on the lip of the valley to guard the pack train and baggage.

The same volley that killed Captain Johnston killed Kit Carson's horse, vaulting Carson into the dirt and breaking the stock off his rifle. The air quickly filled with the violent racket of gunfire and the clang of steel against steel, the staggering thunder of hoofbeats, the screeching and snorting of horses, and ferocious hollering and frantic cursing.

Right then, as Kearny's little party arrived at the fray, about forty of Pico's lancers lurched up out of the gully on the left side of the road. Seeing this, many of the Americans began to dismount and tried to fight from the cover of large rocks, only to find that their paper cartridges were often damp and would not fire. Worse, they had outrun their main force, the First Dragoons, who hearing the shooting were desperately goading and kicking their mules in order to catch up. Behind them were the frustrated horsemen of Captain Gillespie, who had been ordered by General Kearny himself to stay in rear formation behind the mule-slow dragoons.

For a few intense minutes it appeared the Americans were doomed. Carson scrambled forward into the battle scene and, snatching a rifle and ammo box that lay next to a dead private, crouched behind a boulder and began firing away. Out of the ditch to the right came more Mexican lancers. Just when it looked like the end was near, Captain Moore and the leading elements of his strung-out dragoons arrived on their mules and pitched into the battle. An insolent-looking Mexican rode slowly in front of Lieutenant Beale, as if defying him to shoot. Beale shot him dead.

From Pico's perspective, the arrival of Moore's dragoons apparently

*It has been said that Lieutenant Davidson strongly advised Kearny to place the howitzers at the head of the column, but that request was denied due to the slowness of the caissons.

put a new complexion on things. In the misty morning light the Mexican commander could see more and more Americans appearing ghostlike out of the ground fog, and he must have wondered just how many more they were. Because just then he told his bugler to blow retreat, seizing defeat from the jaws of what might have been a complete victory, seeing as how all his men were on the field, better horsed, better armed, and outnumbering the Americans about two to one at that point. He might have killed or captured the whole bunch. Instead, the Mexicans began falling back on the Indian village, behind a rocky point, which masked the scene beyond it.

Seeing this, horse-mounted Captain Moore corralled a couple of dozen dragoons and went flying off after the Mexicans, perhaps in a bid to cut off their route of escape. Instead, as he rounded the rocky point, Moore caught up short and immediately realized two things: he had completely outrun his mule-mounted dragoons and the Mexicans were not escaping. In fact there were scores of them, including Pico himself, waiting behind that rocky point.

Moore apparently fired his pistol and drew his sword, but was lanced a dozen times or more by the overwhelming force of enemy soldiers, who finally killed him, making orphans of his two young children. Lieutenant Hammond, Moore's brother-in-law, arrived moments later and received the same treatment; he died shortly afterward, but somehow he was able to stagger off to the rear where reports have him pleading, "For God's sake, men, come up!"

Charging after Captain Moore, General Kearny and his people arrived on the scene, where it must have also become suddenly clear that they had made a terrible mistake. Not more than twenty Americans faced nearly a hundred Mexican lancers, whose spears were more than a match for a three-foot American cavalry saber. The battle soon took on an almost medieval character as multiple lancers swarmed around lone dragoons, often stabbing them several times before they fell, and all too often finishing them off as they lay on the ground.

The dragoons soon began a fighting retreat back down the road from whence they'd come—only to be met by the furious and determined marine captain Archibald Gillespie, finally coming onto the battlefield, who now flew into the bloody chaos with his well-armed, horse-mounted volunteers of the California Battalion, shouting at the top of his voice to the crushed Americans, "Rally men, for God's sake rally! Show a front, don't turn your backs! Face them, face them, follow me!" But they paid him no heed and continued to the rear.

All this had taken place in under ten minutes, and the battlefield already littered with the dead, dying, and wounded, but there was more butchery to be done. Late as usual, the two six-pounder howitzers appeared on the field and were immediately attacked by the lancers before they could be unlimbered. The crew of gun number one fired a rifle volley at the Mexicans, which spooked the mules, who bolted away off the road. The lancers closed in, slaughtering the three-man crew as they pleaded for their lives. The young artillery commander, Lieutenant Davidson, was lanced several times but fought off his tormentors, shooting one with his pistol.

Kearny, who had thus far suffered a bad cut on his arm, saw some of this and started toward the gun with Captain Emory and Lieutenant Warner, but they were immediately assailed by a dozen lancers, one of whom stabbed the general in his rear end and would have stabbed him in the back, too, but for Emory intervening with a fatal pistol shot just as the lance was thrust. Captain Griffin, the surgeon, told the general to go to the rear where he could be treated, but Kearny refused and dashed back into the battle.

Other Mexican lancers massacred the crew of gun number two but were soon driven off by dragoons who were just now coming up to the fight. They began to unlimber the howitzer in preparation for bringing it into action when they encountered a dreadful sight. Lurching toward them afoot was red-haired Captain Gillespie, his uniform in tatters and smeared with blood from head to toe. He had been attacked by eight lancers in a savage confrontation that left him stabbed in the back, neck, arm, chest, and mouth. The lance to the chest had punctured a lung and the one to the mouth sliced his lip in two and broke off a front tooth. As he staggered up to the gun, almost faint from loss of blood, he heard someone shout, "Where is the match?" Came the unhappy reply, "There is none." Gillespie reached in his pocket and pulled out a cigar match, which he lit and touched to the firing port, unleashing an instant cannon blast. As he handed the still lit match to a dragoon Gillespie fainted.

Other members of Gillespie's force had by then arrived with the little brass Sutter Gun and, loading it with grapeshot, "cleared the field." Willing and able to engage in mortal human combat, the Mexicans had no taste for standing up to artillery, however small, and Pico withdrew his force, along with its wounded and most of its dead, also dragging along one of the American howitzers by a lasso.

A brief stillness descended upon the battlefield as the panting, pulsing, amazed Americans took stock. Blue-jacketed bodies and dead horses lay in every direction, while riderless horses and mules, most of them lance-wounded and bleeding, wandered aimlessly or stood still, necks bowed low and reins drooping, as if themselves in shock. Meanwhile, more dragoons continued to arrive on the battlefield, appalled by and in despair at what they saw.

It was the kind of shattering experience that would almost have to be endured to be believed. All told, it lasted no more than twenty minutes, but Kearny had lost nearly 80 percent of those actively engaged in the battle, and 20 percent of his entire force. Nineteen Americans lay dead, including three officers, and fifteen men were badly stabbed or sliced with "from two to ten lance wounds," and of these several more would die. Doc Griffin and his crew had set up a triage in a corner of the field and were treating the wounded, including Kearny. He would later characterize it as a victory on the strength of his men still holding the field, but if so it was certainly a Pyrrhic one.

Kearny quickly dispatched mountain man Alexis Godey and two others to San Diego to tell Stockton of the Battle of San Pasqual and that he urgently needed reinforcements. He also ordered that the slain be strapped to pack mules to be brought to San Diego, but he was forced to countermand that when it was pointed out there weren't enough mules for both dead and wounded. It was then decided to bury the dead on the battlefield, which they did, around midnight, to "the distant howling of wolves," in a common ditch beneath a willow tree.

The rest of the day went to reorganizing, foraging for food—of which none was found—and, with the guidance of the mountain men, building Indian-style travois to carry the wounded. Next morning, what was left of the California contingent of the Army of the West got under way toward San Diego, thirty-nine miles distant. But Pico and his lancers weren't through yet, and figures of Mexican horsemen would appear tauntingly on the hills in front of Kearny's march, then disappear as the Americans approached. This went on all day until they arrived at the Rancho San Bernardo, unoccupied, where they rested, watered their animals, collected some livestock, and "killed a few chickens for the sick."

But as they moved out, "driving the cattle before us," a "cloud of Mexican cavalry dashed from hills in our rear to occupy a hill by which we must pass," recorded Captain Emory. "Thirty or forty of them got possession of the hill, and it was necessary to drive them from it. This was accomplished by a party of six or eight [led by Emory] upon which the Californians delivered their fire; and strange to say, not one of our men fell." Emory was still mourning the loss of his good friend Ben Moore, for whom he had named the big striking bluff way back along the Gila River, an eternity ago, but there was still duty to be done. It was the army way. During a sharp gunfight Emory's men burst over the crest of the hill and the enemy fled, leaving behind several badly wounded.

In the confusion, however, Kearny's men lost their cattle—their only source of food—and upon reflection it was decided that proceeding any farther, through narrow passes and hills, would constantly subject them to ambush and "lose[ing] our sick and our packs." Worse, Dr. Griffin concluded that moving the wounded along the rough bouncing road with only the rude travois was not only cruel but endangered their lives. Any hope that Stockton had received their plea for help was dashed next morning when Pico appeared under a flag of truce and informed them he had captured Alexis Godey and the other two messengers and wanted to exchange them for a high-ranking Mexican prisoner the Americans had taken.

The situation had become dire; there was no more food, the wounded needed proper care, and fast, and they were certainly in no condition for another battle with the Mexicans. It was decided as a last-ditch measure to send out another courier party toward San Diego. It was composed of their best scout, Kit Carson; Lieutenant Beale of the navy, in hopes that he might hold special sway with Commodore Stockton; and Beale's servant, an Indian, who they presumed would keep his ear to the ground for trouble.

Theirs was a daunting mission. Before sunset they could make out distinct lines of Mexican pickets surrounding the hill to prevent just the sort of escape they were planning. There was almost no food and precious little water, but the dragoons gave up what they had to fill the messengers' pockets with a few parched peas and kernels of corn and small strips of dried mule meat. At dusk these men began crawling across the rocky, cactus-strewn desert, and soon after dark, as they approached the first line of pickets, Carson suggested they remove their shoes and stick them under their belts so as not to make noise against the rocks.

The next hours were among the most harrowing imaginable for the little party, since they were unarmed and the lancers were edgy to begin with. It was freezing cold again and a flutter of breeze often carried whiffs of the enemy sentry's cigarette smoke. They could also hear them talking and laughing. They slithered on for hours until they thought they were beyond the final line of pickets when suddenly two Mexican horsemen rode up just ahead, dismounted, and lighted *cigarrillos.* Carson signaled Beale to lie perfectly still, which they did for what must have seemed an eternity. When the pressure became too much and Beale said into Carson's ear, in the faintest whisper, "We are gone. Let us jump up and fight it out," Carson replied, "No—I have been in worse places than this," which must have had a soothing effect on the young navy lieutenant, because he continued to lie still and quiet and presently the sentry mounted his horse and rode away, leaving them in the cold, lonely desert.

When they finally stood up they realized their shoes were gone, having worked their way out of their belts somewhere back along the Mexican picket line. There was nothing for it but to set out barefoot through the cactus and hard, sharp stones—not that shoes would have much mattered, but the desert at night was also alive with rattlesnakes. San Diego was a long thirty-six miles away.

They traveled all day, and the next night the lights of the town finally appeared on the horizon, but Pico's scouts also prowled the outskirts. Carson decided to split them up, giving Beale, who was suffering terribly with his feet, the most straightforward path, while the Indian was to circle south and Carson went north, the farthest route. To give an idea of the abusive nature of the shoeless forced march, Carson had to be hospitalized afterward for more than a week, and Beale could not stand on his own for three months and, in Carson's own words, "had become deranged by his excessive exertions and did not fully recover his health for two years."

All three reached safety to tell Stockton of Kearny's misadventure. The commodore, already annoyed at the Mexican uprising, was doubly displeased over the news of the army's predicament, but he immediately assembled a relief force of 160 U.S. Marines and sailors, along with a cannon, "which the men hauled along by means of ropes."

Back at what they came to call Mule Hill, Kearny's troops were on their final legs. They had practically no water and were eating the last of their mules. Kearny faced a wrenching decision. On December 9, a Sergeant Cox of the Dragoons, "a gallant fellow," succumbed to his wounds, leaving a "pretty wife," whom he had just married before leaving Fort Leavenworth. On the morning of December 10, the Mexicans attacked the Americans' camp "driving before them a herd of wild horses which they hoped would cause a stampede." The Mexicans chased the horses toward the camp, but the gambit failed because the Americans were ready, and the dragoons even managed to kill a few of the horses to eat. To Captain Emory, "the sufferings of the wounded were very distressing." In particular he recalled a moment with one of the mountain men, Antoine Robideaux, who was so badly lanced that Emory did not think he would live out the thirty-eight-degree night. Suddenly the fifty-two-year-old scout sat up and asked Emory if he smelled coffee. Huddled under a blanket, Emory said he did not.

"I supposed a dream had carried him back to the cafes of New Orleans and St. Louis," the captain said, but when Emory stuck his nose outside his blanket, "it was with some surprise I discovered my cook heating up a cup of coffee over a small fire of wild sage." Emory lifted the cup to Robideaux's trembling lips and "his warmth returned, and with it hopes of life. In gratitude," Emory said, "he gave me what was then a great rarity, a half of a cake made of brown flour, almost black with dirt, which had, for greater securing, been hidden in the clothes of his Mexican servant, a man who scorned ablutions. I ate more than half without inspection," Emory went on, "when, on breaking a piece, the bodies of the most loathsome insects were exposed to view."

Scenes like this were being played out all over the American camp, and when the men's minds weren't on food they were on how to deal with the fix they were in. Considering the demise of the last message party, nobody gave Carson's group much of a chance. They had been fought to a frazzle but surrender was a prospect too horrid to contemplate. Emory ate the rest of his cake anyway.

Then, in the darkest hours just before dawn, one of Emory's sentries came in breathless with an extraordinary report. Out in the desert, he said, he had clearly heard someone speaking in English. As this was being absorbed, there "came the tramp of a column, followed by the hail of a sentinel." They were saved.

CHAPTER THIRTEEN

The Death Trap

From the moment they peeled off on the Hastings Cutoff, bad luck overtook the Donner-Reed wagon train. First was a shocking murder, likely prompted by the frustration and fear that had begun to nag the emigrant party, the dark and nervous sensation that they had made a mistake in following Lansford Hastings's advice. They were now utterly on their own among the misshapen mountains and deserts of what is now northern Utah. There was often no marked trail to follow and the leaders and scouts found themselves flummoxed in box canyons or up against massive granite walls, losing entire days or more, as leaves browned and shriveled and the deathly breath of winter closed in around them. They wasted three precious weeks fumbling around in the Wasatch Range, where amity receded into acrimony as they fell farther and farther behind, knowing they must get across the High Sierras before the big snows came or . . . or what? Perish, probably. It was certainly on their minds.

It quickly became apparent that the Hastings Cutoff was no place for ladened wagons. Parties coming afterward recorded that the desert trail along the Donners' path was strewn with "highly waxed heirlooms," a chair here, a table there, incongruous in the sandy sage; a trunk of ladies' clothes or Grandma's chifforobe, promiscuously tossed aside with or without tears but never without grim determination.

On October 6, 1846, wagon master James Reed killed his young friend John Snyder; witnesses' accounts differed but the killing was a fact. It was said Reed's big "Palace Car" was trying to pass Snyder's wagon on a hill somewhere along the Humboldt River in Nevada when their ox teams tangled up. Threatening words were exchanged. In a fit of original road rage, Snyder hit Reed with the heavy leaded butt end of his bullwhip and Reed stabbed him to death with his butcher knife. Or Reed stabbed first, or Snyder also hit Reed's wife, Margaret, who tried to intervene. Whatever the truth, Snyder lived but a few minutes before his heart pumped out the last of its remaining blood on the desert floor, and Reed, a principal organizer of the company, became a pariah. The Graves family, who had employed Snyder as a driver, called for Reed's execution. Lewis Keseberg, a German ghoul about whom we will hear more later, offered to hang Reed from the tongue of his wagon. Reed's friends interceded, armed to the teeth.

A trial or drumhead court was held and banishment from the company, without gun, was Reed's punishment—there in the wilds, a fate just about corresponding to death. The bullwhips cracked, the dogs barked, and the caravan moved on with the sorrowful Reed standing alone in the wagon tracks. Later that night his thirteen-year-old step-daughter, Virginia, sneaked away from the party and brought Reed a rifle and some food—at least a fighting chance. Seeing the distress of her mother "seemed to make a woman of me," she recalled later.

Swinging wide around the train, Reed overtook George Donner and his party of a dozen wagons who were a day ahead of the others. He said he was riding on for supplies and never mentioned the killing. He would never mention it, even in his diaries and writing, for the rest of his days.

Here was enough drama for a lifetime but their furies were just beginning. The wagons became mired in deep beds of loose sand. Digger Indians stole the emigrants' horses and cattle—once eighteen head at a fell swoop, a dangerous rate. At dusk their camps were often showered with arrows from surrounding clumps of sage. It was soon determined that the Reed family's wagon was too heavy to negotiate the weak trail and must be abandoned. Other families took in the Reeds, and the Palace Car was left to the desert and the Indians.

In the excitement over the murder it was overlooked that old man Hardcoop was missing. He was a sixty-something-year-old Belgian who had been riding with Keseberg, the German. Two boys working cattle next day had seen him sitting beside the tracks nursing his feet, which had become enormously swollen and the skin had split. Hardcoop told them that Keseberg had put him out of his wagon and told him to walk. Keseberg was not well liked in the company. Once chastised by Reed for risking everyone's life by rifling an Indian grave to get a buffalo robe, the tall, thirtyish Westphalian sported a long beard that gave him somewhat of a theatrical countenance. A group went to Keseberg and urged him to return and look for Hardcoop but he flatly refused. Two men, William Eddy and Milford (Milt) Elliott, stayed up all night tending a fire, hoping it would guide Hardcoop into camp. They would have gone looking for him themselves but the Diggers had stolen all their horses.

In the morning a party, including Mrs. Reed, approached Franklin (Uncle Billy) Graves and Patrick Breen, who owned the only horses left, and asked them to help. They also refused on grounds that it was dangerous and that by now Hardcoop was probably dead anyway. The idea of waiting for him was out of the question. By then the threat of snow in the mountains and starvation were "already hanging upon them like a death-sentence."

The wagons rolled on, leaving Hardcoop to his fate. The Humboldt River disappeared, and along its sink a vast belt of stinking alkali dust arose to cover everyone and everything in a foul white powder. The mood of the emigrants matched their environs. Families had become withdrawn and distrustful. On October 13, twenty-one head of cattle were killed by Diggers' arrows and more wagons were abandoned. They were already low on food. Another German—one Jacob Wolfinger—stayed behind to hide his wagon in brush, apparently hoping to retrieve it later, but he failed to return. Two fellow Germans, Spitzer and Reinhardt, claimed the elderly man was slain by Indians, but everyone suspected he was murdered by the pair for a stash of gold coins he was known to possess. The lead wagon came across a note tacked to a tree. It was a warning from the exiled Reed that hostile Indians lay ahead.

On October 23, the day the first snow fell, what had now become the Donner party began its ascent of the Sierra Nevada Mountains, a seventy-mile-wide wall of granite that rears out of the desert for four hundred miles along what is now the California-Nevada line. It is one of the most striking terrain features in the world and a place of great beauty, but in winter it can also be a death trap. The mountain peaks rise from 10,000 to 14,000 feet, but there was an Indian pass that Frémont took, and that Hastings also mapped, a gap at 7,085 feet with relatively easy access provided you came before late autumn. If not, you faced an average yearly snowfall of 400 inches, or more than 30 feet—much higher in drifts—and below-zero temperatures, where in big storms winds can easily reach a hundred miles per hour. In short, it is no place for fools or foul-ups.

The bad luck seemed to cling to them like a pall. That same day they reached the mountains, a man named William Pike was accidentally shot in the back by his brother-in-law, whom he had just asked to hold his pistol while he put another log on the fire. Pike lived for two hours, then died and was buried in a shallow grave beside the trail, leaving a wife and two babies. Two days later things took a better turn. On the trail they met one of their number who had gone ahead weeks earlier and crossed the mountains to Sutter's Fort for provisions.

His name was Charles Stanton, and he came with two of John Sutter's "civilized" Miwok Indians, Luis and Salvador, and seven mule-loads of food—enough to get them across the Sierras if they hurried. It was already late in the year, and as they climbed higher the ponderosa pines were snow-dusted and dark storm clouds hovered over the peaks to the northeast. Cresting a final rise on the final day of October, they could see snow already clogging the pass above. That was not supposed to be. They'd been told the pass was generally open till mid-November. And perhaps it was—generally.

Three days later in a driving rain they reached a mountain lake. What they did not know, but would soon find out, was that rain at that altitude meant snow up at the pass. Scouts sent ahead reported chest-deep snow approaching the pass. Panic set in; suddenly it became obvious that the wagons could never get through, that they were trapped, and that they would have to crash through on mules and oxen alone or perish in the cold and snows. They plowed on but it was no good. The snow went from knee deep to waist, and from waist to chest. Animals plunged into ravines masked with drifts, not to be seen again. They floundered through it most of the day until they were exhausted, then returned to the lake where they camped for the night among the huge ponderosas, ghostly with their blankets of snow, like stark white sentries guarding the mountain pass. Tomorrow, they said, they would cross; tomorrow they would find a way. It was only one, maybe two miles, then the trail began slowly descending into the lovely valley of the Sacramento that Frémont had written about so eloquently, a cornucopia of fruits and honey, of brilliant sunshine and gentle rains. They built fires from pine limbs and settled in for the night. Around bedtime it began to snow.

It snowed for eight days straight, leaving the emigrant party trapped at both ends of the trail. They could not move forward through the pass and they could not move back down the mountain from whence they had come.

The exiled James Reed, riding a week ahead of the company, had made it through the pass in the nick of time and arrived at Sutter's to acquire provisions to take back—despite his banishment—for his family and others. Sutter, now a captain in Frémont's California Battalion, had generously provided Reed with food, mules, and two Indian guides—wholly on credit—as he had with Charles Stanton. As Reed ascended the mountains in the first week of November, the big north Pacific storm crashed into the coast and spread across the Sacramento valley with driving rain and howling winds. In the Sierras it had clogged the mountain passes with fifteen feet of snow that had stranded the Donners flat.

As the drifts became deeper and wider climbing up the eastbound slope, Reed's Indian guides counseled that going farther would be useless because the drifts would only become worse, even dangerous, since another large snowstorm could trap them, too. Reed plowed on anyway in snow shoulder deep, sometimes so deep he had to dig his horse out of it. But it was useless. Finally, reluctantly, he turned back, which was probably a lucky thing for the Indians and also the mules. Something very nasty was brewing up beyond the dark, low-hanging clouds that wreathed the jagged peaks. Consider the earlier party of relief, led by Charles Stanton, with its mule train of provisions and Indian guides. At first the Donners gratefully devoured the food, but as the weeks went by and things went from bad to worse they ate the mules, and then they ate the Indians.

Back at the fort, Sutter informed Reed there was no hope of getting through to the Donner party till spring, February at the earliest. He wanted to know how many cattle and other livestock they had; when Reed gave him the numbers the wilderness-savvy Swiss declared the Donners would survive the winter, provided they killed their beef and preserved the carcasses beneath the snow. But what Sutter didn't know, and Reed couldn't tell him because he hadn't been there, was just how many of the Donners' livestock had been stolen or killed by the Indians in those frightful days along the Humboldt. In fact, there wasn't enough beef or mule meat on that mountain to last them much more than a month.

Unaware of this, and unwilling to sit around waiting for spring, James Reed—like nearly every other able-bodied American in the Sacramento valley—joined Frémont's California Battalion, which had just been called back into service due to the uprising of General Pico and the Californios. In due time he was elected captain, and imagine his surprise at finding out that among his fellow captains was none other than the huckster Lansford Hastings.

Up in the mountains it had begun to penetrate to the people of the Donner party that there might not be any way to get down before the snow thawed, in three or four months. They all began taking inventory of their food, since starvation was a real danger. It soon became apparent that now food was to be the principal currency, and those who had brought along their wealth in gold, jewelry, or other tender began to trade and exchange with the others who owned more food. Inflation quickly set in, and the price of flour, beef, and mutton rose dramatically, generating even more bitterness and rancor among the stranded refugees.

There were a few rude log huts or log cabins in the area, hastily cobbled together by earlier parties or trappers. Members of the Donner company moved into these, while others built lean-tos, or other hovels with cowhide for roofs and doors. They had separated into two main groups: the Breens, the Graves and Murphy families, and about fifty of their cohorts settled down by the large tarn that would later become Donner Lake. The other group, the Donners and about thirty of their people, camped six miles away on Alder Creek. Of the entire number of the party, just about half were children.

On November 13 the weather cleared and fifteen of the fittest decided to try to get down on foot, led by Charles Stanton and with the two Indians, Luis and Salvador, as guides. By nightfall they returned worn-out, "used up," and frustrated. They had sunk in snowdrifts ten and fifteen feet deep and the trail was completely obliterated. Next day William Eddy tracked and shot a grizzly bear but nearly got eaten up in the process. That night at least some of them dined on bear meat and Eddy had himself the makings of a fine bearskin robe.

At the end of November it was plain that food would not last till spring and once more Stanton assembled twenty of the stoutest, including several women and a few of the older children, and tried to make it off the mountain. After packing Sutter's seven mules with provisions, the expedition got off to a good start; a week of sun had melted much of the snow and turned the top to crust. They actually got through the pass after breaking through six feet of snow and camped in a valley. But they had had an awful time of it, and in many places all they could see "was the snow with the tops of pine trees sticking out of it."

That night there arose the gravest kind of controversy. The party had been able to slide over the crusty tops of snowdrifts that day, but the mules could not and sank down, mired, and it was only with unsustainable exertions that they could be brought down the mountain. William Eddy, one of the two men who had stayed up all night tending the fire for old Hardcoop to see, was determined to go for broke, to take food from the mule packs, leaving the mules, and break out down the mountain now, while the getting was good.

But Stanton, the leader, was one of those characters imbued with an antique sense of honor, which fixed itself upon those seven mules that Sutter had lent him. They were not his, he said, and he would not leave them to starve and die, and since it was obvious the mules could not make it through the snows, there was nothing else but to return with them to the camp back up the mountain. So said Stanton. Eddy was aghast and furious, and the discussion nearly became violent. But Stanton held the upper hand: he and the two Indians were the only ones who knew how to navigate the fifty miles through the mountains down to Sutter's Fort.

Back at the camp, some remained angry and all were frustrated. William Eddy decided to try once more next day, but in the morning it commenced to snow and did not let up for the next ten days. Instead of slaughtering their livestock immediately—as Sutter had assumed they would, and as any competent mountain man would have known to do—the Donners left them to run free, apparently thinking they could be butchered as needed. But during this fierce and unrelenting snowstorm the remaining cattle and few horses and mules wandered off, and while the Donner party huddled in shelters against the storm their livestock starved or froze to death and became buried beneath snow six to ten feet deep, never to be found again. It now became a race against time and starvation.

While the storm raged outside, Charles Stanton, who grew up in New York State, and a man of the Graves family from Vermont, were feverishly fashioning snowshoes from oxbows and rawhide to facilitate another escape attempt. On December 11, the very day of Kearny's deliverance following the Battle of San Pasqual, half a dozen members of the Donner party entered the last phases of starvation sickness. They were all young men. The symptoms were malaise and hallucinations, followed by coma and death. They were buried beneath the snow.

Before he died, thirty-year-old Joseph Reinhardt had a confession to make. He told George Donner and others that he and Augustus Spitzer murdered Jacob Wolfinger back along the Humboldt River. They killed him for his gold and blamed it on Indians, he said.

Many were down to their final morsels and began to eat rats, mice, and insects like the Digger Indians. Others boiled raw cowhide, producing a kind of glue they believed had nutrition. At the Donners' camp at Alder Creek, twelve-year-old Lemuel Murphy climbed a tree to search for any sign of a rescue party. All he could see was snow.

On December 15, the party of seventeen snowshoers—fathers, mothers, boys, and girls, including three without snowshoes—began the long trek down the mountain. They were led by Stanton and the two Miwoks and came to be known as the Forlorn Hope. Misinformation in Hastings's book led them to believe a ranch was thirty miles to the west; in fact, it was twice that distance. On the first day two grown men of the three without snowshoes gave up and returned to the camp, but the twelve-year-old Murphy boy struggled on.

By Christmas Day, when Colonel Doniphan and his First Missouri Volunteers were scattering Mexicans during the Battle of the Brazito, the Forlorn Hope had run into serious trouble. They had made it across the pass but a huge new storm had obliterated the trail. They had run out of food three days earlier. Three members expired from starvation—Charles Stanton was one of them. The thirty-five-year-old bachelor had contracted snow blindness, a serious affliction. When the group collected themselves to continue that morning, Stanton remained by the campfire smoking his pipe. Nineteen-year-old Mary Ann Graves asked if he was coming. He nodded cheerfully and replied, "Yes, I am coming soon." But he would not. He was exhausted and blind. Stanton's death would be keenly felt. He was a true hero, having crossed the mountain, then returned with food. The Indians, Luis and Salvador, spoke some English, but it was Stanton who best knew the path down and could communicate it.

With no food the surviving members were going fast now. Some were already in the delirium or raving madly and flailing. Thirty-year-old Patrick Dolan lost consciousness. Others wailed and cried. No one could really sleep, the hunger hurt too much. Dolan died; so did Antonio the Mexican, who slumped into the fire, and fifty-seven-year-old Franklin Graves. Young Lemuel Murphy appeared to be next. He was out of his mind and fading fast.

The day after Christmas, with the three bodies lying in snow around the campfire, the surviving members were faced with a choice for which they felt there was no alternative. They began cutting the flesh from the arms and legs of Patrick Dolan and roasting it on sticks in the flames, "averting their faces from each other, and weeping."

Only William Eddy, who had discovered a pound of bear meat his wife had hidden in his pack, and the two Miwok Indians abstained from the practice. When faced with hard situations such as this, the will to survive is perhaps the most potent, compelling force in human nature. But it would get worse than this. Much worse. They tried to feed a piece of cooked flesh to Lemuel Murphy, but he was too far gone to eat it, and he died shortly afterward.

Next morning, they turned to the grisly task of butchering the four bodies and roasting and drying the flesh for their journey. By now the Indians had decided to join the others in eating the dead.

While all of this transpired, General Kearny and the tattered remnants of his Army of the West staggered into the fortified city of San

Diego without further incident. General Pico could not persuade himself to tangle with Commodore Stockton's tough-looking relief force of
nearly two hundred sailors and U.S. Marines and took his lancers north
toward Los Angeles. After so long in the wilderness, Kearny's woe-
begone troops were flabbergasted by the never-ending bawdiness and
debauchery in the town—drunkenness, cockfights, fandangos—but
this did not last for long.

On the evening of December 22, 1846, Kearny sent a letter to
Stockton, having just spoken with him that morning, which apparently
sparked a friction between the two men that ultimately exploded into
the most sensational court-martial trial of the century.

Kearny's letter seemed harmless enough. It began "Dear Commodore" and advised that it would be a good thing if Stockton could
"take from here sufficient force to oppose the Californians," who were
believed to be waiting for Frémont and the California Battalion. After
offering to accompany such an expedition and serve in any capacity,
Kearny then added a sentence stating, "I do not think that Lt. Col.
Fremont should be left unsupported to fight a battle upon which the
fate of California may for a long time depend." Here is where Stockton
seemed to take umbrage, for the next day Kearny received a message
from the commodore, asserting that Stockton had proposed just such
a mission that very morning in personal conversation between the two
men. Stockton suggested, somewhat cattily, that "if the object of your
note is to advise me to do any thing which would enable a large force
of the enemy to get into my rear & cut off my communications with San
Diego . . . you will excuse me for saying I cannot follow such advise."

Now it was Kearny's turn to be perplexed, for he responded in a note
the same day that he'd never understood in the morning's conversation
that it was Stockton's intention to move on the enemy, and further that
he certainly never made any suggestion about "enabl[ing] a large force
of the enemy to get into [Stockton's] rear" and cut him off.

Stockton immediately replied with a note of his own acting as if the
matter never happened, and stating that "nothing would be more grati-
fying to me personally than your presence" on the march.

These were murky times. By all rights, as a general, Kearny was
the ranking officer in California. In addition, he had direct orders from
President Polk to take control of the province. Stockton, on the other

hand, was officially a captain in the navy but held the temporary rank of "commodore," a title designated for captains who commanded more than one ship—in Stockton's case, the U.S. Pacific Squadron—but below the rank of admiral. But Stockton was also of a separate service than Kearny, and had far more men directly under him than Kearny's poor decimated command. So Kearny accepted, at least temporarily, his secondary role, but the commodore nevertheless seemed to harbor ill feelings toward his army counterpart.

After counting noses, Stockton was able to assemble a 550-man force consisting of 345 marines and sailors acting as infantry, 47 of Kearny's healthy dragoons, 48 of Captain Gillespie's California volunteers, 40 sailors manning the artillery, and various officers and noncommissioned officers, as well as detachments such as Captain Emory's topographical group. It was Stockton's expressed intention to march this small army on Los Angeles, 125 miles distant, retake the city, and, if possible, capture the rebel leader José Flores and, he said, hang him for violating his parole of the previous August.

On December 29, the same day that the Donners' Forlorn Hope began the descent into cannibalism, Stockton's army, with Kearny in charge of the infantry and accompanied by a dozen or so wagons, departed San Diego and camped at Soledad, watched closely but not molested by Pico's mounted lancers. Captain Emory reported that the navy tars, because of "close discipline aboard ship, made a very good infantry soldier." However, their lack of marching experience made them footsore, and the column scarcely managed ten miles a day; all the while the ferocious Californio lancers hovered around them at a distance. On January 7, 1847, they came to a ranch owned by "a rich widow lady" who said the Mexicans would attack next day as they crossed the San Gabriel River, about a day's march south of Los Angeles.

Sure enough, the following afternoon when they reached the river, Captain Emory said, "It became quite apparent the enemy intended to dispute our passage."

The San Gabriel was about a hundred yards across and knee deep. The Americans' approach was level, but on the opposite side, where the Mexicans had gathered, the land rose in a bluff, or hill, about fifty feet high. Kearny had arranged the marching force in a version of the British "hollow square," with infantry on the outside, artillery at each of the four ends, and the livestock and supply wagons protected inside. It was Emory's opinion that the Mexicans, who were mounted, intended to break into the square with a cavalry charge and "deprive us of our cattle."

Just as the Americans were about to cross the river, 250 Mexican cavalry appeared on the bluff opposite, and about 200 more appeared to their left. The Americans began to take fire from enemy sharpshooters, and just then the Mexicans rolled out four pieces of artillery and commenced firing.

Kearny ordered a hundred-man company under Captain Turner to deploy as skirmishers and ford the river. When the company reached midstream the Mexicans opened fire with grapeshot and cannonballs, sending geysers of water into the air. Remarkably, no one was hit. Then Stockton ordered his own artillery across, where "it was unlimbered and placed in counter-battery on the enemy's side of the river." The commodore personally assisted in this maneuver, which involved man-handling the guns through the water.

Emory wrote, "Our people, very brisk in firing, made the fire of the enemy wild and uncertain. Under this cover the wagons and cattle were forced with great labor across the river, the bottom of which was quicksand."*

On the north side of the river where the Mexicans held ground there was a little bluff or overhang at the bottom of the hill where the Americans took cover and returned fire. Emory credits this terrain feature with the low number of casualties. A large detachment of Mexican cavalry somehow got to the Americans' rear and charged down, threatening to envelop Stockton's force, but his sailors, as Emory had predicted, proved very effective marksmen indeed, and the charge was repulsed. In an hour and twenty minutes of rattling gunfire, the entire U.S. column hauled itself across the river. Meantime, the American artillery fire had taken its toll on the Californios, whose guns were soon silenced.

Flores then ordered a charge on Stockton's left flank, which was repulsed, and threatened his right flank, where Kearny ordered the men into a square. But Stockton countermanded the order and directed the

*What he meant, apparently, was that there were patches of soft sand on the bottom.

men to rush the Mexican positions atop the hill. This they did, chanting, "New Orleans! New Orleans! New Orleans!" in commemoration of Andrew Jackson's famous victory over the British army at the Battle of New Orleans, which took place January 8, 1815, exactly thirty-two years to the day. Thus inspired, the Americans charged upward with bayonets fixed and blood in their eyes, ready for the hand-to-hand combat they considered inevitable at the top of the hill, "but great was our surprise," Emory concluded, "to find it abandoned."

It was so. Flores had tried everything he knew but, unable to break or even penetrate the American formation, he drew off his forces to fight another day, which happened to be the next one.

The following afternoon, only two or three miles from Los Angeles, Stockton's men were marching across the wide, empty mesa between the San Gabriel and San Fernando rivers when Flores reappeared and began shooting at them with his artillery from a long distance. The Americans ignored this as a nuisance and marched on, even though some men were wounded and animals hit. At some point Flores "addressed his men, and called upon them to make one more charge; expressed his confidence in their ability to break out line; said that 'yesterday he had been deceived into supposing that he was fighting soldiers.' "

As the Americans came closer, the Mexican artillery "was so annoying that we halted to silence them," Emory said, which took about fifteen minutes, but just as they resumed march Flores's lancers came down simultaneously on their left flank and rear. The soldiers, sailors, and marines opened a terrific fire, emptying many Mexican saddles. Meantime, Stockton's artillery laid on the grape. "We all considered this the beginning of the fight," Captain Emory wrote, "but it was the end of it."

It was also—though they could not know it at the time—the end of Mexican control of California. That night they camped outside Los Angeles and saw about four hundred enemy horsemen and their artillery draw off toward the town, but next morning three prominent Los Angelenos appeared in the American camp with a flag of truce. Flores, realizing that he could not beat the Americans, agreed that Andrés Pico and his cavalry lancers would move north to surrender to Colonel

Frémont, who was nearby, at what today is Pasadena.* Flores, concerned about his own fate for having broken parole, headed his force south toward Mexico. Or as Emory understood it: "Towards the close of the day we learned very certainly that Flores, with 150 men, chiefly desperadoes of the country, had fled to Sonora, taking with them four or five hundred of the best horses and mules in the country, the property of his own friends. The silence of the Californians was now changed into deep and bitter curses upon Flores."

Stockton and Kearny accepted the surrender of the city, the capital of California, and marched the army into town where they were received with a sullen and gloomy silence by the residents. Even if neither of the two final skirmishes rose to the dignity of a battle, it does not diminish their importance. Once more, Old Glory flew from the flagstaff in the Los Angeles plaza, and flies there still today, lo these many years.

---

*It has been suggested that Pico, whose family had large land holdings in the area, wished to surrender to Frémont's contingent because he was concerned that the U.S. Army might hang him for the business at San Pasqual.

CHAPTER FOURTEEN

The Horror

On January 10, 1847, the same day Stockton and Kearny marched victorious into Los Angeles, Luis and Salvador, the two Miwok Indians accompanying the travelers of the Forlorn Hope in their attempted escape from the Sierra, were killed and eaten by starving members of the party.

On New Year's Eve, two days after they stripped the first flesh from companions who had perished, the snowshoers remained high in the mountains, exhausted, frightened, and out of provisions. Whether from squeamishness or oversight they had not fully butchered the corpses for travel, and as they sat around a common campfire in the snow—five men and five women—they ate the last of the dried human meat and wondered what the next day would bring. So far, there seemed no end in sight, day after day of floundering through drifts in their snowshoes, sometimes crawling or plowing, or sliding down crevasses, then hauling themselves over another hump by the roots of trees or rocky outcroppings. All of them suffered from frostbite of various severity. They had descended far enough that a few live oaks now began to appear, scattered among the usual cedars and pines, but as far as the eye could see there was nothing but a frigid, empty wasteland, an unbearable desolation of rock and snow and ice. A man named Jay Fosdick, twenty-three, was on his last legs, but no one knew when he might die. His new, twenty-one-year-old wife, Sarah, was unable to help as he lagged far behind, crashing over the broken ground, nearly blind and beginning to have delusions.

Starvation is one of the more excruciating ways to die; the pangs of hunger magnify terribly and exponentially with the passing days, then hours, and finally minutes and seconds as the brain and body conspire in crying out for nourishment. Desperation sets in, then panic, along with anguish and pain, before the system begins to shut down for good. Starving people have been known to do bizarre things, eat the unimaginable, do the unthinkable. So it was with the Forlorn Hope of the Donner party. In their extremity they resorted not only to cannibalism but to murder.

It was said that a man named William Foster raised the idea of killing the Indians. The fact that they had risked their lives with Stanton, coming up from Sutter's to bring food, did not seem to enter into their favor; they were Indians, to the frontiersman's mind a subspecies not quite so low as game animals but low enough on the human scale to be sacrificed if need be. It did not help that many of their brethren made careers of stealing from and killing white men, but one senses that it wouldn't have made much difference if they hadn't.

It was also said that William Eddy was appalled by the notion and suggested that instead everyone draw lots to see who would be killed. When he was overruled, it was later said Eddy warned the Indians what the discussion was about, and they quickly disappeared into the forest.

Meantime, Jay Fosdick died, and his wife, Sarah, wrapped him in a blanket and slept beside him through the night. They had been married only hours before the wagon train left Kansas. Next morning, despite her pleas and protests, the others cut out his heart and liver and stripped his bones for sustenance. But soon they were out of food again. Even though they had descended below the snow line there was still nothing to eat, and they began to boil their shoes, boots, and moccasins for whatever nourishment remained in them. They continued on, wrapping rags around their bare feet, which soon swelled until the skin burst.

On January 10 they came across bloody footprints that could only belong to Luis and Salvador. Foster, with his rifle, tracked them while the others waited. Soon they heard shots. Foster maintained they had been too weak to move. Later, Sutter would claim they were gathering acorns when they were killed.

Two days later, fueled by the flesh of the Indians, they stumbled upon an Indian trail and soon came to a village of Diggers, where, ironically, the astonished inhabitants fed them ground-up acorns, and assisted Eddy—who was on his last legs but the only one capable of further travel—to the home of an American farmer in Bear Valley. It had been a twenty-five-day nightmare since departing the Donner camp.

A rescue party was quickly organized by Americans in the area who rode out to collect the remaining six members of the Forlorn Hope, five women and one man. Because of the Californio rebellion, however, an immediate rescue of the Donners was out of the question; the valley was virtually destitute of able-bodied men, gone off to fight with Frémont. While he recovered, Eddy learned that his best bet to organize a party of relief would be at Sutter's, another thirty-five miles south. He sent off an Indian runner with a letter for the American *alcalde* of the Sutter's region outlining the urgency of the catastrophe. The first impulse of the *alcalde*'s wife was to send the Indian back with a bundle of underclothing for the wretched women of the Forlorn Hope, who had been practically naked when they emerged from the wilderness.

Word of the Donners' plight quickly spread throughout northern California. In San Francisco a money-raising drive produced $700 for horses, pack animals, and food for the stranded sufferers. A party of ten was cobbled together led by James Reed, who had been released from service with the California Battalion.

Likewise, another relief party was organized from the region around Sutter's, which was closest. Led by a man named Aquilla Glover, and riding either horses or mules, it was composed of fourteen men, about half of them recent American emigrant farmers and the rest a strange assortment of refugees from around the world—European adventurers, ship jumpers, vagrants, gamblers, and would-be artists. Also along, though still weakened by his ordeal, was William Eddy, whose wife, three-year-old son, and one-year-old daughter were among those marooned. These men got under way on February 1, 1847. High in the mountains it had begun to snow again.

On the day Luis and Salvador were killed, Margaret Reed, James Reed's wife, left her three youngest children with another family and took thirteen-year-old Virginia, her eldest daughter, and began walking toward the pass with another woman and a man. She was out of food, except for boiled hides and bones, and in desperation decided to follow after the Forlorn Hope. Within two days all had returned, exhausted, frostbitten, and famished.

In the beginning, young men died first,* then the elderly and children. Most of the emigrant company were members of families, who took care of their own. Single travelers, or those whose spouses had died, in their distress often sought to attach themselves to one of the families, with differing levels of success. Everyone prayed, even the heathens.

When someone died they were buried in the snow, which also preserved them. So far there had been no cannibalism within the camps atop the mountain, but nearly all the pet dogs had been killed and eaten. Commerce continued in food, principally hides but sometimes pieces of beef or mule. It was often an undignified process. For example, Margaret Reed had apparently borrowed some food from the Graves family and on January 30: "The Graves seized Mrs. Reid's [sic] goods until they would be paid. Also took the hides that she and her family would live on. She got two pieces of hides from there and the balance they have taken. You may know from these proceedings what our fare is in camp." So according to Patrick Breen's diary.

Each day men went out into the fields and poked sticks deep into the snow in hopes of finding their dead cattle or horses, but not a sign. Ever since they had blundered onto the Hastings Cutoff, a kind of curse had hovered over the Donner party, as if they had suddenly begun following the wrong star. The starvation and their miserable living conditions were making them pathetic and depraved. With the exception of their praying, the last vestiges of civilization seemed to be passing them by.

The first relief party, the one from Sutter's, reached the snow line February 10; soon they would be climbing up on foot in drifts ten to twenty feet deep. The plan was to cache provisions along the way so as to make them available on the trip back down. There was no way to carry sufficient food up to the camp by backpack. At a stopping point named Mule Springs two men were left to guard the provisions against bears and wolves. Two others, including William Eddy, were selected to

---

*It has been suggested this was because they had a higher metabolism and required more nourishment.

take the empty pack mules back down the mountain. Everybody could see that Eddy was not up to climbing the mountain; he was still not recovered from the ordeal with the Forlorn Hope. He didn't know that his wife and year-old daughter were already dead of starvation. ("She had lived until the baby died and then flickered out.") They were buried together in the snow. Eddy's three-year-old son was hanging on by a thread, tended to in one of the cabins by old and failing Mrs. Murphy.

Ten men of the rescue party were left to continue climbing upward, not a guide or experienced mountain man among them. It was appalling and dangerous work, wading through the drifts, fighting across freezing streams in bitter cold and with fifty-pound packs on their backs. At one point they came across human remains beside the ashes of a fire and guessed what must have happened there. On the mountain, people continued to die.

Eleven days into it three of the rescuers up and quit, turned around and went back to the valley. The remaining seven continued. Bold men—heroes—they pushed on, straining every sinew against the raw, cold, snow white granite mountain. It snowed again and covered their tracks; above, through holes in the clouds, they could see the jagged, serrated peaks, as if they were climbing toward some monstrous maw. Each day it became steeper and more deadly.

At last on February 18 they reached the pass, still clogged with snow. By superhuman exertions they struggled across it, descending to the lake where Eddy had told them many of the party had encamped. At first they saw nothing but snow and forest but then some stumps and felled trees and unnatural-looking snow-covered lumps in the ground. They called out "hello," but for the longest time there was no answer; then a woman's head appeared from one of the lumps and searched the seven unfamiliar faces, wanting to know, "Are you men from California, or from heaven?"

Soon other scarecrow apparitions began to appear, rising raggedly and agog from their snowbound hovels as if they were leaving their own tombs. At first there was shock and disbelief, which quickly turned to joy and tears of relief. By then, of the original eighty-one there were only thirty-three left on the mountain; twenty-four had died, including seven with the Forlorn Hope. "Some were so broken by long suffering," wrote their chronicler George Stewart, "that they seemed to have lost all sense of self-respect, pride, or principle." What they did not know was that it was going to get a lot worse.

The rescuers carefully distributed what little food they had been able to carry up the mountain and sized up the situation. The condition of the Donner group was shocking; most were emaciated beyond words. Many were so weak they could scarcely walk or even rise, their skin hanging down from drawn faces and hollow, vacant eyes. There were those who raved and cursed and others who simply cried or whimpered. It took the rescuers, who themselves were in great need of recuperation, three days to get it sorted out. There were some, including children, far too weak to attempt a move off the mountain. Some of the stronger would have to stay and care for them. Among the weak were the Donners themselves. George was too feeble to move and Tamsen refused to leave him. She would also try to fend for the children. The rescuers promised that another relief party was right behind (though they had no way of knowing it). Nor did they provide details of the gruesome fate of the Forlorn Hope.

On February 21 they started down the mountain and had not gone far when it became apparent that Patty Reed, James and Margaret's nine-year-old, and their son Thomas, three, were too weak to continue and there was nothing else but to return them to the camp. Margaret went on, brokenhearted, with daughter Virginia and five-year-old James. As they parted, Patty said to her mother, "Good-bye, Ma. If I don't see you again, do the best you can." That night when they reached the spot where they'd cached a bale of food, they found it was broken open and saw bear tracks leading into the forest. The next food was four days down the mountain.

Back at the lake, Patrick Breen killed his pet dog, the last one in camp. Others left behind were not so fortunate, if that is the word. Breen wrote in his diary: "Mrs. Murphy said here yesterday that [she] thought she would commence on Milt [Milt Elliott, who had died two weeks earlier] & eat him. I don't [believe] she had done so yet, it is distressing. [The Donners] told the California folks that they commenced to eat the dead people 4 days ago. I suppose they have done so ere this time."

.   .   .

As the first relief party feebly ground its way down the mountain several of the survivors finally succumbed to starvation. But on February 27 the second relief party, led by James Reed, met up with the first just above the snow line. Here Reed was reunited with Margaret, Virginia, and James, whom he had not seen since his banishment from the wagon train after the Snyder killing.

Next day Reed and his people continued up the mountain, in hopes of finding his two remaining children alive. The survivors, strengthened somewhat by provisions they received from the second relief, trudged down toward Bear Valley, in the process losing a twelve-year-old boy to starvation sickness. Reed's party arrived at the lake camp March 2 and were even more appalled then their predecessors by what they saw. Milt Elliott's body was butchered, lying in the snow. Other areas of the camp "looked like a battlefield," with human parts strewn about. They found the body of Jacob Donner, brother of George, with the head cut off, faceup, "the snow and cold having preserved all his features unaltered." The arms and legs had been severed and the heart and liver cut out; "the leg and thigh had been thrown back, upon [learning] of the party of relief coming up." It was a scene out of Dante's worst nightmares: sitting on a log, one man reported, were several Donner children, "their faces and breasts smeared bloodily as they innocently tore and ate the half-roasted heart and liver."

At least there was this: Reed, overjoyed, came across his daughter Patty "sitting on a cabin roof with her feet dangling in the snow." His son Tommy, he quickly learned, was in the good care of the Breen family.

A triage again had to be conducted to see who was strong enough to make it down the mountain and who must be left behind for a third relief party, which this time they believed was close behind them. George Donner had only been getting worse, and a cut he received on his arm months earlier repairing a wagon had never healed and was now gangrenous. He was still too weak to travel and again Tamsen would not leave him. When all was said and done seventeen of the survivors were judged strong enough to try an escape down the mountain. Those remaining were either too enfeebled to go or decided to stay and care for their kin.

Reed's group left camp March 3 in a vaguely lighthearted mood.

They camped across the pass and atop a twenty-five-foot snowdrift, and around the campfire that night diarist Patrick Breen played a fiddle. Tomorrow, they were told, there would be a cache of food five miles below. But that night the temperature dropped and it began to snow. It did not quit for two days.

What hit Reed's people was one of the severest snowstorms of the year. Shrieking winds reached hurricane force and the thermometer plummeted. The snow was blinding and the children began to wail in terror, caught out in the open. Two days later they were still there and out of food. They had built a platform around the fire pit but, as time wore on, the fire and the platform began to melt into the drift and sink. They barely were able to keep the fire going and some of the party began to blame Reed for taking them from the relative safety of their camps. On the second day Isaac Donner, age five, died on a blanket between his sister Mary and Patty Reed.

On March 7 the sun finally reappeared and Reed prepared his family to move out. But the Breens and their five children, Elizabeth Graves and her four, and seven-year-old Mary Donner and her dead brother decided not to expose themselves to the elements again, but opted to wait for the third party of relief, which was supposed to be coming up any time.

Reed argued that was crazy, but to no avail, and he started down the mountain. Within two days Elizabeth Graves and her son Franklin, age five, were dead. The fire pit had sunk deeper in the snow, out of sight, but the remaining sufferers huddled to it, praying and crying; they had been without food going on four days. In Donner lore, this became known as Starved Camp.

On March 11, long after it was to have gotten under way, the seven-man third party of relief left the base of the mountain for what by then everyone knew was a ghastly situation. Led by a rancher, big John Starks, the party included William Eddy of the Forlorn Hope and William Foster, who had murdered the Indians, each desperately anticipating that he would find his remaining son alive atop the mountain. Not far above the snow line they discovered beside the ashes of a fire the body of John Denton, an Englishman who was left behind by the first relief party after he could not go on. In his hands Eddy found a pencil and a piece of paper, on which in his final hours in the snow he'd been writing down pastoral poems of his native soil.

Next afternoon they came upon the spot where Reed had told them he'd left Breen and the others. "Suddenly they stood upon the brink of a great cup, twenty-five feet deep, melted into the snow. At the bottom a fire burned on a piece of bare ground about the size of an ordinary room, and about it was a jumble of blankets and children and hideous things." In the center were Patrick and Peggy Breen, alive, but lost in some kind of macabre reverie. "The body of Mrs. Graves lay there with the flesh nearly all stripped from arms and legs. Her breasts were cut off and her heart and liver taken out, and all of these were boiling together in a pot upon the fire. Her year-old baby sat wailing, with one arm resting upon the mangled body of its mother. Little remained to be seen of the corpses of two children." Such was the description given by Donner chronicler George Stewart and cannot be improved upon. The rescuers fished the sufferers out of their pit of death, fed them, and sent them down the mountain in the care of Starks and two other men, while Eddy, Foster, and two others continued up to the camps at the summit.

Traveling light, they crossed the pass next morning and reached the camps by midday. They saw what the earlier parties had seen, only worse. After the Breens left, Lavinia Murphy, a fifty-year-old grandmother, had been looking after four-year-old Georgie Foster and three-year-old James Eddy, but both boys were now dead. And gone.

The story was horrendous and confused, for Lavinia was half out of her mind from starvation. But as they pieced it together the wretched German Keseberg had taken young Georgie to bed with him one night and in the morning he was dead. An account later given by the young Donner girls tells that Keseberg "hung the body up in the cabin," then ate it, and did likewise to young James Eddy.

Keseberg, whose children had starved but whose wife had gone out with the first relief, was probably the most execrable participant in the entire Donner affair. It will be recalled that he had endangered the entire wagon train by robbing an Indian grave for a buffalo robe, abandoned old Hardcoop to his fate along the trail, and finally offered the tongue of his wagon to hang James Reed. Of course Keseberg denied wrongdoing with the children, but William Eddy, for one, did not believe him and later told an interviewer he would have killed him on the spot if he had not been such a pathetic creature—filthy, emaciated, and cringing.

Again there was need for more triage, and Eddy knew he had to move fast. The problem with all the parties of relief was that because the pass was clogged with snow they could not bring up wagons, or even pack animals with food, but only the small amounts they could carry on their backs. Salvation, then, lay in moving the sufferers off the mountain. So Eddy wanted to start down that very afternoon, before another storm might assail them.

Six survivors left with the third relief: children aged from four to sixteen and one adult member of the second relief who had stayed behind. The younger children had to be carried on the backs of the rescuers. They got beyond the pass that same day. Left behind were Tamsen Donner, who again would not leave her dying husband; her son George, four, who was too sick to move; Lavinia Murphy, who took care of the children and was blind and too sick; and Keseberg, who said he was also too ill to go.

By March 18 all relief parties had returned to safety and the survivors were being cared for in ranches all over the Sacramento River valley. Two more youngsters would die of complications as a result of their ordeal. Young Virginia Reed, who had secretly taken the gun to her father when he was banished, finally got to see the Eden that California was supposed to represent. She wrote to a cousin back east, "California is a beautiful country. We have left everything but I don't care for that—we got through."

CHAPTER FIFTEEN

Political Treachery, Military Insubordination, Discovery of Zion, and the Salvation of Children

After Colonel Doniphan and his Mounted Missouri Volunteers defeated the Mexican army at the Battle of the Sacramento they marched triumphantly twenty miles south into the state capital of Chihuahua City. There they remained for two months—while the Donner party underwent its ordeal in the California mountains—in splendid debauchery: gambling, wenching, bathing in the public water fountain, and carving their names into trees in the town plaza. They had no money to finance most of these activities because they had not received a red cent of government pay since leaving Fort Leavenworth, but luckily there was the captured Mexican army money chest from the Sacramento battle, which was barely enough to see them through. In addition to the requisite chicken fights, card games, and fandangos, the Missourians also drank excessively, fought among themselves, attacked citizens, boasted, ravished females, and abused property. Doniphan lamented that his men were "wholly unfit to garrison a town or city."

But as all good things must end, just when the fragrance of Chihuahuan jacaranda began to waft on April breezes, Doniphan received orders to join General Wool at Saltillo, a monthlong, 600-mile march, complete with *jornadas*, exhausting mountains, and other unpleasant features. Even so, the men were glad to go and "everyone, to express his joy, got drunk," for time was drawing near to the expiration of their one-year enlistment. During their term of service, the First Missouri Mounted Volunteers had achieved great distinction in the annals of Missouri and the U.S. Army.

When they reached Saltillo they would have marched more than 3,500 miles from Fort Leavenworth—longer even than Kearny—and heaven only knew how many more by the time they got home. In the vernacular of the day they had "seen the elephant": had come down the Santa Fe Trail and chased the Mexican army out of Santa Fe; continued on into the frozen mountain wastes of New Mexico to (temporarily, as it turned out) subdue several tribes of wild and murderous Indians. They marched down El Camino Real, scuffled across desolate *jornadas*, won resounding victories at the Battles of the Brazito and the Sacramento, and captured the huge Mexican state of Chihuahua. Not bad work for a rabble of Missouri farm boys who, just a year ago, were off to see the world.

Even so the army, and the war, were not quite finished with the First Missouri; it had one final—and completely noble—task to attend to, which involved great danger, but the Missourians did not shirk and neither did they quail.

Ahead of Doniphan's main column, the irrepressible Captain Reid and nineteen of his cavalry troopers were scouting and patrolling near the city of Parras when they came upon a distressing scene. A band of sixty-five Comanches* had descended upon the town from the mountains, murdered eight or ten citizens, robbed their houses, and made off with two hundred horses and three hundred mules. They also kidnapped nineteen girls and boys of the town who, considering standard Comanche practices at the time, would be either ransomed, enslaved, or tortured to death.

As in New Mexico, Indian depredations in northern Mexico had reached a crisis level. Captain Hughes summed it up in his diary. "Since 1835† the Indians have encroached on the frontiers of Mexico and laid waste many flourishing settlements, waging a predatory warfare and leading women and children into captivity. Cavalry scouts

---

*Some chronicles have them as Lipan Apaches.
†This was the year Santa Anna took power and closed down the church missions that had made inroads in socializing the Indians.

were told that the residents of Parras were in much distress . . . and besought Capt. Reid to interfere in their behalf." Even though Mexico was at war with the United States, said the town leaders, "it did not become the magnanimity of the American soldiers to see them robbed and murdered by a lawless band of savages." Reid agreed with the logic in this plea and set out tracking the band toward the mountains. They came upon a hacienda where fourteen other Doniphan troopers under Lieutenant George P. Gordon were drawing water for the army and Reid enlisted them in the posse.

Then a cloud of dust on the horizon revealed a party of Indians and a large herd. Servants at the hacienda said this was the same band that had attacked Parras and that the kidnapped children were with them. They said the Indians intended to water their stock there. Reid, now in command of thirty-five men, quickly set up an ambush, sending out the owner and several of his servants "to decoy the Indians into the hacienda. The feint succeeded. When the Indians came within half a mile, the order was given to charge upon them, which was gallantly and promptly done."

A desperate battle ensued, and a number of Indians were killed during the initial onslaught. The others dismounted and defended themselves from behind rocks using steel-tipped arrows, two of which painfully wounded Captain Reid, who, nevertheless, led three charges against the horse thieves. The fighting went on for more than two hours, with no sign of the Indians giving up, when the stalemate was broken by the fortuitous arrival of the New Mexico trader, Manuel X. Harmony, a U.S. naturalized Spaniard, and twenty-five of Doniphan's troopers who had been guarding his caravan. They pitched into the fight and the Indians fled, leaving behind seventeen dead—including their chief—many more wounded, a pile of stolen housewares, most of the horses and mules, and most importantly the kidnapped children, unharmed. For this Reid received a certificate of appreciation from the *alcalde* of Parras, in the name of the people. No Americans were killed.

One of those along for the adventure with trader Harmony was a German botanist, Dr. Frederick A. Wislizenus, who had the misfortune to be traveling in Mexico at the outbreak of war and had been held prisoner in Chihuahua until Doniphan came along. He noted that after the fight the Mexican servants had dragged the dead Indians into a pile and left them to rot in the sun. Never one to waste a scientific opportunity, Wislizenus "hacked off the head [of the chief] and displayed it on the wagon pole during the day and boiled it each evening to take the flesh off," with the intention of presenting it eventually "to that distinguished craniologist, Professor Samuel G. Morton of Philadelphia."* Even Doniphan's men gave Wislizenus a wide berth.

When they reached Saltillo the Missourians learned that John Wool and Zachary Taylor had won a stunning victory over Santa Anna and a force three times their size at the Battle of Buena Vista. Not only that, but Winfield Scott and a large American army—including nine thousand troops taken from Taylor's force—had made an amphibious landing at Veracruz, captured the city by siege, then defeated Santa Anna's army again at Cerro Gordo, well down the road to Mexico City itself. Taylor by law could have kept Doniphan's regiment in Mexico, but instead he sent them home with commendations for a job well done—even gave the sun-bronzed tatterdemalions a full military parade in review before they departed for the Gulf Coast to board steamships for New Orleans and points north.

Susan Magoffin and most of the Santa Fe traders had been following along with Doniphan's force for protection from the Indians and Mexican *banditti*. They had sold most of their wares between Santa Fe, El Paso, and Chihuahua and would dispose of the rest at Monterrey and along the Rio Grande. For her part Susan, a devout Protestant, began attending Catholic Mass in El Paso, for want of any other organized religious options, and continued the practice in Chihuahua, secretly worrying whether she had become an idolatress. She didn't know, as yet, that so many of the young officers of Kearny's First Dragoons, the ones who gaily courted her friendship during the Santa Fe days and on the long ride down the trail, now lay dead and buried in the valley of the San Pasqual.

When Doniphan's men took Chihuahua Susan and her husband, Samuel, were elated to learn that brother James had been removed

---

*Craniology, or phrenology, a popular pseudoscience of the nineteenth century, asserted that it was possible to understand and even predict human behavior by examining the shape of the skull.

south to Durango—still a prisoner but not executed as they'd feared. What they could not know then was that James was bribing his way out of his predicament and it would ultimately cost him "3,392 bottles of good champagne," which so captivated his jailer that he handed over to Magoffin the incriminating letter from Kearny that fingered him as a spy. "If it is so unimportant," the Mexican suggested, "then why don't you burn it in the fire," which is what Magoffin promptly did. The evidence thus consumed, he returned to the States to present the U.S. government with a bill for $50,000. Upon examination, it was discovered that Magoffin had billed the U.S. government for 3,392 bottles of champagne wine, and even Secretary of War Marcy was taken aback, according to the account of Colonel Cooke, who had vouched for Magoffin.

"Mr. Magoffin," Secretary Marcy is reported to have said, "ten thousand dollars is a very large sum for wine."

"Yes," responded Magoffin, with gravity. "But Mr. Secretary, champagne at $37.50 a basket counts up pretty fast. Try it yourself sometime."

When last we left Colonel Cooke and his Mormon Battalion they were slouching out of the Sonoran desert toward God knew where, building a wagon road, of sorts, as they went. God knew where was at last revealed to be the intersection with General Kearny's route near the cheerful Pima Indian villages, which they struck December 21, just as Kearny and Stockton were preparing to march out of San Diego to put down the Mexican uprising. All along, Cooke had been following a southern but parallel route to Kearny, but now he rose up out of the desert to what was the straightest path to southern California.

The Pima were good enough sorts to bring Cooke three-week-old letters left for him by Kearny and also Major Swords, Kearny's quartermaster, who informed Cooke they had left eleven broken-down mules for him in care of the Indians. Lo and behold the Indians also brought the mules, now recuperated, minus a few that had died. The colonel appraised the Pima in his journal thusly, and their neighbors the Maricopa too: "They had the simplicity of nature, and none of the affected reserve and dignity characteristic of other Indians, before whites. At the sound of a trumpet, playing of a violin, the killing of a beef, they rush to see and hear, with delight or astonishment strongly exhibited."

Cooke followed Kearny's trail for the next month, deviating from time to time to break a new road—sustenance was a constant worry since there was little game, few plants, and sparse watering holes—before landing at Warner's Ranch and learning of the distressing events in California and the deaths of so many friends. Cooke hurried on best he could, but he was burdened by the wagons and still charged with making a road. On January 21 his trusty guide Charbonneau returned from San Diego to report that the way "was unsafe from hostile Californians, and communication with General Kearny was now cut off."

At that moment Kearny was marching on Los Angeles from the south, while Frémont's battalion was marching from the north, "so that a direct march on Los Angeles from the east [by Cooke and the Mormon Battalion] was evidently the proper course." The battalion quickly set out but three days later a dispatch rider appeared with news that it was over—Los Angeles secured, the Californios in retreat, and Kearny on his way back to San Diego. So Cooke altered his march and presented himself at San Diego four months and 1,095 miles from Santa Fe.

A few days later Cooke issued a proclamation that began in part: "History may be searched in vain for an equal march of infantry. Half of it has been through a wilderness where nothing but savages or wild beasts are found, or deserts where, for want of water, there is no living creature. With crowbar and pick and axe in hand we have worked our way over mountains which seemed to defy aught but the wild goat, and hewed a passage through a chasm of living rock more narrow than our wagons."

These self-congratulatory "orders" went on in the etc., etc. fashion for a while, but the significant point was that they had "brought these first wagons to the Pacific" on an overland southern route, which meant that they had to build a road to do it, which in that day and time was like conquering worlds unknown, almost akin to discovering a new continent. And if one is tempted to point out that both Kearny and Doniphan shared equal or superior marches in terms of distance or hardship, it must be remembered that, as Cooke emphasizes, his men marched as infantry, afoot, not as mounted troops as had the other two. There is something to be said for that.

In any case Cooke was there in California with his Mormons, who so far had not fought anything but bulls, minus twenty-two who had died from illness or accidents along the way. More important, the money they had earned by their strenuous labors would soon help set into motion the greatest single human migration in American history up until that time—the descent of the Latter-Day Saints upon the Utah Territory.

Back at Winter Quarters in the frozen wastes of Nebraska, six thousand Mormons were encamped praying for spring, while six hundred had perished from the living conditions. It was Brigham Young's intention to take the Saints forever out of reach of the United States, even if it meant living among Lamanites, who were beginning to look not so bad in comparison with the hated Gentiles.

With the $70,000 in pay and allowances earned by the Mormon Battalion and the proceeds from the fire sale of their homes and property in Nauvoo, the Saints were able to purchase supplies and some wagons for the great crossing.* The group was organized military-like into divisions right down into companies of several hundred each. Brigham Young and seven of the twelve apostles would go ahead in the pioneer company. Nobody, including Young, knew exactly where they were going, but they went on the theory that some divine revelation would tell them when they got there. Since they considered themselves the lost tribe of Israel, they already understood that what they were looking for was nothing less than Zion itself.

They got as far as what is now Wyoming when who should appear but old Jim Bridger, the famous mountain man, with his trading post by the Hastings Cutoff, ready to share the gospel news. Bridger pointed them toward the Great Salt Lake valley: good soil, timber, water, just a few Digger Indians. (You could "drive the whole of them off in twenty-four hours," he said, or better yet "make slaves of them.")

The pioneer company went off toward the valley for a look-see and had not gone far when they met a Mormon named Brannan, on his way

*Because of the circumstances of their hasty departure, the Mormons were able to recoup only a fraction of the value of their various properties.

back east from San Francisco, who had early news of the tragedy of the Donner party, starving and turned cannibal in the mountains. Word had it that the unfortunates were from Missouri, which was not so. Still it soon got around among the Mormons that these were the murderers of Joseph and Hyrum Smith, a fable that went on "growing until it became a permanent part of Mormon mythology," says De Voto. Among Mormons it became a parable about what happens to the wicked who persecute God's chosen people.

On July 21, atop Little Mountain, the pioneer party "looked out on the full extent of the valley where the broad waters of the Great Salt Lake glistened in the sunbeams." Dumbstruck, they knew they'd arrived at their Zion, which they named Deseret, a Mormon neologism meaning "land of the honeybee"—symbol of economy, obedience, and industriousness. "About two hours after our arrival," remembered Orson Pratt, one of the founders, "we began to plow the ground."

This new Canaan that the Saints claimed remained neither Deseret nor Mormon territory for long; within three years it became a part of the United States, which named it Utah Territory instead, after the Ute Indian tribe. But for the next two decades, until the building of the transcontinental railroad, some 70,000 Mormons would make their way there through the wilderness, many pushing handcarts with their meager belongings, over what is now known as the Mormon Trail.

James K. Polk had been furious since August 1846 when David Wilmot, a fellow Democrat, injected his infamous proviso into the president's Mexican War appropriations bill, which would have banned slavery in any territory the United States acquired from the war. The bill had died for lack of time, but Polk was furious again now, six months later, as New York representative Preston King, another Democrat, had the gall to reintroduce the incendiary measure. The source of the president's fury was not merely what he considered treacherous behavior by fellow Democrats, although that was certainly a great part of it. Polk was a thoroughly political creature; he always thought politically, and understood everything politically, including his ham and eggs for breakfast, so that all matters great or small took on a political hue, ranging from the golden celestial aspirations that radiated from his Democratic Party to the noxious fulminations of the despised, bottom-dwelling Whigs, whom he continued to refer to as "Federalists."

Ever since the days of Jackson and the Nullification Crisis, slavery had been the hot potato for U.S. presidents because the notion of disunion that it raised was almost too monstrous to contemplate. Like the ten commanders in chief that had preceded him, Polk considered slavery "settled law," unshakably ingrained in the Constitution. But in the 1820s the abolitionist movement began to strengthen so that, by Polk's time, it was blowing a gale, if not yet a hurricane. By the 1840s the movement had gone beyond campaigning against the South's peculiar institution as a mere social evil, which heretofore had been the bedrock of their opposition; by now they had concluded that slavery was a moral wrong and began to agitate on that basis. The effect was beginning to unsettle the foundation of the country.

In this debate Polk found himself dancing on the edge of a very sharp knife, inasmuch as he did not intend to preside over the dissolution of the United States of America, which was becoming a real possibility. Polk's opposition to Wilmot's proviso, and King's proviso, was not a practical one. In fact he was convinced that slavery would never be feasible—economically or otherwise—in the territories he intended to acquire. What he objected to, and justifiably so, was "the agitation of a question that might sever and endanger the Union itself." And what was even worse, in Polk's myopic view, was the politicization of that selfsame question, on the one hand, by his old enemy the South Carolina Democrat and celebrated nullifier in chief John C. Calhoun, who promptly got up a "paper" opposing the very notion of the Wilmot Proviso and was going around buttonholing prominent southerners to sign it, including members of Polk's cabinet. Polk interpreted this as a blatant attempt by Calhoun to "seize on this agitation of the slavery question" in order to further "his aspirations for the Presidency," a motive that was "not only unpatriotic and mischievous, but wicked."

On the other hand Polk perceived that the aim of Wilmot and King was to promote the presidential aspirations of the New York governor Silas Wright, who was assembling a constituency centered on "opposition to slavery.'"* In both of these activities the president saw a positive danger to the compact adopted in 1787. "The slavery question is assuming a fearful and most important aspect," Polk told his diary on January 4, the day King introduced his proviso. "[It] will be attended with terrible consequences to the country, and cannot fail to destroy the Democratic Party, if it does not ultimately threaten the Union itself.

"The truth is there is no patriotism in either faction of the party," Polk went on. "Both hope to mount slavery as a hobby, and hope to secure the election of their favorite upon it. They will both fail, and ought to fail. The people of the United States, I hope, will cast off all such intriguers, and make their own selection of the Presidency."

Nothing came of the Wilmot Proviso at the time—it was quickly killed in the Senate—but it planted a savage seed in the minds of southerners, which germinated into an immutable conviction that their northern brethren planned to use the Congress of the United States to destroy their economy and way of life—an especially critical plank in the bridge to war.

Meantime, Polk had an immediate war to fight and the proviso business made him peevish. "I had recommended [to Congress] a vigorous prosecution of the war," he told his diary. "Instead of acting upon the great measures of the country, they are spending day after day, week after week, in a worse than useless discussion about slavery." On Thursday, January 28, he wrote, "It is two years ago this day since I left my residence at Columbia, Tennessee, to enter on my duties as President of the United States. Since that time I have performed great labor and incurred vast responsibilities. In truth, I occupy a very high position, I am the hardest working man in the country." So there.

The trouble was that politics was fogging Polk's vision about the course of the war, or at least about the commanders he had sent to fight it. Both Zachary Taylor and Winfield Scott were Whigs—or in Taylor's case, "probably" a Whig. Furthermore, they were both winning battles, which made them presidential material, and Polk foresaw—or thought

---

*Wilmot vehemently denied this and insisted the proviso was designed ultimately to end slavery, which was viable only for cultivation-intense crops such as cotton, tobacco, and rice that ultimately wear out the soil, "so that after 10 or 15 years the planter finds himself with his slaves doubled in numbers and his land worthless." Upkeep of the slaves, Wilmot asserted, would eat up owners' savings and ultimately end the practice.

he did—that politics was causing them to whipsaw each other. Taylor, for instance, had written letters that found their way to the newspapers, indicating he thought the best policy would be simply to occupy Mexico's northern provinces until the Mexicans cried uncle. It would be less expensive in terms of both lives and treasure. Scott, on the other hand, was planning to bowl hell-for-leather down Mexico's main east-west highway with a 20,000-man army and force the war to an early conclusion. This last was something Polk yearned for, because he knew a long and protracted war would sink him, but it galled him that it might at the same time propel a Whig such as Zachary Taylor or Winfield Scott into the presidency of the United States. By the end of February he had this to say about it: "I have good reason to believe that General Taylor's camp has been converted into a political arena, and that great injustice has been done to officers who happened to be Democrats. General Scott, since he assumed command, has commenced the same tyrannical course."

Clearly the president needed to catch his breath, an opportunity for which presented itself in the midst of a complicated discussion with his cabinet regarding an emissary he was intending to send to the Mexicans in case they wanted to settle for peace after all the American victories. Let Polk tell the story.

"Tuesday, 13th April, 1847. About two o'clock p.m. it was announced to me that General Tom Thumb, a dwarf, who is being exhibited in this city and who has become quite celebrated by having been exhibited in all the principal courts of Europe, was in the parlor below stairs, and desired to see me.

"I invited the cabinet to take a short recess and to walk down with me, and they did so. We found a number of ladies and gentlemen in the parlor. Tom Thumb is a most remarkable person. After spending twenty or thirty minutes in the parlor I returned with the cabinet to my office."*

Happenings such as this were not all that uncommon in the White House of those times.

The first news that Polk received about the successful conquest of

---

*Thumb was a famous dwarf in the employ of the circus impresario P. T. Barnum, who had managed to introduce him to England's Queen Victoria among other European crowned heads.

California came in late April and brought with it a whiff of trouble. "An unfortunate collision has occurred in California," said the president, "between General Kearny and Commodore Stockton, in regard to precedence in rank. I think General Kearny was right. It appears that Lt. Col. Fremont refused to obey General Kearny, and obeyed Commodore Stockton, and in this he was wrong."

It was too true and even then Polk must have smelled the trouble that was brewing because he brought it up before his cabinet with a mind toward "having the matter . . . passed over as lightly as possible."

But it was not possible. Because of the personalities involved they were playing with political fire. Frémont, as we know, was no ordinary army officer; he remained one of the nation's most popular heroes. And whatever the trouble might be, he was sure to be backed up by his father-in-law and most ardent supporter the redoubtable Thomas Hart Benton, the so-called Lion of the U.S. Senate. Here is how it started.

On January 13, 1847, two days after Kearny's and Stockton's forces retook Los Angeles, Frémont was about twenty miles north of the city with the five hundred men of his California Battalion. He had been on the march for six weeks and was preparing to catch the Mexican rebels in a pincers movement. On that day, however, Californio emissaries rode into Frémont's camp to ask his terms of surrender.

When Los Angeles fell it became clear to Pico and Flores that further resistance was futile, and they felt that surrendering to Frémont would give them a better deal than surrendering to Stockton, who had refused to treat with Flores and instead offered "to have him shot" for violating his parole. Unaware of this, Frémont, who had Stockton's promise to appoint him governor of California—but no authority as yet—nevertheless drew up articles of capitulation that, among other things, forgave the Mexicans for all parole violations. The terms were generous and sensible. The rebels would lay down their arms and swear to abide by the laws of the United States but were not required to swear allegiance to it, until hostilities ended and a treaty was signed. In return they would be given protection under all U.S. laws. That, in effect, ended resistance to American rule in California. Flores, as we know, absconded to Sonora, never to return, and Pico retired to his country property. Frémont and his battalion ambled into Los Angeles.

At this point Kearny, acting on orders from President Polk and Secretary of War Marcy, tried to assert his authority over Frémont and his people in order to consolidate the conquest of the province. But for some inexplicable reason Stockton immediately appointed Frémont governor of California, and Frémont in turn rebuffed Kearny's efforts to take charge of the province. This was despite the fact that the general carried on his person, and produced for both men, the explicit orders from the president and secretary of war appointing him governor as soon as power had been consolidated in the region, which it had. Except not by Kearny, Stockton contended. It was *he*, he said, who had conquered California, and *he* who would select its governor. Frémont foolishly assented to this blatant act of insubordination, which was soon to inspire a national uproar.

Kearny found himself in a highly peculiar situation. He was in fact a general, who outranked Stockton no matter the separation of services, but between Stockton's navy sailors and Frémont's five hundred frontiersmen he was utterly outgunned, with only his depleted dragoons to enforce his orders.

So he bided his time, wrote an account of how matters stood, and then sent it to Washington aboard a U.S. Navy ship in the care of Captain Emory, who saw it to the War Department. But that would take months, as Kearny knew, and months more to receive a reply. Meantime, Stockton sailed away, leaving Frémont to contend with things.

Kearny sent Frémont a letter calling on him to produce the authority under which he was assuming the position of governor, but the Pathfinder's reply was arrogant, flippant, and vague, noting that during the advance on Los Angeles Kearny had maintained "deference" to Stockton and thus had acknowledged the commodore's superior rank. Frémont compounded the insult by delivering the letter in person to Kearny in his tent.

The general had been in the army a long time, and he was known as a stern taskmaster. But either out of desire to give his subordinate a chance to redeem himself or out of respect for Frémont's father-in-law, Benton, whom Kearny counted as a friend—or both—Kearny offered Frémont a way out. He counseled the Pathfinder to take the letter back and destroy it and he would forget the whole matter.

Frémont refused the advice, saying that Stockton would back him up.

"I told him," Kearny later testified, "that Commodore Stockton could not support him in disobeying the orders of his senior officer, and that if he persisted in it, he would unquestionably ruin himself."

Instead, Frémont began to argue, continuing to insist that Stockton had the authority in California. Then he left. Next morning Kearny marshaled his remaining dragoons and headed south for San Diego while Frémont sat in Los Angeles, issuing edicts, invoices, bills, and letters, all under the signature of "J. C. Fremont, Governor of California."

In one particularly self-aggrandizing epistle to Benton he claimed that Stockton had named him governor and that Kearny had offered him the same position "in four or six weeks." He said, "I was proclaimed governor and immediately proclaimed peace and order restored to the country." He told of children singing his praises in street songs. "Throughout the Californian population," Frémont wrote, "there is only one feeling of satisfaction and gratitude to myself."

Meanwhile, down in San Diego Kearny stewed for a month until, on February 13, he received a courier packet from Washington containing copies of dispatches to Stockton from not only the secretary of the navy but the chief of the army himself, Winfield Scott. These documents made it perfectly clear that Kearny was to be in charge of all civil and military activities in California, including governor.

Frémont became aware of these same documents but apparently came to believe that since they were dated November 5, 1846, there surely would be further orders from Washington upholding his governorship. It was an unfortunate gamble.

On March 1 Kearny, who by then had moved his headquarters to Monterey, had an order delivered to Frémont, telling him to come to Monterey personally and bring with him any and all archives and records of the California Battalion. He signed the letter, "S. W. Kearny Brig. Gen. & Governor of California."

But Frémont ignored the orders and continued doing business in Los Angeles as governor, surrounded by his fierce and faithful California Battalion and generally behaving in a Kurtzian fashion.

Kearny soon followed up by publishing a "circular" in which he advertised himself as the governor of California under official orders from Washington. In response, Frémont issued a circular of his own, denying it.

Kearny then ordered Frémont to muster into the regular service the members of the California Battalion so that they could receive government pay, after which they would be put under the command of Colonel Cooke and then be disbanded.

Frémont refused. The situation was becoming not only ridiculous but confusing and even dangerous, with two persons claiming to be governor, each with his own little army. But Kearny was gaining the upper hand; among other things, he now had under his command not only Cooke's five hundred Mormons but another infantry regiment of volunteers from New York, which had recently begun arriving by ship. Those First Dragoon officers who kept diaries or notebooks all wrote, some furiously, that they thought Kearny should have long since clapped Frémont in irons.

Finally, on March 28, in response to another Kearny order, Frémont made a hard 125-mile-a-day ride to Kearny's headquarters in Monterey, where things immediately went off to a bad start. Upon entering the general's room Frémont objected to the presence of Colonel Richard B. Mason, of the First Dragoons, who had brought the confirming orders out from Washington by ship. Frémont intimated that Mason might be some kind of spy for Kearny, which infuriated the general, who replied that he could not believe Frémont would "come into my quarters and intentionally insult me." He explained that Mason was to be his replacement as head of the civil government in California as soon as Kearny felt it proper to go back east, that it was perfectly proper for Mason to be there.

Kearny demanded to know if Frémont was going to obey his orders and disband the California Battalion. In response, Frémont offered to resign his commission but Kearny would not hear of it. Kearny asked again if Frémont was ready to start taking orders, but the explorer could not get his answer together. Kearny suggested that he take some time to think it over, emphasizing that it was going to be an important decision in Frémont's life. Frémont departed but was back within the hour. Yes, he said, he was ready to disavow the governorship and obey Kearny's orders.

Frémont then returned to Los Angeles to relinquish his duties as governor of California, but he was followed by Colonel Mason, his superior in rank as well as in civil authority. Now thoroughly alarmed at his future, Frémont wrote Kearny asking if he could take sixty men and ride to meet Winfield Scott's army in Mexico. Now it was Kearny's turn to start refusing things—permission denied. Frémont must have suspected then that his goose was cooked. Flush with the exhilaration of the California conquest, he had hitched his wagon to the wrong star. For years he had been a freewheeling American icon in buckskin, an explorer in the western wilds reporting to political authorities in Washington's highest circles, including his powerful father-in-law. Now he was about to get a taste of the real army—the hierarchy of rules and regulations, of chain of command and West Point spit-and-polish yessir-nosir-whatever-you-say-sir!

As if that wasn't enough, Frémont got into a squabble with Mason over various demands the colonel made regarding documents Frémont had issued, which escalated into, of all things, a duel.

It was Frémont's challenge, and therefore Mason's call as to weapons. He picked double-barreled shotguns and buckshot at twenty paces, a sporty choice. Mason, in fact, was said to be expert with a shotgun, but when word of the affair got around the consensus was that these were not exactly considered gentlemen's weapons. But it was a sordid affair from the beginning. Distasteful as they were to begin with, duels at least were supposed to concern matters of personal honor, not peevishness over bureaucratic irritations. It led some people to think Frémont had spent too much time in the woods.

CHAPTER SIXTEEN

Last Roll Call:
A Warm Salute

Frémont's duel never came off, but his troubles had just begun. The day after he issued the challenge, Colonel Mason wrote Frémont that he needed several days' time to go to Monterey before the duel, a request that Frémont granted—in writing. In the meantime Kearny got wind of the affair and wrote Frémont that he had ordered Mason not to engage in any duel, and that "the necessity of preserving tranquility in California, imperiously requires that the meeting above referred to [the duel] should not take place at this time, and in this country, and you are officially directed by me to proceed no further in this matter."*

Meanwhile, Kearny had other plans for the Pathfinder, which did not bode well for his military career. On May 29 the general announced that he was leaving California for Washington in two days. Frémont was to turn over all of his topographical instruments to Lieutenant Henry Wager Halleck of the engineers and assume a place at the rear of Kearny's party on the long march home.

Frémont asked if he could go to San Francisco for some botanical and biological specimens he had been collecting. Permission denied. When Kearny's entourage reached Sutter's Fort on June 11, Frémont again applied for leave to return home under his own steam, which, he said, "with my knowledge of the country, would allow me to reach the States some forty or fifty days earlier than yourself." Permission denied.

---

*Kearny appears to have been of the old school on this subject. As the editors of the Frémont correspondence correctly point out, Kearny's apparent postponement of the duel "was a strange proceeding, since his duty by military regulations was to arrest both parties."

Next he asked if he could take "a party of sixty men and 129 horses" and join the Mounted Rifles in Mexico, under General Winfield Scott. Permission denied. Instead, Kearny prepared to push on across country with Frémont deliberately assigned to bring up the rear, apparently for purposes of his humiliation. By now it must have been apparent to Frémont that he was more or less a prisoner.

What had caused the bizarre hubris on Frémont's part remains a mystery. Perhaps it had to do with the Latin aspects of his French heritage, but he hardly gave anyone the impression that he was a practicing Frenchman. The duel challenge, however, was revealing. Could it be that his sudden acceleration from captain in command of a sixty-man party of mountain men to lieutenant colonel in charge of a combat battalion had somehow gone to his head?

Doubtless Frémont regarded Kearny's entrance into California a surprise and unwelcome intrusion, but surely he considered that to defy a general and hope to remain in the army was a risky business at best and might even lead to an encounter with the wrong end of a rope. Stockton, an eccentric and known troublemaker, obviously had much to do with it, and in fact he had egged on the whole thing by appointing Frémont governor in the first place, then hiding behind the navy to solidify his position. But from what Frémont published afterward, it can be fairly said that he had come to think of himself as a man of destiny who was disposed as such to take action, right or wrong. It was as if he were looking into a tarnished mirror that caught only a fractured glimpse into his future and had failed to reflect the fine, thin line between the heroic and the ignoble.

Kearny's party learned at Sutter's of the grisly end to the Donner tragedy, as Keseberg was at last brought out of the mountains by a relief party that reached the pass April 17, 1847, when the snows had subsided. This fourth relief actually had a dual mission of rescue and plunder, after the custom of the times. They knew from the previous relief that three people had been left on the mountain alive, and if any of them remained alive they would be brought out. At the same time, they knew there were many valuables left up there—money, jewelry, weapons, tools, utensils, clothes, and so forth—abandoned to the elements like so much flotsam and jetsam. The party of seven, led by a self-styled mountain man named William "Le Gros" Fallon, met at Sutter's, where it was agreed they could keep one half the value of what they found, the other part going to the survivors or the survivors' children.

Upon their arrival at the Donner camps the party "was obliged to witness sights from which we would have fain turned away, and which are too dreadful to put on record." So said Fallon in his journal, where he put them on record anyway. The patchy snow was strewn in all directions with human remains and bones and no one was alive but Keseberg, half deranged, who was "reclining in his cabin, smoking his pipe," surrounded by bodies that had been carved up, and their livers, brains, and eyes removed and placed in a large pan. On the floor beside him, they said, was a kettle containing what Keseberg claimed was human blood. George Donner had finally died a week earlier and Tamsen Donner, faithful to the last, had wrapped his body in a sheet and laid it out in the snow, then came to Keseberg's cabin, wanting to go after her children, but she died that same night. According to Fallon, Keseberg told them he had eaten her.

Two months later Kearny's return march, with Fallon acting as guide, "reached the scene of these horrible and tragical occurrences," noted Edwin Bryant, the newspaper editor who had crossed the mountains, fought with Frémont's California Battalion, and was now going home to tell his tale.*

"A more revolting and appalling spectacle I never witnessed. The remains were, by order of Gen. Kearny, collected and buried under the superintendence of Maj. Swords. They were interred in a pit in the centre of one of the cabins for a *cache*. These melancholy duties to the dead being performed, the cabins by order of Major Swords, were fired, and everything connected with this horrid tragedy consumed.† The body of Mr. George Donner was found at his camp, wrapped in a sheet. He was buried by a party of men detailed for that purpose."

Soon as word of the Donners' plight got out, the rumors and exagger-

---

*Bryant's book, *What I Saw in California*, published in 1848, has become a classic of the genre.

†Not quite. Frémont's party of disgrace, traveling a day or two behind, finished the job, "burning the broken wagons, ox-yokes, and other sad relics," to "destroy all traces which might operate to the discouragement of emigrants."

ations had begun. By the time Keseberg was rescued the newspapers flaunted the most lurid tales of cannibalism, murder, and depravity. The *California Star*, for example, wrote, "The day before the [rescue] party arrived, one of the emigrants took a child of about four years of age to bed with him, and devoured him whole before morning, and the next day ate another about the same age before noon." Or this: "A woman sat beside the body of her husband who had just died, cutting out his tongue; the heart she had already taken out, broiled, and ate!" Or this: "The daughter ate the flesh of her father, the mother of her children. So changed had the emigrants become," the newspapers reported, "that when the party sent out arrived with food, some of them cast it aside and seemed to prefer the putrid human flesh that still remained."

It was bad enough without all that nonsense, but the nation was both scandalized and mesmerized by the calamity as the story wafted back east, sometimes merely as third- or fourth-hand hearsay. What had happened to the Donner expedition was a great human tragedy that piled up stroke of fate after stroke of fate from the outset, beginning with the devolution of James Reed as wagon master. Reed may have been smart, rich, and tough but what had been needed was an experienced mountain man to lead that caravan across the country; then there was the unwise decision, after being warned against it, to take the Hastings Cutoff, which set them behind a full month so that their climb into the mountains was the same as climbing into a trap.

After Reed was banished the social system disintegrated. In large part the cannibalism must have been dreadful for the cannibals, but not deplorable; the human instinct to survive can trump the mightiest taboos, and who is to say that under similar circumstances Kearny's people, crossing parallel down south, or Cooke and his Mormons, would not have done the same thing. It was a classic example of pragmatism, perhaps the ultimate example of it. What *was* deplorable, of course, was Foster's murder of the Indians and whatever Keseberg was rumored to have done, if he did it. The distinction between their actions and the others' is plain, not blurred.

There were eighty-seven emigrants in the Donner train and thirty-nine of them died, five before reaching the mountain pass and the rest on the mountain or trying to get off of it. Most of these last were cannibalized. Throw in Sutter's two Indians, Luis and Salvador, who had come as rescuers, and you have forty-one souls who perished. That left forty-eight, many of them children, who went on to new lives in California. Over the years journalists and historians tracked most of them down and got them to tell and retell their stories. Keseberg, for instance, lived to the age of eighty-one and became, of all things, a restaurateur. It was said that he often went about the streets of Sacramento like the Ancient Mariner, proclaiming his innocence to anyone who would listen—the only thing missing was the albatross.

The Donner experience was more than just a ghoulish aberration; it quickly became an instructive lesson on how *not* to cross the great American continent. To suggest that the Donners represented the western emigration would be absurd, given what happened to them. In the first place they were probably more financially substantial than other wagon trains, and that alone set them apart. But the legacy they shared was the immense ambition, or wanderlust, that seemed to overtake much of the nation following reports such as Frémont's—not of gold dust and instant riches but of vast fertile lands to be sowed and reaped, a seductive harvest home. A life different, exciting, and a little dangerous was their manifest destiny. That is what the Donners stood for in the beginning, though they won't be remembered for it. But even the horror of their failure underscores the success of countless others who heralded Polk's initiative to expand the United States to the Pacific Ocean.

In the beginning of April, at the height of the Kearny-Frémont set-to, Frémont had sent his faithful scout Kit Carson back east with letters to his father-in-law and to James Buchanan, secretary of state, giving his side of the controversy—though, oddly, nothing was written to the War Department. At last Carson was going to Washington. Among his entourage was the poor navy lieutenant Beale, whose feet were still so damaged from the barefoot walk across the desert that Carson "had to lift him on and off his horse," and he actually thought he was going to die.

Carson took the southern route as before, along the Gila and up to Taos where he was devastated to learn of the uprising that killed his brother-in-law, Charles Bent, and so many of his friends and had nearly killed his wife, Josefa. At least he got there for the hangings of the rebels and had more than a week before he was off again for St. Louis. There he was warmly received by Benton and invited to stay in the senator's home in Washington, which he reached on June 5, 1847. It was said that Carson was greeted at the District of Columbia railway station by Jessie Benton Frémont herself and escorted to the Benton home.

Both Benton and Jessie understood the implications contained in Frémont's correspondence; the Pathfinder was defying a U.S. Army general, his superior, who had been under orders from the president of the United States. Among the many charges possible could be the accusation of mutiny, a hanging offense. They were fearful of the shape of things to come, and on June 7, trying to head off trouble, Jessie accompanied Carson to meet the president. In that capacity, Carson handed Polk the letter Frémont had written to Benton, which explained his decision to accept and retain the governorship of California and to defy Kearny. Basically, Frémont laid it all on Commodore Stockton, with whom, Frémont said, he had "contracted relations" from which "it would be neither right nor politically honorable to withdraw my support." The letter went on to say that Kearny might be apt to make trouble and that Frémont wanted the president to appreciate his position.

In fact, Polk already knew Frémont's position and didn't agree with it one bit, for Kearny's messenger Captain Emory had lately arrived with Kearny's side of the story, in which the general had written to the War Department, "I am not recognized in my official capacity, either by Commodore Stockton or Lieutenant-Colonel Fremont, both of whom refuse to obey my orders, or the instructions of the president."

"Mrs. Fremont," the president wrote in his diary, "seemed anxious to elicit from me some expression of approbation of her husband's conduct, but I evaded making any. In truth, I consider that Col. Fremont was greatly in the wrong when he refused to obey the orders issued to him by General Kearny. It was unnecessary, however, that I should say so to Col. Fremont's wife, and I evaded giving her an answer."

Polk met with Carson again that night, alone, with further discussion about the "unfortunate collision between our land and naval commanders in that distant region." Knowing that the scout was close to Frémont, the president remained inscrutable as the Sphinx. But the next day he met with his cabinet, which was unanimous in deciding to send Carson back immediately with dispatches affirming that Kearny was in charge in California. The fact that Kearny had already taken charge and was on his way back to Washington was notwithstanding; it was the issue of disobedience that mattered.

Next morning Jessie Frémont returned to the White House with Kit Carson in tow, again to plead her husband's case, a matter that was becoming tiresome for James K. Polk. He informed her that the dispatches he was sending back to California with Carson would thoroughly clarify the situation.*

Kearny's column reached Fort Leavenworth, Kansas, on August 22, 1847, from whence it had departed one year and two months earlier. Much had happened in that space of time. On the same day, Kearny called Frémont into the post commandant's office and told him to consider himself under arrest and to report to the adjutant general in Washington. The charges were mutiny, disobedience of orders, assumption of powers, and other military offenses, down to and including insubordination. Kearny had thrown the book at him.

Soon as the telegraph wires began to sing with news of Frémont's arrest, a blizzard of mostly anonymous articles began to howl in the press, either in his defense or in his disparagement. Benton charged that some of them were the defamatory work of Captain Emory and Colonel Cooke of the Mormon Battalion, both of whom he charged with envy over Frémont's fame and of holding the characteristic disdain of West Pointers for non–Military Academy officers. Both men denied the charges. Because of Frémont's renown, the months leading up to the court-martial devolved into a media circus, with scarcely a day passing that some new aspect of the case was not headlined in the press, then flayed in next day's papers with opposing views. Naturally Frémont's mountain men—for instance, Godey, Carson, Walker, Dick Owens, and Bill Williams—stood by him and doubtless would have entered the letter-writing contest in his favor if they hadn't been illiterate. Thus far, it was shaping up to be the most dramatic trial of the century.

---

*As a token of gratitude for his service, before Carson left, Polk conferred upon him a lieutenant's commission in the army's Mounted Rifles, a regular army regiment. This would pay him roughly $100 a month, or about $32,000 a year in today's money.

Benton, meantime, seemed to have come nearly unhinged. Each week he penned a torrent of letters to anyone and everyone involved in the matter, chiding, threatening, blustering, wheedling. His capacity for hatred seemed boundless. He treated the charges against his son-in-law as a matter of family honor. One night before a fireplace in the White House a vitriolic Benton seethed to the president that if justice were not done, he would use his powers to court-martial Kearny, Emory, Cooke, and Captain Henry Turner, Kearny's adjutant, causing the president later to groan to his diary that the senator "is a man of violent passions, and I should not be surprised if he became my enemy."

On November 2, 1847, at straight-up noon, Frémont's trial got under way in the Washington Arsenal, presided over by a general of infantry—not a good sign for Frémont. Seated behind their leader was a cluster of Frémont's mountain men in their buckskins, and on the opposite side of the aisle a detachment of Kearny's loyal officers, in full dress.

After the charges were read, Frémont opened his own defense by brushing aside all technicalities and announcing that the whole case against him boiled down to three issues. First, that the orders to Stockton and Kearny by their respective military bosses in Washington were imprecise; second, California had already been conquered when Kearny arrived, and thus Kearny's orders were obsolete; and, third, the prosecution was unable to appreciate the great issues at stake. Frémont argued that at all times he had acted in good faith, that he had been a good governor and military scientist, prevented civil war, and conquered California bloodlessly. In essence Frémont painted himself as a respectful soldier trying to do his duty for his country during a difficult time.

When his turn came, Kearny said that it came as news to him that California was already conquered by Frémont and Stockton, since the day he arrived there he was violently attacked by Mexicans at the Battle of San Pasqual, which killed or wounded most of his men. He painted Frémont as an opportunist and testified that Frémont had basely attempted to "sell himself to the highest bidder" by asking if Kearny would also be willing to appoint him governor, just as Stockton had, thus offering to switch sides.

At length Benton's great hour came round. With Kearny still on the stand he puffed himself up in the manner of an actor, his face reddened with rage, turned his great head and beetle brows toward the witness chair, and launched into a tirade of disdainful maledictions, as though the general had become some bottom-dwelling misfit. He implied that Kearny was lying about selected events, that his memory was consciously "faulty." He accused Kearny of coming to California "to steal the laurels and material benefits" that had been so hard won in battle by Frémont and Commodore Stockton.

He charged that Kearny was jealous of Frémont's youth and fame and was deliberately out to ruin him. He informed the court that the general had "looked insultingly and fiendishly" at Frémont, apparently to intimidate him, and it "was therefore his duty to glare" at Kearny "till his eyes fell—till they fell upon the floor!"

His voice cut the air like a saw. Benton might have thought of himself as an American Cicero, but rarely, if ever, had a general officer of the armed services such as Kearny been so scurvily treated in a court-martial proceeding. Naturally, the court took this into consideration, the newspapers lapped it up, and Frémont's trial vied for front-page coverage with flashes of the victorious American battles in Mexico.

The court-martial continued for three months while the press "tried the case on a country-wide basis," eclipsed only by news that Winfield Scott's army had at last taken Mexico City and that peace was at hand.* It had been a remarkable achievement, with Scott fighting his way across the interior of Mexico with an army half the size of what Santa Anna could throw at him, and testimony to the amazing skills and ingenuity of America's military establishment, which would be put to such terrible use little more than a decade hence.

It didn't do Frémont's case much good that he attempted to portray General Kearny as pretentious and overbearing; officers of the regular army understood that lieutenant colonels do not refuse to obey the

---

*Captured in the city fighting were seventy-two of the Irish deserters alluded to in an earlier footnote, who had formed the St. Patrick's Battalion in the Mexican army. Lured by pleas from their fellow Catholics and the promise of high pay and Mexican land, most had deserted from Taylor's army. Scott ordered them court-martialed and had forty-eight publicly hanged.

orders of their superiors on grounds that they may have been pretentious or overbearing.

Nor was it helpful that he had agreed to let Benton be his lawyer.
The fiery old politician had argued as he would in the Senate, fulminating with provocative and sometimes insulting rhetoric, especially
against Kearny, which caused the court to admonish him on more than
one occasion. After all those years of nearly freelance exploring, it
appeared that Frémont had fallen out of touch with traditional army
customs and standards; how else can one explain such an incendiary
defense?

In any case the court found him guilty as charged and sentenced
him to be dismissed from the service, which caused not just a national
but an international uproar. That was not quite the end of it, however,
though it might as well have been.

Half of the court recommended clemency by President Polk, and
while the others did not the matter went to the president's cabinet, half
of whom recommended clemency and half did not. Polk split the difference. He dismissed the most serious charge of mutiny but concluded
that Frémont was guilty of the lesser offenses. He canceled the punishment and ordered Frémont to "resume his sword."

However, Frémont's egocentric personality would not admit to any
guilt whatever, and he immediately presented his resignation from the
army. He had just turned thirty-five years old.

Benton used the occasion to launch a rancorous vendetta against
Polk—as Polk himself had predicted—the U.S. Army in general, and
Stephen Watts Kearny in particular. He stopped speaking to the president, tried to pass a law to change courts-martial procedures, and voted
against the administration in almost all of its war measures. When
Kearny's bill for brevet major general came up for approval in the Senate, Benton's was not only the lone vote against it, he also threatened a
filibuster.

To redeem his slightly tarnished reputation, Frémont went back to
exploring but his good luck seemed to have run out. This time he was
without the backing and subsidy of the U.S. military and had to finance
his own expedition, which he did by enlisting wealthy St. Louis men
who were interested in an exploration of the south-central Rockies for
purposes of establishing their city as the eastern terminus of a trans-

continental railroad line. In the meanwhile Jessie had a baby, a boy, but he was sickly and soon died, which crushed her. She blamed it on the court-martial, and on General Kearny.

Frémont nevertheless set out, taking a party of thirty-three— including many of his old regulars—though not Carson this time. They went from Independence down the Santa Fe Trail to Bent's Fort where it was already winter, and everyone was talking about the extraordinary snows for that time of year. Against the advice of the fur traders there, Frémont decided to push on anyway, perhaps overanxious to redeem himself, and got trapped on Boot Mountain in the San Juan Range. In winter this was some of the most savage terrain on earth. A big storm hit; mules began to die, then men. They sent out for help but they were starving. By the time it was over a dozen men were dead and there had been a pragmatic cannibalism of the Donner variety. The expedition had been a disaster and one reason undoubtedly was Kit Carson's absence.

Just as Frémont began his ordeal in the mountains, Polk sent Kearny to Mexico, first as governor of Veracruz, then as governor of Mexico City. But a few months after he arrived the general came down with yellow fever and was returned to St. Louis in fragile health, to the home of his brother-in-law Meriwether Lewis Clark, who had commanded Doniphan's artillery so well. There the fever killed him on the last day of October 1848, with his wife and children by his side. Because of the sensational press reports emanating from Frémont's trial, many dead cats had been thrown Kearny's way by a public that disliked being told its hero may have feet of clay. Nevertheless, a few weeks before he died, Kearny had sent for Jessie Benton Frémont, whom he'd known and befriended in St. Louis since she was a girl. But she refused to come, blaming him for the strain she thought had caused the death of her child. "I could not forgive him," Jessie told Kearny's doctor. "There was a little grave between us I could not cross."

Benton's vicious attacks on Kearny during the court-martial were of course spread throughout the land and hurt Kearny personally, because before the rift Benton had been a longtime friend, and also professionally since he never responded to the slander. De Voto mounts his high horse on the subject nearly a hundred years later, but his proofs are good and fair. He wrote in 1942: "Benton could be a gigantic hater

[and] turned demagogue on a cosmic scale. His attack on Kearny was dishonest, it was absurd, and it was puerile. "Few of those in high places were capable of putting the republic before themselves. Kearny served it without trying to serve himself. He was a man, a gentleman, and a soldier. The enmity of an adventurer's father-in-law should not be permitted to obscure his achievement any longer."

After his catastrophic fourth expedition, Frémont went to California where he had acquired a huge piece of property below the Sierras and intended to start a ranch. In 1850 he was elected senator from the new state, where gold had been discovered three years earlier and emigrants were pouring in at an astonishing rate.* There was even gold on Frémont's place but he was somehow cheated out of it through his employees' misfeasance or malfeasance while he was away in Washington. In 1856 he was an unsuccessful presidential candidate for the fledgling antislavery Republican Party, and financial troubles plagued him until the Civil War, when he was taken out of mothballs and commissioned a major general.

Benton had died in 1858 at the age of seventy-six, having been defeated for office in Missouri seven years earlier after he came out against slavery. He had subsequently been censured for misbehavior on the Senate floor. His autobiography, *Thirty Years' View*, a lengthy screed fulminating against everything and everyone, from paper money to President Polk, was published in 1854.

During the Civil War Frémont did not distinguish himself; in fact, quite the opposite. His first duty in 1861 was as commander of the Union Army of the West, headquartered in St. Louis. It was an enormous responsibility, but for some reason Frémont surrounded himself with a bunch of cronies and a company of brass-helmeted troops dressed like French chasseurs, and he became ensconced in an expensive mansion where he refused to see anyone. Dispatches came to the house, and

---

*The gold was first discovered at a mill Sutter was building, and the "rush" lasted less than a decade, but it saw more than 300,000 people—mostly Americans—pour into California during that time and extract precious metals worth billions in today's dollars.

dispatches left the house, but nothing of consequence occurred until Frémont issued an edict under his own authority freeing all the slaves of anyone suspected of having Confederate sympathies. This happened to be the very last thing that President Lincoln wanted at the moment, since he was trying frantically to hold the slaveholding border states Missouri, Kentucky, and Maryland to the Union politically rather than by force. The president tactfully ordered Frémont to modify his order but the Pathfinder refused, even after another urgent appeal by Jessie, who again marched on the White House with her indignant swishing of skirts. On November 2, 1861, Lincoln relieved Frémont of command.

Four months later he was given charge of the Mountain Department of Virginia, Kentucky, and Tennessee and in this capacity in June of 1862 he engaged, or endeavored to engage, the redoubtable Thomas J. "Stonewall" Jackson, who made a fool of him all over the Shenandoah Valley. Again relieved, after refusing to serve under General John Pope in the Army of Virginia, Frémont went to New York but never received another command. In the election of 1864 hard-line abolitionists once more pushed Frémont into the Republican primary, but he quit in the middle of it. As a regular soldier, it seems Frémont was a wash, no matter how brilliantly he had performed in the mountain wilds as explorer par excellence. Benton had doubtless been accurate when he accused such West Point officers as Emory and Cooke of being disdainful of Frémont because he had no formal military training. In retrospect their assessment seems to have been quite correct.

After the war Frémont became involved in railroad building but lost everything in that dicey business. In 1878 he secured an appointment as governor of the Arizona Territory, but when that ended he had to rely on Jessie's literary career for their living. They remained in New York, where he died in 1890, at the age of seventy-seven. Afterward, Jessie moved to Los Angeles, where she died in 1902 at the age of seventy-eight.

Frémont has turned out to be a controversial and contradictory personality in American history. Headstrong, and at times imprudent, he inspired the utmost loyalty from his subordinates—those fabled mountain men—no mean feat in itself. He was curious, fearless, and had a decisive presence of command, even when he was wrong. During the Civil War his status as national hero was diminished, and he became lampooned in the press for his Civil War blunders and his radical politics.

He nevertheless will be remembered by more than a score of western plants that are named after him (as well as *by* him), and numerous counties, cities, mountains, rivers, high schools, streets, hospitals, libraries, parks, and bridges, mostly in the West, bear his name. In addition, innumerable children were named after him during his most famous exploration years in the 1840s, including, I suspect, as noted, my great-grandfather Fremont Sterling Thrower.

Of the other characters in the drama, Kit Carson became a national folk hero through Frémont's expedition reports, and his stature was further expanded by the publication of dozens of pulp fiction Westerns—then called dime novels—purporting to recount his fabulous exploits. After the Frémont years, he became a rancher in New Mexico and later served the U.S. government as an Indian agent and fighter during numerous uprisings. During the Civil War he was recalled to service, commanding a 500-man battalion of mounted infantry against a Confederate invasion of New Mexico and fought at the Battle of Valverde.

Following that he was once more preoccupied with "Indian troubles," the Indians having used the Civil War as an occasion to run amok. In the spring of 1864 he forced the surrender of 8,000 Navajos who were marched three hundred miles to Fort Sumner, New Mexico, a trek known then, as today, in Navajo lore as the "Long Walk."

By the end of the war Carson was breveted a brigadier general with headquarters in Ute territory in Colorado. Afterward he continued to ranch until the death of his wife, Josefa, in childbirth in 1868. He followed her a month later, on May 23 of that year, from a rupture of his abdominal aorta. His last words were *"adios compadres!"* Their eight orphaned children were parceled out to relatives and Carson soon passed into legend. His reputation remained solid as an honest, decent, fearless, sympathetic frontiersman, as well as a cold-blooded killer of Indians that he felt threatened by. He was a man of his time.

Interviewers of Carson have stated that, like Andrew Jackson, he believed the Indians needed to be separated from white men for their own good, that for the most part the trouble started when whites confronted Indians in what the Indians considered to be their territory.

Unlike for Frémont, there are no botanical specimens named after Carson, but in the West one might justifiably conclude that almost everything else under the sun has been: the state capital of Nevada is Carson City, and there is Fort Carson, Colorado, as well as Carson Park, Peak, Pass, National Forest, River, Valley, Trail, and untold Carson streets, roads, expressways, and schools; there is even a Kit Carson Parking Lot in Kentucky, his home state.

The mountain men who accompanied Frémont and Carson also found themselves the subjects of dime novels and likely the made-up tales weren't even the half of it. Trapping beaver had gone out of style and most of them turned to such occupations as wagon train guides, border traders, outpost operators, and buffalo hide and meat hunters. Their day had lasted only about a quarter century, but in that time they made an indelible impression on the American landscape.

The English adventurer Lieutenant George Frederick Augustus Ruxton, who gave so much literary grief to the Missouri Volunteers, went on to become a respectable mountain man himself, and after a year or so he went to St. Louis and began writing articles for a British magazine as well as a fine book, *Adventures in Mexico and the Rocky Mountains*. But he was terribly unwell from dysentery he had contracted somewhere along the way, a disease for which, often, there was no cure. Weak and resigned to his fate at the (comparatively) fashionable Planter's Hotel in St. Louis, he wrote home.

"My dear Mother," he began. "I always think it better not to say goodbye, and therefore only tell you to keep a lookout for me one of these days."

He died there shortly afterward, at the age of twenty-eight. His works on the American West are still well worth reading.

Commodore Robert F. Stockton resigned from the navy in 1850 and the following year was elected to the U.S. Senate as a Democrat from New Jersey. He served three years, and then resigned to become president of a canal-building company. In 1863, when the Confederate army invaded Pennsylvania, Stockton took charge of the New Jersey militia. He died in 1866, at the age of seventy-one, and his name has been honored on no fewer than four U.S. Navy vessels, as well as the cities of Stockton in California, Missouri, and New Jersey, and Fort Stockton, Texas.

Captain Archibald Gillespie of the U.S. Marines returned to Washington and testified for Frémont at his court-martial. There, he married into a wealthy family—a cousin, in fact, of the socially prominent Captain William Emory. For the next several years Gillespie held various posts but was ill much of the time; then, in 1854, he became embroiled in a disgraceful scandal. Officers of the USS *Independence*, flagship of the U.S. Pacific Squadron, accused Gillespie of "swindling his messmates and brother officers out of the money paid him by them for the mess stores." Sobered by this shameful incident, Gillespie abruptly resigned his commission, and around the same time he separated from his wife. He found his way to California where his brother practiced law and lived an obscure and shadowy life there until August 1873, when he died at the age of sixty-three. There are no public monuments to his name.

Alexander William Doniphan and his regiment returned to Missouri via New Orleans, where they were feted and fawned over until they resumed their boorish behavior and were nearly asked to leave town. By then, their clothing and appearance were deplorable. A description of one of these men by General Wool seems typical: "He was almost naked, dirty and bearded like a pirate, hair unkempt and falling over his shoulders." Doniphan arranged on his personal credit to buy civilian clothing for the entire bunch, to the tune of $60,000 (about $60 per man), after which, on June 28, 1847, they were assembled in formation for a final time and mustered out with honorable discharges. Most, but not all, returned to Missouri, by steamboat, up the Mississippi, greeted enthusiastically along the way by the flag-waving occupants of its fabulous plantation homes, which lined both banks of the river for hundreds of miles. In St. Louis, especially, they were received with parades, dinners, and fireworks.

Doniphan was much celebrated and even asked to address the Corps of Cadets at the United States Military Academy. He was so popular it has been said by his biographers that "he could have sought national office in the Congress or perhaps even the presidency." But despite the efforts of political insiders and pundits he resisted running for office and quietly resumed the practice of law. As the Civil War approached he counseled loyalty to the Union, and later, as things grew heated, at least neutrality for Missouri.

He was offered a high commission in the Union army but like many Missourians refused to fight against the South. In 1861 he attended the much ballyhooed "Peace Conference" in Washington, which accomplished nothing. He died in 1887 in Richmond, a small town outside St. Louis, still practicing law, at the age of seventy-nine, having outlived his wife, as well as both of his sons, who were killed in accidents. Alexander William Doniphan, too, has a county, a city, and various byways in Missouri honoring his name.

And when his thousand ragamuffins gathered on the boat decks headed home, could anyone among their number see within a dozen years those river flagpoles draped in Stars and Bars, the banner of a new and angry nation gouged out from the old? Being from Missouri, they probably would have said, "Go show me"—but in the end the story turned out well.

The intrepid cavalry captain John Reid, who led the charge at the Battle of the Sacramento and saved Mexican children from Indians, also returned to his law practice in Missouri. Unlike Doniphan he became a state representative and then a U.S. congressman, but in 1861 he withdrew, and was later expelled, for siding with the Confederacy. He served as an aide to the Confederate general Sterling Price, who had put down the Taos rebellion in New Mexico. After the war Reid resumed law and died in 1881, aged sixty.

Price, for his part, returned to become a wealthy governor of Missouri but also threw in his lot with the Confederacy during the Civil War. He became a major general and commanded an army but his battle record was undistinguished. At the end of the war he took the remnants of his army into Mexico rather than surrender, but an attempt to begin an American colony at Veracruz failed when Price contracted cholera, or some similar disease, which ultimately killed him in 1867, at age fifty-eight. He was buried in St. Louis in what was one of the cities largest funerals at the time.

After his trading expedition to Mexico, Samuel Magoffin also retired to Missouri. He "acquired a sizable estate near Kirkwood," where he took up the life of a cotton planter and real estate man. His wife, Susan, our diarist, gave birth to his daughter in 1851, but the strain seemed to have ruined her health and, as was all too common in those times, she died during her next childbirth in 1855, at the age of twenty-seven, and is buried in St. Louis. In addition to her family, she left behind her priceless memoir, first published in 1926 as *Down the Santa Fe Trail and into Mexico.*

James Magoffin, Susan's narrowly escaped brother-in-law, finally received a healthy claim settlement from the federal government for his part in securing the peaceful American acquisition of Santa Fe and the New Mexico Territory. He later established an outpost in what is now the city of El Paso and became a wealthy entrepreneur until his death in 1868, at the age of sixty-nine.

Of the other men on Kearny's march, Colonel Philip St. George Cooke had one of the most colorful careers. After mustering out his Mormon Battalion, Cooke returned east where he became an Indian fighter during the early 1850s uprisings, defeating the Jacarilla Apaches in 1854 and the Sioux in 1855, then he tried to keep the peace in "bleeding" Kansas. He was an observer for the United States during the Crimean War and wrote a famous two-volume manual on cavalry tactics.

When the Civil War began, Cooke's family of Virginians was consumed in a perfectly dreadful schism. His daughter was married to the soon-to-be legendary Confederate cavalry chieftain J. E. B. Stuart, and Cooke's son, John Rogers Cooke, became a brigade commander in Lee's Army of Northern Virginia.

But Cooke remained loyal to the Union, despite Stuart's gibe that "He will regret it only once, but that continually." As a general, Philip St. George Cooke commanded the federal cavalry during the 1862 Yorktown Peninsula Campaign up toward Richmond, along with then Major General George Stoneman, who had been Cooke's lieutenant during the Mormon march and was wounded in the hand during the "Great Bullfight."*

The Yorktown Peninsula was where J. E. B. Stuart made his storied

---

*Stoneman's name was immortalized for his prowess at tearing up Rebel railroad track in the 1969 song "The Night They Drove Old Dixie Down."

"ride around the Union army," in which the infamous Rebel horseman led his cavalry in a devastating and humiliating raid completely encircling McClellan's huge army, even leaving a note addressed to his mortified father-in-law—"Sorry I can't stay for dinner."

After that Cooke, who was then fifty-two, withdrew from service in the field and assumed desk and administrative duties for the remainder of the war. He was promoted to major general toward the end, and later he returned to western commands until his retirement in 1873, after some fifty years of service. Like most southerners who had sided with the Union, Cooke never returned to the South and lived out his remaining years in Detroit, where he died in 1895, peacefully in bed, at the age of eighty-six.

The road across the Southwest that Cooke's Mormon Battalion built was so perfectly constructed topographically, due to his flawless engineering and astronomical calculations, that in 1853 the United States paid Mexico an additional $10 million for the Gadsden Purchase, some 30,000 square miles of southern New Mexico and Arizona that Cooke had laid out, for the transcontinental railway line. It is presently the route of Amtrak's famous Sunset Limited, a scenic train, begun in 1894 by the Southern Pacific Railroad.

When Cooke disbanded the Mormon Battalion in California many of the men went to work temporarily for Sutter, who was then hiring and paying high wages. They were there when gold was discovered at the mill Sutter was building, and many lined their pockets with gold dust and nuggets. When word finally came that Brigham Young had found a place to settle the colony on the banks of the Salt Lake in Utah, these men crossed the mountains to their new home. With them went the so-called Sutter Gun, a gift, presumably, from Captain Sutter. Lore has it that when the Mormons built their great temple, they used the cannon as a sort of battering ram or wrecking ball to tamp down the stones by continually hauling it up, then dropping it from a gun hoist. It is said that the Sutter Gun remains there today, buried in the foundation of the Mormon Tabernacle.

As for the Mormons themselves, the tiny sect that Joseph Smith started in 1830 has grown to nearly 14 million today, worldwide, and counts among its prominent members such notables as Governor Mitt Romney, Glenn Beck, and Senator Harry Reid.

Captain William Emory went back to Mexico with a Maryland regiment and fought until war's end; then he directed the U.S.–Mexican boundary survey of 1848–55. During the Civil War he, too, sided with the Union and as a brevet major general commanded the Nineteenth Corps in the Shenandoah Valley Campaign of 1864. He retired in 1876 and died in Washington, D.C., in 1887 at the age of seventy-six. Emory Peak in Big Bend National Park, in Texas, is named in his honor.

As President Polk had predicted the war heroes and political Whigs Zachary Taylor and Winfield Scott, the two leading American commanders, vied for the U.S. presidency in the election of 1848. Taylor handily won the Whig nomination and the presidency as well.

Until the election, Taylor had never publicly discussed his politics, or for that matter even voted in a presidential election, an omission of which he was proud. Aside from being a general, he was also a Louisiana planter and slaveholder, which made him attractive to Whigs looking for southern support. For all the campaign knew he might as well have been a Know-Nothing, too, since he was utterly noncommittal on political issues, including those of his own party.

The slavery issue consumed most of the nation's political discourse by the time Taylor took office, but congressional Whigs were infuriated when he turned against some of their favorite domestic programs, in particular "internal improvements, a national bank, and protective tariffs—basically, the entire Whig economic platform." On slavery, Taylor was, like Polk, of the opinion that it would not spread to the territories acquired from Mexico due to sheer impracticality. Maybe so, but what of Kansas and the interior states?

Under the bitterly contested Compromise of 1850, citizens of U.S. territories would be allowed to vote on whether they wished to be free or slave states, but Taylor died before it passed. He had served only a year in office when he became ill watching the Fourth of July groundbreaking for the Washington Monument and died five days later from what doctors diagnosed as gastroenteritis. He was replaced by Vice President Millard Fillmore.

From then until now assassination theories have abounded, implying that Taylor had been deliberately poisoned by some food brought

to the groundbreaking ceremony. By then of course he had made enemies enough on both sides of the political spectrum, but in 1991, when
rumors at last forced the exhumation and examination of his remains,
no traces of arsenic or any other poison could be found.

Winfield Scott remained chief of the U.S. Army until 1861, the first
year of the Civil War, by which time at the age of seventy-five he had
become enormously corpulent and unable to mount a horse. Before his
resignation, however, Scott undertook to offer Robert E. Lee command
of all the Union armies and, failing in that, devised perhaps the single
most important strategy of the war, the so-called Anaconda Plan to
seal off the South with a blockade. He lived to see the Union victorious
but died in 1866, just shy of eighty, and is buried at the U.S. Military
Academy at West Point, New York.

The Mexican-American War concluded with the Treaty of Guadalupe
Hidalgo in February 1848. By then the United States was so divided
over the aims of the war and the possible spread of slavery that it was
doubtful whether the pact could attract ratification by two-thirds of the
Senate, but ultimately it passed muster on March 10, by a vote of 38–14.
In exchange for more than $18 million, Mexico ceded a total of approxi-
mately 600,000 square miles of territory, including what are now New
Mexico, Arizona, California, Nevada, and parts of Colorado and Utah.

This acquisition has subsequently been the subject of much criti-
cism and revisionist history, including that of luminaries such as
Ulysses Grant, who condemned the action as "one of the most unjust
ever waged by a stronger against a weaker nation." Many Whigs were
equally outspoken even as the conflict was raging. There is something
to be said for both sides.

First, Mexico had threatened war, and loudly, ever since the U.S.
Congress voted to accept Texas into the Union. Earlier, actually; the
Mexicans said there was going to be war if the United States even *tried*
to annex Texas. They recalled their ambassador in Washington and
refused to see the peace commissioner sent by Polk to mitigate the
issues. And they attacked and massacred a company of U.S. cavalry on
what Texas had long claimed was its soil.

On the other hand, Polk made no secret that he wanted not only

Texas but California and New Mexico in the Union. He offered to compensate Mexico, and well, but the offer was refused, even though Mexico was broke and, as we have seen, unwilling or unable to properly protect or care for the citizens of its northern territories, practically all of whom were being terrorized by the Indians. Neither was it any secret that sending Zachary Taylor's army to Matamoros would be interpreted by Mexico as a provocation.

In the event, Mexico tried to bell the cat and got slapped down, as we have also seen. The trouble that nags is: was it improper for the U.S. government to bait Mexico into a war of acquisition? This forces us to question whether said "provocation" actually amounted to "baiting." After all, if Mexico had not moved an army to its border with Texas and attacked the bait, there probably would have been no war. That is one view, with substantial gravitas.

Was the United States a bully, being larger and more powerful than its southern neighbor? Certainly it was larger and more powerful, but it was fighting on foreign soil a long way from home, and the casualty rate in the American army—nearly 13,000 dead of all causes—was horrendous in relation to the numbers serving. With better leadership it is certainly possible that Mexican armies could have destroyed the U.S. forces at Monterrey, Buena Vista, and possibly Cerro Gordo. But because they did not have better leadership the question becomes moot.

John Eisenhower writes quite astutely that "The fact is that Mexico stood in the way of the American dream of Manifest Destiny." It is best left to the scholars and pundits to argue the morality or rightness of it. One thing to ponder through is this: if the war had not been fought and won, would the United States have found a second chance to create a nation from sea to shining sea? Such opportunities do not often present themselves to democracies and, after the 1848 war, it is hard to imagine when or how the United States could have acquired these territories. Which leaves us with this: but for the Mexican-American War—be it right or wrong—citizens of the American West, from Denver to Phoenix, from Reno to San Francisco and points in between, today just might be speaking English as a second language and paying their taxes to Mexico City.

Another enduring legacy of the war was that it proved once and for all the efficacy of martial training at West Point, which had been called into question on numerous occasions since the U.S. Military Academy was established in 1802. A large number of the junior officers who did the actual fighting were West Pointers, who time and again out-maneuvered and outfought their Mexican counterparts, never losing a battle. For better or worse, this improved their confidence and warrior spirit and, more ominously, served as grim preparation for nearly all of the top generals in the American Civil War, which of course lay just over the horizon. In addition to the aforementioned Robert E. Lee, Ulysses S. Grant, John Pope, Joseph Hooker, George B. Meade, Thomas J. "Stonewall" Jackson, Ambrose Burnside, Braxton Bragg, P. G. T. Beauregard, and James Longstreet served in the conflict with Mexico, as did Jefferson Davis, the first and only president of the Confederate States of America.

Eighteen forty-six was a remarkable year in United States history. It was a year when a great number of people set themselves in motion; Americans en masse suddenly became agitated enough to haul across the next ridge west, and the next, in such numbers that it began to shake and shift the national equilibrium.

With every step the Wilmot Proviso echoed like the clang of the log splitter's wedge; antislavery literature and abolitionist screeds in newspapers were one thing but acts of Congress were a powerful gauntlet. (Versions of the proviso were soon regularly appended to any legislation regarding new territories, in hopes that one would stick. An outraged Thomas Hart Benton compared it to the biblical plague of frogs: "You could not look upon the table but there were frogs, you could not sit down at the banquet but there were frogs, you could not go to the bridal couch and lift the sheets but there were frogs!" So it was with Wilmot's proviso—"this black question, ever on the table, on the nuptial couch, everywhere!" so Old Bullion roared.)

And the southern slavers sat and thumbed their noses. Yet at least it got the question of slavery out of the drawing rooms and into the political arena for good. After that, it was only a matter of time. Toward the end of the Mexican-American War, Ralph Waldo Emerson sized it up: "The United States will conquer Mexico, but it will be as the man swallows the arsenic, which brings him down in turn. Mexico will poison us." He was not alone in saying it; many wise men of the day said the same but were powerless to prevent it.

The political consequences of the war were immediate and seismic. A coalition of northern Democrats and so-called Conscience Whigs split off from their respective parties and, with members of the Liberty Party, formed the Free Soil Party for the upcoming elections. Martin Van Buren was its presidential candidate. Things were already beginning to fall apart, rarely a good sign. In time the victory glow of Monterrey, of Buena Vista, Cerro Gordo, Sacramento, and Veracruz, shrank back into the stormy chaos that was Mexico, and in its place an awful dazzling hatred glared across the newfound continental map, driving men mad until they grasped the sword and nearly dealt themselves a mortal blow.

What of Polk, the political cipher who set it all into motion? He had promised from the start that he would seek only one term, and he was good to his word. On the evening of the same day that Polk accompanied Zachary Taylor to the Capitol to be inaugurated, he and Sarah boarded a steamboat on the Potomac for a monthlong trip through the South before returning to Nashville. However, what began as a restorative vacation for the ex-president quickly became a relentless orgy of speeches, luncheons, dinners, parades, balls, and galas that sapped Polk's energy instead of restoring it.

At New Orleans he was taken ill by an intestinal bug that left him drained. He cut the trip short and headed up the Mississippi, remaining aboard ship and attended by doctors at ports along the way. At Nashville, where he was met by cheering crowds, he seemed to rally and soon took an active part in preparing the library of their new home in the former Grundy mansion, now renamed Polk Place. But in less than two months he was struck down during a cholera epidemic that was sweeping the South and died on June 15, 1849. He was fifty-three years old. His last request had been to be baptized, which he was, into the Methodist Church.

Many modern historians disparage Polk, mainly because of his drab personality. I don't know why that is. It sometimes seems as if all it takes for a president to be accepted is that he play golf and tell good jokes. When Polk went to the White House, he went knowing precisely what he wanted to accomplish, a rarity of course. Even

Harry S. Truman thought so a hundred years later. "A great president," he remarked. "Said what he wanted to do and did it."

Indeed, Polk did it, accomplished each of the four things he wanted, although it took a war to achieve the last one. As Eisenhower astutely points out, "Manifest Destiny was not Polk's invention, but he was its ideal agent."

Polk died believing that the acquisitions in the West would make the United States stronger, but in one of the great quirks of history it did no such thing, at least for the then foreseeable future.

When the dust of Mexico had settled and the treaty papers were signed, America did not return to the so-called Era of Good Feelings. Politicians, preachers, editors, and leaders on almost all sides became averse to listening; instead they barked louder and more profanely above the rising din. And so the nation shuddered into a kind of "era of agitation," ending only with the curse of civil war.

That might have been the end of it, and of the United States as one people, but it wasn't.

The whole remains today as immutable testimony to the perseverance of such men as Polk and Kearny, Frémont and Doniphan, Scott and Taylor, and the hundred thousand more who served under them in war, and their descendants, down to the present day. It remains because another hundred thousand pioneers on horse or muleback, or in their Conestoga wagons—including the Donners and the Mormons with their hand carts—struck out across those thousand or two thousand miles and braved the parching deserts, treacherous mountains, lethal snowstorms, open plains, gloomy forests, and a hundred other places where death came within a wink. They were the ones who first made the American West; then came the railroads and the multitudes, who may have been settlers but they weren't the pioneers.

All those in the story played their roles and Kearny's march, of course, is just a part, but it looms large when the history of the West is told. From the day Stephen Kearny rode out of Fort Leavenworth on that bright June morning in 1846, wherever he went became the United States of America.

My first acknowledgment is to the dogged historians who have gone before, providing information, illumination, context, and insight into the diverse themes and threads of this story. My thanks to them is profound and heartfelt.

In a note regarding the sources of my previous book about the Civil War battle of Vicksburg, I remarked on the explosion of bureaucratic documentation that had taken place between the setting of my book *Patriotic Fire*, about the War of 1812, when only the barest of government records were kept, and the 1860s. Moving on to the 1840s, when the present story is told, I found a sparseness of documentation more akin to 1812 than to the Civil War, just fifteen years hence. Commanders such as Kearny, Doniphan, Price, and Taylor submitted straightforward, almost cursory accounts of their campaigns to the War Department and these, more or less, comprise the official record. However, those documents are supplemented by an abundance of personal diaries, journals, memoirs, and letters alluded to in the text, allowing us to flesh out the portrait of this extraordinary time in American history.

Not the least of these is the diary of President James K. Polk, as edited and annotated by Allan Nevins, which provides remarkably candid insights into the problems Polk faced and the solutions he endorsed. My friend John Sigenthaler's fine, concise biography of Polk and Walter Borneman's more elaborate *Polk: The Man Who Transformed the Presidency and America* are solid guides to "Young Hickory" Polk. Otherwise, the politics of the times is amplified by such works as Thomas Hart Benton's *Thirty Years' View*, Frederick Jackson Turner's *The Significance of the Frontier in American History*, George Bancroft's *History of the United States*, Allan Nevins's *Ordeal of the Union*, and Bernard De Voto's *The Year of Decision: 1846*. Of the modern accounts, Hampton Sides's *Blood and Thunder*, Robert Leckie's *From Sea to Shining Sea*, and Robert Merry's *A Country of Vast Designs* provide a good overview of the age.

John C. Frémont was his own best advertiser in *Memoirs of My Life*, but Tom Chaffin's *Pathfinder* and Allan Nevins's *Frémont: Pathmarker of the West* bring clarity to Frémont's bold and complex personality. One has to wend one's way through the various arguments and counterarguments about what, or what not, Frémont was charged with doing, vis-à-vis California; I just followed my instincts, which is about as much as anyone can do until yet further information is brought forth.

Of the mountain men, there are more than a dozen books on Kit Carson alone; among the best are Harvey Lewis Carter's *Dear Old Kit* and *Kit Carson: A Portrait in Courage* by M. Morgan Estergreen.

There are many, many fine works on Native Americans, or Indians, among them Robert Utley's *The Indian Frontier of the American West: 1846–1890* and, of course, Dee Brown's *Bury My Heart at Wounded Knee*, the latter covering a later period in Indian history.

David Dary's *The Santa Fe Trail*, Henry Inman's *The Old Trail to Santa Fe*, and Francis Parkman's *The Oregon Trail* are excellent reading for what life was like out on the plains. William Keleher's *Turmoil in New Mexico, 1846–1848* is a fine primer for the situation at the Santa Fe end of the trail as General Kearny found it. And General John S. D. Eisenhower's masterful *So Far from God* is by far the best piece of writing on the Mexican-American War itself. *Niles' National Register*, a journal of the times, proved to be a fount of information, since it collected and published numerous contemporary reports of every important issue of the day.

The best of the numerous books on the Donner Party is still George R. Stewart's 1948 *Ordeal by Hunger*. Edwin Bryant's *What I Saw in California* and James Clyman's memoir *Frontiersman* are two of the best contemporary accounts of crossing the mountains and descending into the turmoil that was California in 1846–47, in addition to the Englishman George F. A. Ruxton's 1847 *Adventures in Mexico and the Rocky Mountains*, which is simply a pleasure to read.

My profound thanks also goes to my editor, Andrew Miller, for his careful attention to the manuscript, and to his assistant, Andrew Michael Carlson, whose fine line editing improved the story immensely—as did that of my long-time copy editor, Don Kinneson, whose eagle eye and keen mind saved me from myself more times than I can count.

My wife, Anne-Clinton, and Wren Murphy are professionals when it comes to locating and acquiring photographs and other images, research materials, and permission to use or quote from them. In the course of those pursuits, I would like to extend my grateful thanks not only to them, but also to Valerie Moore at the Library of Congress; Daniel Kosharek, Photo Archives, Palace of the Governors, the New Mexico History Museum; Jaime Bourassa, Missouri History Museum; Tom Price, curator, James K. Polk Memorial Association; Doug Misner, Utah History Research Center; Erika Castano, University of Arizona Libraries, Special Collections; Bonnie Coleman and Dennis Trujillo, State Historian's Office, New Mexico; and Ray John de Aragon of Albuquerque, who graciously allowed me to use the portrait of General Armijo from his private collection. Each of them was kind enough to go beyond the normal courtesy, and made a special effort to locate difficult-to-find images.

BIBLIOGRAPHY

(*) denotes primary source material

Adams, James. *The Epic of America.* New York: Blue Ribbon Books, 1931.

Allie, Stephen J. *All He Could Carry: U.S. Army Infantry Equipment, 1839–1910.* Leavenworth, Kans.: Leavenworth Historical Society, 1991.

Anderson, Donald Jack. *Goodbye Mountain Man!* New Castle, Pa.: Summit House, 1976.

(*) Atocha, Alejandro Jose. "Comments on reports of his dealings with Mexico." *Niles' National Register,* vol. 72, May–June 1847.

Bacon, Melvin, and Daniel Blegen. *Bent's Fort: Crossroads of Cultures on the Santa Fe Trail.* Brookfield, Conn.: Millbrook Press, 1995.

Bancroft, Hubert Howe. *The Works of Hubert Howe Bancroft. Vol. 18.1, 2: History of California 1542–1800.* A. L. Bancroft and Co., 1884.

Barney, William L. *The Road to Secession: A New Perspective on the Old South.* New York: Praeger, 1972.

Benet, Stephen Vincent. *Western Star.* New York: Farrar and Rinehart, 1943.

(*) Benton, Thomas H. "Benton's Card about Gen. Stephen Watts Kearny and . . . Fremont." *Niles' National Register,* vol. 72, May–June 1847.

(*) ———. *Thirty Years' View: A History of the Working of the American Government for Thirty Years. 1820–1850. Vol. 2.* New York: Appleton and Co, 1881.

(*) ———. "Thomas Hart Benton's remarks . . ." *Niles' National Register,* vol. 72, May–June 1847.

Bonsal, Stephen. *Edward Fitzgerald Beale.* New York: G. P. Putnam's Sons, 1912.

Borneman, Walter R. *Polk: The Man Who Transformed the Presidency and America.* New York: Random House, 2009.

(*) Brewerton, George Douglas. *Overland with Kit Carson: A Narrative of the Old Spanish Trail in '48.* New York: A. L. Burt, 1930.

(*) Brooks, N. C. *A Complete History of the Mexican War.* Baltimore: Hutchinson and Seebold, 1849.

Brown, David E. *The Grizzly in the Southwest.* Norman: University of Oklahoma Press, 1994.

Brown, Dee. *Bury My Heart at Wounded Knee: An Indian History of the American West.* New York: Holt, Rinehart, 1970.

Brown, Kenneth A. *Four Corners: History, Land and People of the Desert Southwest.* New York: HarperCollins, 1995.

(*) Bryant, Edwin. *What I Saw in California.* New York: D. Appleton, 1848. (University of Nebraska Press, 1985.)

(*) Buchanan, James. "Letter on his Sentiments on the Wilmot Proviso." *Niles' National Register,* September–October 1847.

Calabro, Marian. *The Perilous Journey of the Donner Party.* New York: Clarion Books, 1989.

(*) *The Californian.* "Affairs in California." *Niles' National Register,* vol. 72, May–June 1847.

(*) Calvin, Ross, ed. *Lieutenant Emory Reports.* Albuquerque: University of New Mexico Press, 1951. From: *Lt. W. H. Emory's Notes of a Military Reconnaissance from Fort Leavenworth, in Missouri, to San Diego, in California, including Part of the Arkansas, all Norte and Gila Rivers. Presented to the 30th Congress, lst Session, Senate Document No. 7. 1848.*

Camp, Charles L., ed. *James Clyman Frontiersman. 1792–1881. The Adventures of a Trapper and Covered Wagon Emigratas Told in His Own Reminiscences and Diaries.* Portland, Ore.: Champoeg Press, 1960.

(*) Carleton, Lt. J. Henry, Louis Pelzer, ed. *The Prairie Logbooks: Dragoon Campaigns to the Pawnee Villages in 1844 and to the Rocky Mountains in 1845* Lincoln: University of Nebraska Press, 1983. (First published in *New York Journal* in two series: 1844–45.)

Carter, Harvey Lewis. *Dear Old Kit: The Historical Christopher Carson, with a New Edition of the Carson Memoirs.* Norman: University of Oklahoma Press, 1968.

Carter, Jack I. *Trees and Shrubs of New Mexico.* Boulder, Colo.: Johnson Books, 1988.

(*) Castro, José, Manuel Castro, et al. "Frémont's Operations in Upper California, correspondence . . ." *Niles' National Register,* vol. 71, November–December 1846.

Chaffin, Tom. *Pathfinder: John Charles Frémont and the Course of American Empire.* New York: Hill and Wang, 2002.

Chambers, William Nisbet. *Old Bullion Benton: Senator from the New West, Thomas Hart Benton, 1782–1858.* Boston: Little, Brown, 1956.

Chronic, Halka. *Roadside Geology of New Mexico.* Missoula, Mont.: Mountain Press, 1987.

Clark, Laverne Harrell. *They Sang for Horses: The Impact of the Horse on Navajo and Apache Folklore.* Tucson: University of Arizona Press, 1966.

(*) Clark, Maj. Meriwether Lewis. "Official Report on Action at Sacramento." *Niles' National Register,* vol. 72, May–June 1847.

Clarke, Dwight L. "The Final Roster of the Army of the West 1846–1847." *California Historical Society Quarterly,* March 1964.

———. *Stephen Watts Kearny, Soldier of the Old West.* Norman: University of Oklahoma Press, 1961.

(*) Clarke, Dwight L., ed. *The Original Journals of Henry Smith Turner: With Stephen Watts Kearny to New Mexico and California. 1846–1847.* Norman: University of Oklahoma Press, 1966.

(*) Cooke, Philip St. George. *The Conquest of New Mexico and California in 1846–1848.* (New York, 1878.) Albuquerque, N.M.: Horn and Wallace, 1964.

(*) ———. *Scenes and Adventures in the Army, Or, Romance of Military Life.* Philadelphia: Lindsay and Blakeston, 1859.

Coy, Owen C. *The Battle of San Pasqual.* Sacramento: California State Printing Office, 1921.

Curtis, George Ticknor. *Life of James Buchanan.* New York: Harper, 1883.

Cutts, James Madison. *The Conquest of California and New Mexico.* Albuquerque, N.M.: Horn and Wallace, 1965.

Dary, David. *The Santa Fe Trail: Its History, Legends, and Lore.* New York: Knopf, 2000.

Del Castillo, Richard Griswold. *The Treaty of Guadalupe Hidalgo: A Legacy of Conflict.* Norman: University of Oklahoma Press, 1990.

De Voto, Bernard. Introduction by Stephen E. Ambrose. *The Year of Decision: 1846.* Boston: Little, Brown, 1942, 1943.

Dobie, J. Frank. *The Longhorns.* Austin: University of Texas Press, 1984.

———. *Rattlesnakes.* Austin: University of Texas Press, 1988.

(*) Doniphan, William Alexander. "Letters on his Operations . . ." *Niles' National Register,* vol. 72, May–June 1847.

(*) ———. "Reports . . ." *Niles' National Register,* vol. 72, May–June 1847.

(*) ———. Letter to Maj. E. M. Ryland, who sent to Editors of *St. Louis Republican,* June 10, for publication. "Doniphan's achievements, casualties, . . ." *Niles' National Register,* vol. 72, July–August 1847.

(*) ———. "State of Affairs at Santa Fe." *Missouri Republican,* Nov. 26, 1846. *Niles' National Register,* vol. 71, November–December 1846.

(*) Drumm, Stella M., ed. *Down the Santa Fe Trail and into Mexico: The Diary of Susan Shelby Magoffin, 1846–1847.* Lincoln: University of Nebraska Press, 1962.

Duffus, R. L. *The Santa Fe Trail.* Albuquerque: University of New Mexico Press, 1975.

Dunlay, Tom. *Kit Carson and the Indians*. Lincoln: University of Nebraska Press, 2000.

Durand, John. *The Taos Massacres*. Elkhorn, Wis.: Puzzlebox Press, 2004.

Dyer, Brainard. *Zachary Taylor*. Baton Rouge: University of Louisiana Press, 1946.

Earle, Jonathan H. *Jacksonian Antislavery and the Politics of Free Soil, 1824–1854*. Chapel Hill: University of North Carolina Press, 2004.

Eisenhower, John S. D., *So Far from God: The U.S. War with Mexico, 1846–1848*. New York: Random House, 1989.

Ellison, William H. "San Juan to Cahuenga: The Experiences of Frémont's California Battalion." *Pacific Historical Review*, 1958.

Estergreen, M. Morgan. *Kit Carson: A Portrait in Courage*. Norman: University of Oklahoma Press, 1962.

(*) Flores, José María. "Mexican Account of the Seizure of Chihuahua." *Niles' National Register*, vol. 72, May–June 1847.

Forbes, Jack. *Apache, Navaho and Spaniard*. Norman: University of Oklahoma Press, 1960.

(*) Frémont, John Charles. *Memoirs of My Life. American West* (1887). Introduction by Charles M. Robison III. New York: Cooper Square Press, 2001.

(*) Garrard, Lewis H. *Wah-to-Yah and the Taos Trail* (1850). Norman: University of Oklahoma Press, 1955.

George, Issac. *Heroes and Incidents of the Mexican War: Containing Doniphan's Expedition*. Written from Dictation by J. D. Berry, Greensberg, Pa.: Review Publishing Co., 1903. (Hollywood, Calif.: Sun Dance Press, 1971.)

Gerson, Noel R. *Kit Carson: Folk Hero and Man*. Garden City, N.Y.: Doubleday, 1964.

(*) Gibson, George Rutledge. *Journal of a Soldier under Kearny and Doniphan. 1846–1847*. Edited by Ralph P. Bieber. *Southwest Historical Series III*. Glendale, Calif.: Arthur C. Clark, 1935.

Goetzmann, William. *Army Exploration in the American West, 1803–1863*. New Haven, Conn.: Yale University Press, 1959.

Going, Charles Buxton. *David Wilmot, Free Soiler*. New York: Appleton and Co., 1924.

Goodwin, Cardinal. *The Establishment of State Government in California, 1846–1850*. New York: Macmillan, 1914.

Gordon-McCutchan, R. C., ed. *Kit Carson: Indian Fighter or Indian Killer?* Niwot: Univeristy Press of Colorado, 1996.

Grivas, Theodore. *Military Governments in California, 1846–1850*. Arthur C. Clark & Co., 1963.

(*) Gudde, Erwin G., ed. *Bigler's Chronicle of the West: The Conquest of California, Discovery of Gold and Mormon Settlement as Reflected in Henry William Bigler's Diary.* Berkeley: University of California Press, 1962.

Guild, Thelma S., and Harvey L. Carter. *Kit Carson: A Pattern for Heroes.* Lincoln: University of Nebraska Press, 1984.

Hamalainen, Pekka. *The Comanche Empire.* New Haven, Conn.: Yale University Press, 2008.

Harlow, Neal. *California Conquered: The Annexation of a Mexican Province.* Berkeley: University of California Press, 1982.

Hart, E. Richard. *Pedro Pino: Governor of Zuni Pueblo, 1830–1878.* Logan: Utah State University Press, 2003.

Hawgood, John A. *America's Western Frontiers: The Exploration and Settlement of the Trans-Mississippi West.* New York: Knopf, 1967.

Haynes, Sam W. *James K. Polk and the Expansionist Impulse.* New York: Addison Wesley Longman, 2002.

(*) Heredia, Maj. Gen. José A. "The Battle of Sacramento." *Niles' National Register,* vol. 72, May–June 1847.

Herr, Pamela. *Jessie Benton Frémont.* New York: Franklin Watts, 1987.

(*) Herr, Pamela, and Mary Lee Spence, eds. *The Letters of Jessie Benton Frémont.* Urbana: University of Illinois Press, 1993.

(*) Holmes, Kenneth L., ed. Introduction by Anne M. Butler. *Covered Wagon Women: Diaries and Letters from the Western Trail, 1840–1849.* Lincoln: University of Nebraska Press, 1955, 1983.

Horgan, Paul. *Great River: The Rio Grande in North American History.* Austin: Texas Monthly Press, 1984.

Houghton, Eliza P. Donner. *The Expedition of the Donner Party and Its Tragic Fate.* Introduction by Kristin Johnson. Lincoln: University of Nebraska Press, 1997.

Howe, Daniel Walker. *What Has God Wrought: The Transformation of America, 1815–1848.* New York: Oxford University Press, 2007.

Hughes, J. Patrick. *Fort Leavenworth: Gateway to the West.* Newton, Kans.: Mennonite Press, 2000.

(*) Hughes, John Taylor. *Doniphan's Expedition: Containing an Account of the Conquest of New Mexico* (1847). College Station: Texas A & M University Press, 1997.

Hussey, John A. "The Origins of the Gillespie Mission." *California Historical Society Quarterly* 19, no. 1 (1940): 43–58.

Inman, Henry. *The Old Trail to Santa Fe: The Story of a Great Highway.* Topeka, Kans.: Crane and Co., 1916.

Irving, Washington. *The Adventures of Captain Bonneville: In the Rocky*

Mountains and the Far West. Norman: University of Oklahoma Press, 1986.

Jackson, Hal. *Following the Royal Road: A Guide to the Historic Camino Real de Teirra Adentro*. Albuquerque: University of New Mexico Press, 2006.

James, Marquis. *Sam Houston*. New York: Blue Ribbon Books, 1929.

(*) James, Thomas. Introduction by A. P. Nasatir. *Three Years Among the Indians* (1846). Lincoln: University of Nebraska Press, 1984.

Jameson, W. C. *Legend and Lore of the Guadalupe Mountains*. Albuquerque: University of New Mexico Press, 2007.

(*) Jefferson (Missouri) Enquirer. "Affairs at Santa Fe," including a letter from Lieut. Eastin. *Niles' National Register*, vol. 72, July–August 1847.

Jenkins, John S. *History of the War Between the United States and Mexico*. Auburn, N.Y.: Derby, Miller, 1849.

Johnson, Kenneth M. *The Frémont Court Martial*. Los Angeles: Dawson Book Shop, 1968.

Johnson, Kristin, ed. *Unfortunate Emigrants. Narratives of the Donner Party*. Logan: Utah State University Press, 1996.

Kavenagh, Thomas W. *The Comanches: A History, 1706–1875*. Lincoln: University of Nebraska Press, 1996.

(*) Kearny, Gen. Stephen Watts. "Kearny's Proclamation . . ." *Niles' National Register*, vol. 71, November–December 1846.

(*) ———. "Kearny's Proclamation." *Niles' National Register*, vol. 72, July–August 1847.

(*) ———. "Letters . . ." *Niles' National Register*, vol. 72, May–June 1847.

Keleher, William A. *Turmoil in New Mexico, 1846–1868*. Santa Fe, N.M.: Santa Fe Press, 1952.

Krakauer, Jon. *Under the Banner of Heaven*. New York: Doubleday, 2003.

Krober, A. L. *Handbook of the Indians of California*. Berkeley: California Book Co., 1953.

Launius, Roger D. *Alexander William Doniphan: Portrait of a Missouri Moderate*. Columbia: University Press of Missouri, 1997.

Lauritzen, Jonreed. *The Battle of San Pasqual*. New York: G. P. Putnam's Sons, 1968.

Laycock, George. *The Mountain Men and the Dramatic History and Lore of the First Frontiersmen*. Guilford, Conn.: The Lyons Press, 1988.

Leckie, Robert. *From Sea to Shining Sea*. New York: HarperCollins, 1993.

(*) Letter. "About the Cause for Losses at Monterrey . . ." Correspondent's communication over the signature "L.," writing from Matamoros. *Niles' National Register*, vol. 71, November–December 1846.

(*) Letter. "Arrival of Gen. Kearny . . ." *Niles' National Register,* vol. 73, September–October 1847.

Logghe, Joan, and Miriam Sagan, eds. *Another Desert: Jewish Poetry of New Mexico.* Santa Fe, N.M.: Sherman Asher Publishing, 1998.

Lotchin, Roger W. *San Francisco 1846–56: From Hamlet to City.* New York: Oxford University Press, 1974.

(*) Lynch, James. *The New York Volunteers in California. With Stevenson to California 1846–1848;* and Francis Clark. *Steven's Regiment in California.* Glorieta, N.M.: Rio Grande Press, 1970.

Maguire, James H., Peter Wild, and Donald A. Barclay, eds. *A Rendezvous Reader: Tall, Tangled, and True Tales of the Mountain Men, 1805–1850.* Salt Lake City: University of Utah Press, 1997.

Marti, Wernes H. *Messenger of Destiny: The California Adventures, 1846– 1847, of Archibald H. Gillespie, U.S. Marine Corps.* San Francisco: John Howell-Books, 1960.

Merk, Frederic. *Manifest Destiny and Mission in American History.* New York: Knopf, 1963.

Merry, Robert W. *A Country of Vast Design: James K. Polk, the Mexican War and the Conquest of the American Continent.* New York: Simon and Schuster, 2009.

Michno, Susan, and Gregory Michno. *A Fate Worse than Death: Indian Captivities in the West, 1830–1885.* Caldwell, Idaho: Caxton Press, 2007.

(*) Miller, Darlis A. *The California Column in New Mexico.* Albuquerque: University of New Mexico Press, 1982.

Morgan, Dale Lowell. *Jedediah Smith and the Opening of the West.* Indianapolis: Bobbs-Merrill, 1953.

Morrison, Chaplain W. *Democratic Politics and Sectionalism: The Wilmot Proviso Controversy.* Chapel Hill: University of North Carolina Press, 1967.

Mullen, Frank. *The Donner Party Chronicle: A Day-by-Day Account of a Doomed Wagon Train, 1846–1847.* Reno: University of Nevada Press, 1997.

McMurtry, Larry. *Oh What a Slaughter: Massacres in the American West, 1846–1890.* New York: Simon and Schuster, 2005.

(*) McNierney, Michael, ed. *Taos, 1847: The Revolt in Contemporary Accounts.* Boulder: University of Colorado Press, 1980.

Nagel, Paul C. *Missouri: A Bicentennial History.* New York: Norton, 1977.

Nevins, Allan. *Frémont: Pathmarker of the West.* New York: Longmans, Green, 1955.

———. *Ordeal of the Union: Fruits of Manifest Destiny. 1847–1852; A House Dividing 1852–1857.* New York: Macmillan, 1992.

(*) Nevins, Allan, ed. *Polk: The Diary of a President. 1845–1849.* New York: Longmans, Green, 1929.

Owens, Kenneth N., ed. *John Sutter and a Wider West.* Lincoln: University of Nebraska Press, 1994.

(*) Parkman, Francis, Jr. *The Oregon Trail.* Garden City, N.Y.: Garden City Books, 1849.

(*) Peck, Lt. William Guy. "News from Santa Fe . . ." *Niles' National Register,* vol. 72, May–June 1847.

Peet, Mary Lockwood. *San Pasqual: A Crack in the Hills.* Culver City, Calif.: Highland Press, 1949.

Philbrick, Nathaniel. *Sea of Glory: America's Voyage of Discovery: The U.S. Exploring Expedition.* New York: Viking, 2003.

Pitt, Leonard. *Decline of the Californios: A Social History of Spanish-Speaking Californians, 1846–1890.* Berkeley: University of California Press, 1966.

Preston, Douglas, and José Antonio Esquibel. *The Royal Road: El Camino Real from Mexico City to Santa Fe.* Photographs by Christine Press. Albuquerque: University of New Mexico Press, 1998.

Price, Glen W. *Origins of the War with Mexico.* Austin: University of Texas Press, 1963.

(*) Price, Col. Sterling. "Col. Sterling Price at Santa Fe." *Niles' National Register,* vol. 72, May–June 1847.

(*) Quaife, Milo Milton, ed. *Kit Carson's Autobiography.* Lincoln: University of Nebraska Press, 1966.

Quinn, Arthur. *The Rivals: William Gwin, David Broderick and the Birth of California.* New York: Crown, 1994.

(*) Report. "Account of the Pueblo Indians in the Fight at Taos." *Niles' National Register,* vol. 72, May–June 1847.

(*) Report. "The Americanizing of Santa Fe." *Niles' National Register,* vol. 71, November–December 1846.

(*) Report. "British Mediation Suggested." *Niles' National Register,* vol. 72, July–August 1847.

(*) Report. "Cavalry ordered to Parras . . . meet Col. Doniphan." *Niles' National Register,* vol. 72, May–June 1847.

(*) Report. "Col. Doniphan attacked . . ." *Niles' National Register,* vol. 72, May–June 1847.

(*) Report. "Col. Philip Saint George Cooke with Mormon Battalion . . ." *Niles' National Register,* vol. 72, May–June 1847.

(*) Report. "Col. Sterling Price at Santa Fe." *Niles' National Register,* vol. 72, July–August 1847.

(*) Report. "Comanche Depredations." *Niles' National Register,* vol. 72, May–June 1847.

(*) Report. "Dismal Picture of Affairs at Santa Fe." *Niles' National Register,* vol. 72, May–June 1847.

(*) Report. "Doniphan's Command Passes Down the Rio Grande . . ." *Niles' National Register,* vol. 72, May–June 1847.

(*) Report. "Doniphan's uncertainty . . ." *Niles' National Register,* vol. 72, May–June 1847.

(*) Report. "Foray upon Santa Fe (Mexico) by Mexican guerrillas." *Niles' National Register,* vol. 72, May–June 1847.

(*) Report. "Frémont Arrested for Disobedience of Orders . . ." *Niles' National Register,* vol. 72, July–August 1847.

(*) Report. "Fruits of the Mexican Seizure of Correspondence." *Niles' National Register,* vol. 71, November–December 1846.

(*) Report. "Gloomy Letter from the California Expedition." From a volunteer in the California Expedition, *North Hampton Gazette. Niles' National Register,* vol. 73, September–October 1847.

(*) Report. "Loss of Wagon Train en route to Santa Fe . . ." *Niles' National Register,* vol. 72, July–August 1847.

(*) Report. "Massachusetts Resolutions on the Expansion of Slavery . . ." *Niles' National Register,* vol. 72, May–June 1847.

(*) Report. "Mexican Clergy Contribute . . ." *Niles' National Register,* vol. 72, May–June 1847.

(*) Report. "More Territory and the Wilmot Proviso." *Niles' National Register,* vol. 73, September–October 1847.

(*) Report. "Mormon Detachment near San Diego." *Niles' National Register,* vol. 72, May–June 1847.

(*) Report. "Movements on the Pacific Coast." *Washington Union. Niles' National Register,* vol. 71, November–December 1846.

(*) Report. "Operations in California." *Niles' National Register,* vol. 72, May–June 1847.

(*) Report. "Pronunciation of Mexican Names." *Niles' National Register,* vol. 72, May–June 1847.

(*) Report. "Stockton's Difference with Gen. Stephen Watts Kearny." *Niles' National Register,* vol. 72, May–June 1847.

(*) Report. "Unenviable Position of Col. Sterling Price's Division." *Niles' National Register,* vol. 72, July–August 1847.

Reynolds, David S. *Waking Giant: America in the Age of Jackson.* New York: HarperCollins, 2008.

Richards, Leonard L. *The California Gold Rush and the Coming of the Civil War.* New York: Vintage Books, 2007.

———. *The Slave Power: The Free North and Southern Domination, 1780–1860.* Baton Rouge: Louisiana State University Press, 2000.

Richman, Irving B. *California Under Spain and Mexico.* Boston: Houghton Mifflin, 1911.

Roberson, Jere W. "The South and the Pacific Railroad 1845–1855." *Western Historical Quarterly* 5, no. 2 (April 1974): 164–66.

Roberts, David. *A Newer World: Kit Carson, John C. Frémont and the Claiming of the American West.* New York: Simon and Schuster, 2000.

(*) Robinson, Jacob S. *Sketches of the Great West: A Journal of the Santa Fe Expedition.* Princeton, N.J.: Princeton University Press, 1932.

Roosevelt, Theodore. *Thomas H. Benton, American Statesman.* New York: Houghton Mifflin, 1887.

Russell, Carl P. *Firearms, Traps and Tools of the Mountain Men.* Albuquerque: University of New Mexico Press, 1967.

(*) Russell, Col. "Speech in Favor of Col. John Charles Fremont." *Niles' National Register,* vol. 72, July–August 1847.

Russell, Osborner. *Journal of a Trapper.* Aubrey I. Haines, ed. Lincoln: University of Nebraska Press, 1965.

(*) Ruxton, George Frederick Augustus. *Adventures in Mexico and the Rocky Mountains, 1846–1847.* Glorieta, N.M.: Rio Grande Press, 1973.

Sabin, Edwin LeGrand. *Kit Carson Days, 1809–1868: Adventures in the Path of Empire.* Lincoln: University of Nebraska Press, 1995.

(*) *Sangamon* (Illinois) *Journal.* Correspondent's account in California. "Revolution by Settlers in California . . ." *Niles' National Register,* vol. 73, September–October 1847.

Saxton, Alexander. *The Rise and Fall of the White Republic: Class Politics and Mass Culture in Nineteenth-Century America.* New York: Verso, 1990.

Seigenthaler, John. *James K. Polk.* New York: Henry Holt, 2003.

Shoumatoff, Alex. *Legends of the American Desert: Sojourns in the Greater Southwest.* New York: Knopf, 1997.

Sides, Hampton. *Blood and Thunder: An Epic Story of the American West.* New York: Doubleday, 2006.

Simmons, Marc. *Kit Carson and His Three Wives.* Albuquerque: University of New Mexico Press, 2003.

Spence, Mary Lee, and Donald Jackson, eds. *Expeditions of John Charles Frémont, Vol. 2: The Bear Flag Revolt and the Court Martial.* Urbana: University of Illinois Press, 1973.

Spicer, Edward H. *Cycles of Conquest: The Impact of Spain, New Mexico and the United States on the Indians of the Southwest, 1533–1960*. Tucson: University of Arizona Press, 1962.

Starr, Kevin. *Americans and the California Dream, 1850–1915*. New York: Oxford University Press, 1973.

Stegner, Page. *Winning the West: The Epic Saga of the American Frontier, 1800–1899*. New York: Free Press, 2002.

Stenberg, Richard. "Polk and Frémont 1845–1846." *Pacific Historical Review* 7, no. 3. (1938): 211–27.

Stewart. George R. *Ordeal by Hunger: The Classic Story of the Donner Party*. New York: Pocket Books, 1971.

(*) *St. Louis Republican*. "Accounts on the Situation at Santa Fe . . ." *Niles' National Register*, vol. 72, May–June 1847.

(*) ———. "Frémont Arrives at Angels [sic] . . ." *Niles' National Register*, vol. 72, May–June 1847.

(*) ———. "Kearny in Supreme Condition . . ." *Niles' National Register*, vol. 73, September–October 1847.

(*) ———. "Kearny Orders Part of his Force Back to Santa Fe . . ." *Niles' National Register*, vol. 71, November–December 1846.

(*) ———. "News of Gen. Stephen Watts Kearny." *Niles' National Register*, vol. 71, November–December 1846.

(*) Stockton, Robert F. "Report of Rebellion in California." *Niles' National Register*, vol. 72, May–June 1847.

Tays, George. "Frémont Had No Secret Instructions." *Pacific Historical Review* 9, no. 21 (1940).

Tedlock, Barbara. *The Beautiful and the Dangerous: Encounters with the Zuni Indians*. New York: Viking, 1992.

Twitchell, Ralph Emerson. *The Story of the Conquest of Santa Fe, New Mexico and the Building of Old Fort Marcy, A.D. 1846*. Santa Fe: Historical Society of New Mexico, 1923.

Utley, Robert. *The Indian Frontier of the American West: 1846–1890*. Albuquerque: University of New Mexico Press, 1984.

———. *A Life Wild and Perilous: Mountain Men and the Paths to the Pacific*. New York: Henry Holt, 1997.

Vestal, Stanley. *Kit Carson: The Happy Warrior of the Old West, A Biography*. Boston: Houghton Mifflin, 1928.

Wallace, Ernest, and E. Adamson Hoebel. *The Comanches: Lords of the South Plains*. Norman: University of Oklahoma Press, 1952.

(*) *Washington Union*. "Position of Catholic Church in Mexico with Regard to the War." *Niles' National Register*, vol. 72, May–June 1847.

Webb, Walter Prescott. *The Great Plains.* New York: Ginn and Co., 1931.

Weigle, Marta. *The Penitentes of the Southwest.* Santa Fe, N.M.: Ancient City Press, 1970.

Wills, Garry. *Inventing America: Jefferson's Declaration of Independence.* New York: Vintage Books, 1979.

INDEX

Index

Illustration Credits

Pages 1–6: Library of Congress.

Page 7: *(Top right)* Library of Congress. *(Center)* Courtesy of the James K. Polk Memorial Association. *(Bottom)* State Historical Society of Missouri.

Page 8: *(Top)* Courtesy of University of Arizona Libraries Special Collections. *(Bottom)* From Henry Inman, *The Old Santa Fe Trail* (London: Macmillan and Co., 1897).

Page 9: From Henry Inman, *The Old Santa Fe Trail* (London: Macmillan and Co., 1897).

Page 10: From John C. Frémont, *Memoirs of My Life* (Chicago: Belford, Clark & Co., 1886).

Page 11: *(Top)* From John C. Frémont, *Memoirs of My Life* (Chicago: Belford, Clark & Co., 1886). *(Bottom, left and right)* Missouri History Museum, St. Louis.

Page 12: Missouri History Museum, St. Louis.

Page 13: *(Top left)* W. H. Emory, *Notes of a Military Reconnoissance* [sic] *from Fort Leavenworth, in Missouri, to San Diego, in California, including part of the Arkansas, Del Norte, and Gila Rivers* (Washington: Wendell & Van Benthuysen, 1848). *(Center left)* National Archives and Records Administration. *(Bottom)* Courtesy of Bancroft Library, University of California, Berkeley.

Page 14: *(Top)* Courtesy of Palace of the Governors, New Mexico, MNM/DCA Neg. 70437. *(Center right)* Courtesy of Benson Collection, University of Texas, Austin. *(Bottom left)* Courtesy Utah State Historical Society.

Page 15: *(Top right)* W. H. Emory, *Notes of a Military Reconnoissance* [sic] *from Fort Leavenworth, in Missouri, to San Diego, in California, including part of the Arkansas, Del Norte, and Gila Rivers* (Washington: Wendell & Van Benthuysen, 1848). *(Center left)* Courtesy Utah State Historical Society. *(Bottom)* Courtesy Beinecke Rare Book and Manuscript Library, Yale University.

Page 16: *(Right)* Courtesy of Palace of the Governors, New Mexico. *(Left)* From the Collection of Ray John de Aragon.

FORREST GUMP

Six foot six, 242 pounds, and possessed of a scant IQ of 70, Forrest Gump is the lovable, surprisingly savvy hero of this classic comic tale. His early life may seem inauspicious, but when the University of Alabama's football team drafts Forrest and makes him a star, it sets him on an unbelievable path that will transform him from Vietnam hero to world-class Ping-Pong player, from wrestler to entrepreneur. With a voice all his own, Forrest is telling all in a madcap romp through three decades of American history.

Fiction

PATRIOTIC FIRE

December 1814: its economy in tatters, its capital city of Washington, D.C., burnt to the ground, a young America was again at war with the militarily superior English crown. With an enormous enemy armada approaching New Orleans, two unlikely allies teamed up to repel the British in one of the greatest battles ever fought in North America. The defense of New Orleans fell to the backwoods general Andrew Jackson, who joined the raffish French pirate Jean Laffite to command a ramshackle army made of free blacks, Creole aristocrats, Choctaw Indians, gunboat sailors and militiamen. Together these leaders and their scruffy crew turned back a British force more than twice their number.

History

VICKSBURG, 1863

In this thrilling narrative history of the Civil War's most strategically important campaign, Winston Groom describes the bloody two-year grind that started when Ulysses S. Grant began taking a series of Confederate strongholds in 1861, climaxing with the siege of Vicksburg two years later. For Grant and the Union it was a crucial success that captured the Mississippi River, divided the South in half, and set the stage for eventual victory. *Vicksburg, 1863* brings the battles and the protagonists of this struggle to life.

History

VINTAGE BOOKS
Available wherever books are sold.
www.randomhouse.com